# Pennsylvania German Cookery

## A Regional Cookbook

by Ann Hark and Preston A. Barba

Drawings by
Eleanor J. M. Barba
and
Edward E. Smith

COACHWHIP PUBLICATIONS

Greenville, Ohio

*Pennsylvania German Cookery*, by Ann Hark and Preston A. Barba
© 2015 Coachwhip Publications

  Ann Hark (1891-1970)
  Preston Albert Barba (1883-1971)

  Published 1950, 1956. No renewal.
  No claims made on public domain material.

ISBN 1-61646-292-2
ISBN-13 978-1-61646-292-5

CoachwhipBooks.com

To

The Pennsylvania German Hausfrau

*of nine generations, who silently
and unsung, influenced the cookery
of a great nation, and wrought
better then she knew, this book
is dedicated.*

FAIR PENNSYLVANIA! My people's home!
O'er thy green hills and plains I love to roam;
I love to linger in thy lovely vales,
Where mountain peak the roseate morning hails,
Or where thy rivers hold their ceaseless flow,
And streamlets babble and sweet lilies blow.
A Switzerland, a France, within thee lies,
High over-vaulted by Italian skies.
Peace and prosperity within thee reign,
Thy happy people sing but freedom's strain;
Their thrift has turned thee to a garden fair,
And busy noises lade thy balmy air.
'T was here, exiled across the ocean's foam,
My weeping people sought a peaceful home;
And here, through painful toil, that home they found,
Here still their hearty German accents sound.
My heart pulsates in sympathy with theirs,
I love their virtues and regret their cares.
By adverse fortunes have their souls been tried,
By cruel, bitter trial purified.

*From Ellwood L. Kemp's "The German Exiles"*

*in An Idyl of the War. Philadelphia, 1883.*

# Contents

PREFACE                                                          IX

INTRODUCTION                                                   XIII

Chapter

I       Herbs and Greens                                         1

II      Breads, Rolls, Biscuits, Muffins                        11

III     Soups                                                   23

IV      Meat Dishes and Meat Condiments                         39

V       Cheese and Cheese Dishes                                61

VI      Vegetable Dishes                                        67

VII     Salads and Salad Dressings                              83

VIII    Noodles, Dumplings, and the Like                        91

IX      Pancakes, Waffles, Fritters, etc.                       99

X       Sweets and Sours                                       113

XI      DUNKES: Coffeecakes, Crullers, Doughnuts, etc.         133

XII     Loaf and Layer Cakes                                   147

XIII    Cookies, Drop Cakes and Cupcakes                       161

XIV     Christmas Cakes and Cookies                            173

XV      Pies and Tarts                                         191

XVI     Desserts                                               213

XVII    Candies                                                227

XVIII   Beverages                                              233

*Courtesy,* The Historical Society of York County, Pa.
"NO BETTER AND GOOD COOKS CAN BE FOUND NO WHERE . . . ."
From a drawing by the Pennsylvania German folk artist Lewis Miller (1796-1882)

# Preface

The cookery of a nation is an integral part of its cultural history. Today more than ever there is a lively interest in the study of regional cooking. If our American civilization rests solidly upon an Anglo-Saxon foundation, which no one will deny, one wonders why its preparation of foods is so superior to that of old England, unless it be that it has been influenced by other streams of immigration. Of these none has affected the food habits of our nation as widely and as deeply as that of the Pennsylvania Germans. Tillers of the soil for thirty generations, they had made of the Rhenish Palatinate a garden spot, coveted through the centuries by enemy invaders. And when in the eighteenth century they migrated from that and adjacent territories in throngs to seek across the sea freedom of body and spirit and escape from extreme economic distress, they were not long in turning Penn's primeval forests into productive gardens, fields and orchards. They were and have remained America's best farmers. They not only knew how to till the soil but they possessed rich culinary traditions that reached back as far as Charles the Great (742-814) and the establishment of monastic institutions in their fatherland. Here in Pennsylvania, thanks to a benign government and their own diligence, they prospered and produced food in such plenty and quality as they had not ever known before. It was here that their cookery came to its finest florescence. Where else throughout the American colonies was so much good food eaten steadily through the years by people in all walks of life as among the German settlers in Pennsylvania? Where else did master and servant sit down in democratic dignity at the same table and eat of the same food? A conservative people, the Pennsylvania Germans have retained a preference for certain folkways in cooking throughout two centuries. Although the influence of their cookery is nation-wide, they have in turn also readily adapted themselves to the cooking of other racial groups.

This is a regional cookbook. Its purpose is to set forth the cookery of the Pennsylvania Germans. Since its inception some years ago several books and booklets have appeared on the same subject. However, since none of them transgressed upon our original plans, the work was carried on to its completion. This book does not offer a history of the Pennsylvania German people. That has been done many times elsewhere. Although it contains the most comprehensive list of recipes yet gathered among the Pennsylvania Germans, it is at the same time more than a mere collection of recipes. We believe we have for the first time brought the cuisine of this interesting American racial group into a more comprehensive relationship with its old-world culinary traditions. We have gathered and inserted throughout the pages much old and half-forgotten lore and information pertaining to the individual dishes and a consideration of the significance of their names and origins. In doing so we modestly incline to believe that we have contributed a fascinating, although but small, chapter to our general body of *Americana.*

The recipes were gathered from various sources: from old German almanacs printed in Pennsylvania; from old cookbooks in manuscript and in print; and directly from many persons. German cookbooks printed abroad, but which had circulated among the Pennsylvania Germans, were consulted and recipes drawn from them when they seemed better or more interesting than similar ones in hand. Some few had faded into obscurity and deserved to be restored. We were happy to have had access to that rare little item, *Die geschickte Hausfrau* (Harrisburg, Pa., 1852), the first German cookbook to be printed in Pennsylvania. We also owe inspiration and several recipes to Mathilde Jung's charming little book, *Eine Landschaft kocht. Ein pfälzisches Küchenbrevier* (Saarbrücken, 1941).

Those of our readers who have collected recipes among the Pennsylvania Germans will appreciate the dilemma that confronted us. The modern house-wife, influenced by the home economist, maintains that cooking is a science. For our Pennsylvania German mothers and grandmothers cooking was an art which depended upon intuitive good sense and skillful execution. Their recipes, whether written or oral, left much to the imagination. One took some of this and combined it with some of that! Quantity of shortening and of flour was often left to the feel of the mixture, to the acute tactile sense of the practiced housewife or cook. Recipes of this kind found their way into some previous cookbooks. We have endeavored to bring these recipes into the general cookbook conformity of today and to reduce them to the practical needs of the modern small family, but for a few instances where we left them

intact for the sake of folk atmosphere. In many instances we have preferred
to retain dialect names and phrases, partly for the charm of atmosphere,
partly for the pleasure of those many Pennsylvania Germans scattered nation-
wide who still retain nostalgic memories of the tongue of their ancestors.

We are directly and indirectly obligated to many more people than we
could possibly enumerate here, to all of whom we express our gratitude. We
have throughout the chapters made numerous direct acknowledgments. The
names attached to many of the recipes denote our immediate sources and at
no time the originators of the recipes. One finds occasionally people who
exercise a sense of proprietorship over recipes. But who has created any
particular dishes? It is pleasant to think that some one must have been the
first to make *Fassnachts*, Shoofly Pies, Sauerkraut or Lebanon Bologna. What
intrepid housewife first thought of creating that classic combination of *Schnits
un Gnepp*? What young bride first sought to please her husband by sprinkling
caraway seed in her bread dough or putting fragrant garden herbs in her soup?
What buxom widow with mischievous twinkle first charmed with her onion
pie? What poetic provincial soul was fascinated by the romance of distant
lands and first thought of putting ground cardamom seeds in her honey bread,
or currants from distant Corinth in her coffee cakes? No one will ever answer
these futile questions. We do better to assume that cookery is an evolutionary
process. Indeed we could well apply to our folk cookery what Theodor Storm
said of the folksong in his immortal *Immensee*. We could say that recipes
are not made at all; they grow, they fall from out of the air; they are wafted
across the countryside like gossamers, hither and yon; they are being used
in a thousand places at the same time. Our daily lives and those of our
remotest ancestors are reflected in these recipes. Indeed it is as though we
had all had a hand in them.

Preston A. Barba

# Introduction

WAY back in the year 1681 a strange rumor spread along the reaches of the Rhine in Europe. Across the sea, in a country called America, an Englishman named William Penn had just received a princely grant of land, greater than all Bavaria and Wuerttemberg and Baden put together. To this new province he was now inviting all the peoples of the Rhine—those peoples who for decades past had cowered miserably beneath the heel of a succession of invaders. Hardly a kingdom or a principality that had not felt the cruel impact of war—its homes laid waste, its rich fields ravaged, its inhabitants driven away. To all of these the news that traveled far and wide seemed almost unbelievable. That tall young Quaker who four years before had visited the Rhineland, preaching doctrines not so very different from those held by some of their own sects, was offering them a haven in his adopted land. There good, rich soil was plentiful, he said, and peace abode, and each man worshipped God according to his conscience, under laws in whose dictating everyone had had a hand.

Almost at once the invitation was accepted, at first by small groups, then by gradually increasing numbers, till in 1776 nearly half the residents of Pennsylvania hailed from German states. The majority of the immigrants came from the Palatinate, that fertile pocket of the Upper Rhine. They landed at Philadelphia, then spread fan-wise through the valleys of the Susquehanna and the Schuylkill, up and down the Lehigh and the Perkiomen, into sections known today as Lancaster and Berks and Snyder Counties, York, Northampton, Lehigh, Bucks, Montgomery and surrounding areas.

Among them in outstanding numbers came the farmer folk, who knew good land by instinct and at once set out to claim it for their own. But there were others, too, among their number: scholars, ministers and lawyers, artisans and printers, weavers, potters, turners, gunsmiths — men from every walk of life. They brought their Bibles with them, these staunch seekers after peace and freedom, and their deep religious feeling, and their music that had always played a foremost part throughout their lives. They brought their love of color and of decoration also, of hearts and birds and tulips painted in bright blues and earthy reds and brilliant greens, of animals and suns and moons and stars and trees of life, and other symbols dating back into their far-distant past. Here in a new, free land, with different media and tools not always adequate, they set down once again the old familiar figures, on their birth certificates and tombstones, on their dower chests and pottery, on barns and butter molds and stoveplates, and in the lovely Fraktur-painting that adorned their manuscripts and books.

They brought their love of hearty eating with them also, and their own distinctive recipes, stored carefully away in memory and passed on by word of mouth from one group to the next. They are recipes, most of them, for good, substantial dishes, since the majority of Pennsylvania Germans still, as in the past, are farming people. And there's nothing "sneaky" about farm appetites, as anyone can tell you. With unabashed simplicity your Pennsylvania German will admit it. "Them that works hard," he'll explain quite reasonably, "eats hearty!" And lest you think that quantity is all that counts, he'll add with naive pride: "We live common — but good!"

One glimpse of well-tilled fields and bulging barns throughout southeastern Pennsylvania, or better still, of a repast spread out upon a groaning table in that land of plenty, proves the truth of what he says. For food, good food and plenty of it, is the keynote of every Pennsylvania German home. With silent eloquence it speaks out from smokehouse and "cave-cellar," from outdoor oven and sweet-smelling applebutter shed, from indoor-cellar shelves and summer-kitchen cupboards lined with rows of jars and crocks and glasses filled to overflowing with the products of the good, rich earth.

And hand in hand with all this wealth of food there goes a simple hospitality that reaches out to every comer. Friend, relative or hired man — yes, even the stranger within their gates — is given an ungrudging welcome. And the main part of that welcome, naturally, is food. There's plenty of it and to spare, so shame indeed on any *Hausfrau* who permits a visitor to go away unfed. Shame, too, on any visitor who does not live up to his hostess' expectations. For second only to the glow of satisfaction that a well-filled larder brings her, comes the joy of watching valiant trenchermen do justice to her cooking. There's nothing popular about a pindling appetite among the Pennsylvania Germans!

To many persons not familiar with this school of hearty eating, certain of its dishes may still seem a trifle odd. But on the other hand, a goodly number of the viands introduced here by the Pennsylvania Germans have been so whole-heartedly adopted that their origin has been lost sight of through the years. The humble pretzel, for example, brought here by the early German settlers and still turned out at its toothsome best in areas where their descendants live. This salt-besprinkled twist of golden dough made its appearance first on monastery banquet tables and at ceremonial feasts in Central Europe centuries ago. Its German name was taken from the Latin *pretiola*, meaning "little gift," in recognition of the fact that pretzels formerly were used as prizes for small children learning to recite their prayers. The pretzel's shape, suggestive of a pair of folded arms, was meant to signify the attitude of supplication.

Another favorite food today, of Pennsylvania German origin, is sauerkraut. As far back as the Civil War its fame had spread abroad, and history shows that when in 1863 the town of Chambersburg was captured by the Southern troops, the list of items that the conquerors demanded from the town's inhabitants included twenty-five full barrels of that tempting dish. At first this strange demand seemed to the city fathers like a heartless joke directed at their love of sauerkraut, especially as the time was June and sauerkraut is eaten only in the winter months. But General Harmon, in command of the invading forces, hastened to explain. "No slur has been intended, gentlemen," he said. "I've asked for sauerkraut because my men are suffering from the scurvy, and I understand this vegetable is an effective cure, as well as a preventive, of that troublesome disease." So, even though no sauerkraut could be produced in all of Chambersburg at that time of the year, the incident passed by with no ill feeling on the part of either conqueror or conquered.

Another food of Pennsylvania German origin, whose popularity has spread abroad today, is sun-dried corn, as different from the ordinary canned corn as day from night. It had its start, like many another tasty preparation, in the thrifty German habit of refusing to let even the most trifling remnants go to waste. And so, since sugar corn is always picked when "in the milk," before the kernels have a chance to harden, and a generous surplus is on hand on every Pennsylvania German farm, it seemed no more than reasonable to frugal housewives that the extra grains be laid aside to dry beneath the sun. A portion of the sugar content is thus stored within the kernel, and the rich food value of the grain is much increased.

Apparently the famed explorer, Admiral Byrd, had heard of sun-dried corn, for back in 1939, when he was getting ready for his Third Antarctic Expedition, he sent up to Lancaster for several barrels of this concentrated sunshine. The Pennsylvania German farmer who received the order, with a typically Pennsylvania German disregard for free publicity, refused to be impressed. He had his usual patrons to supply, and who was Admiral Byrd to come ahead of them? So, when the loaded North Star pulled up anchor for her journey to the frozen South, instead of seven barrels of stored sunshine in her hold, a mere three barrels was the total that she carried.

But, even though some Pennsylvania German specialties have journeyed far beyond the boundaries of Pennsylvania, most of them still flourish with the greatest richness in their native states. Each season has its special dishes, too, and everywhere throughout the sections where the Pennsylvania Germans live, each man and woman faithfully observes the old-time customs that go with them. Take Maundy Thursday, for example, known to Pennsylvania Germans as "Green Thursday," when a green of some sort must be eaten to insure good health throughout the coming year. Since dandelion is the first green that appears each springtime, this medicinal tasting weed, delightfully disguised however, with a sweetish-sour dressing and small squares of bacon fried to crunchy crispness scattered on the top, is usually the one that's chosen.

Shrove Tuesday also is a day when Pennsylvania Germans everywhere go in for one distinctive article of food. On every table at least once that day, and sometimes at each meal, a high-piled dish of sugar-sprinkled *Fassnachts* (doughnuts) makes its bow, while restaurants in some places even go so far as to provide their patrons with these plump and fluffy rings of goodness without extra charge.

Another season when the hard-worked kitchens of the Pennsylvania Germans hum with industry is autumn. Then vast quantities of red and green and golden apples are borne off to cider mills to be converted into cider, which, combined with tubfuls of sliced apples ("Schnitz") and spices, is then boiled and stirred and boiled again in mammoth copper kettles till it turns to rich, dark applebutter, ready to be stored away in earthen crocks and used in generous quantities throughout the year. In olden times the applebutter "stirrings" in each neighborhood were lively gatherings, with the young folks and the old together turning into gay festivity a strictly practical event.

And hardly had the applebutter season passed than butchering time rolled round, and once again the neighbors would assemble to extend a helping hand. Before the sun was up great fires would be started in the open yard and pots of scalding water would send forth their steamy clouds of vapor on the frosty air. Each person had his special job as butcher's helper, fire stoker, bristle scraper or whatever else might be required, and proceedings would get under way without delay. A ponderous hog, 300 pounds or more in weight, would trot out on reluctant feet before the executioner, urged on by frenzied shouting from the rear, and suddenly an axe would land with sickening thud upon his hapless head and all 300 pounds of him would drop upon the ground. With practiced skill that came from repetition — for each section of the countryside had experts who officiated at all such events — the stout head butcher would step forward, wielding a ferocious-looking knife, and presto! the poor porker's life blood would gush swiftly from the neatly severed jugular vein.

When finally the body had been almost drained, a visit to the scalding trough was next in order. There the bristles were scraped off and the now denuded animal turned over to the womenfolk for their part of the job — the removing and cleansing of the intestines to be used as casing for the liverwurst and sausages on the following day. With this complex and none too pleasant task accomplished, once again the butcher took the center of the stage, assisted by his various helpers, and the cutting up of the huge carcass was begun. Great, massive quarters were removed and laid aside for smoking, in addition to well-padded chops and spareribs to which clung a liberal store of meat. The roasts and flitches of bacon, too, were cut without a thought of skimping, and the pounds of fat left over were then sliced and relegated to a special cauldron to be rendered into lard. Those sections of the porker not considered edible were placed upon a separate pile and later processed by the women into soap. The bristles, even, were retrieved, and after being washed and combed with thrifty care, were sold to manufacturers of brushes.

Although two hearty meals were served the workers, usually the products of the killing did not figure on the menu and the main dish would be chicken or some other kind of meat. But on the second day, when sights and smells attendant on the slaughtering had faded and the warm flesh of the animal itself had cooled, the company would have a chance to sample what their labor had brought forth. "Pot pudding," liverwurst and *Pannhaas, Zitterli* and sausage, representing the less choice portions of the porker, chopped and ground and seasoned to the proper taste — these were the lusty and distinctive products that resulted from their industry.

But probably the time of all the year that gave the Pennsylvania German housewife the most extensive outlet for her culinary talents was the Christmas season. Then it was that, in addition to her usual weekly output of fresh pies and breads and cakes, she turned her hand to mixing, rolling, baking, and embellishing a mighty store of cookies. Rich and crumbly nut drops were among them, highly seasoned *Pefferniss* and almond-sprinkled *Mandel Spitzen*, heavy fruit cake and delicious, chewy macaroons, thin, brittle sandtarts, fragile ginger wafers, and *Lebkuche* that dissolved in beatific sweetness on the tongue. Each visitor throughout the holidays was offered heaping platefuls of these toothsome Christmas cakes to sample, and exchange of specialties among the various households was the hospitable order of the day.

Each year as Christmas time rolls round again, my mind once more goes back to Bethlehem and the quaint old customs linked so unforgettably with that delightful Pennsylvania town. For Christmas time in Bethlehem, with its *Putzes* and its candle service and its myriad array of Christmas cakes, to me sums up as nothing else the whole heart-warming spirit of that loveliest of seasons. In our own family the exciting preparations started two whole weeks ahead of Christmas Day itself. For then the dough for those particular delights called *Leckerle* (or *Berthelsdorfer*, by those able to pronounce the word) was mixed and set away to ripen in a cool, secluded spot. From Berthelsdorf, in Germany, the recipe had come to us — an old-time giant of a recipe that called for quarts and pounds instead of merely cups and teaspoonfuls of sugar, citron, nuts, and other things. My father, always chosen to officiate (it took real strength to knead in six whole pounds of flour!) would begin by mixing slowly in a mammoth dishpan everything except the flour and the brandy. Then, a little at a time, the former would be sprinkled in, with several drops of brandy every now and then as moistening, till the whole amount of each had been absorbed. As final step, the dishpan would be covered with a clean, white cloth and set away until the time, ten days or two weeks later, when the gala baking process would begin. Then once again my father, usually assisted by my brother and a friend or two, would hold forth manfully above the dishpan. For the dough was tough and hard to manage, and brute muscle came in handy for the hewing of thick slabs that had to be rolled out and flattened to the proper thickness. The final steps — the cutting into three-by four-inch pieces, the brushing of each piece with milk before the big, flat baking sheets on which they were arranged in careful rows would disappear into the oven, and the superintending of the baking process proper — these were taken care of by the women of the household. And when at last the ultimate reluctant morsel had been dug out from the dishpan, and the final tins of red-hot, spicy-smelling cakes had slid into the huge washbasket waiting to receive them, an important prelude to the Christmas celebration had been brought to its appointed end.

There were, of course, still other kinds of Christmas cakes, as well as other preludes to the thrilling holiday. The building of the *Putz* was one of these. A *Putz*, for those not versed in such traditions, is the old Moravian version of the Christmas tree. Its name is taken from the German *putzen*, which translated means "to decorate." In a Moravian *Putz*, however, it is not the tree alone that's decorated, but the spacious platform underneath the tree as well. There is portrayed the old, old Christmas story, told with figures made of wood or papier-maché, with jagged tree stumps and large quantities of moss, with rocks and sand and sometimes running water, and above all with a loving understanding of what most appeals to youthful eyes and hearts.

For, in the last analysis, the *Putz* primarily is for the children, though its building is a grown-up function carried on in secrecy behind closed doors. There gradually takes shape the humble, straw-thatched stable where the Holy Family gathers, with the gentle eyes of sheep and cattle looking out from nearby stalls. There the Three Wise Men, led by the directing Star, make their appearance, and the lonely shepherds on the hillside watch their sheep by night. There deer and other creatures of the wild roam through the woodland, and a mountain torrent tumbles down a rocky precipice, to spread into a smooth, clear lake with snow-white swans serenely floating on its glassy face.

Sometimes the platform where the spectacle is laid is just a few scant feet in measurement and sometimes it takes up a good-sized room. Occasionally a single tree is used as background, while at other times a dozen dark and aromatic beauties tower loftily above the peaceful scene. Sometimes the trees are decorated, sometimes not. Often they glow with small electiric bulbs, or old-time beeswax candles that shine forth from out the shadow of their boughs. But always it's the Christmas picture that stands out as thrilling focal point of the entire scene.

That picture dawns upon the dazzled vision of the younger members of the family for the first time at a certain stated hour on Christmas Eve. For to your true Moravian everywhere, it's Christmas Eve, not Christmas Day, that furnishes the climax and the highlight of this stirring season. Then it is that the now famous candle service, to which annually flock scores of visitors from far and near, is held. To all attending it, the mystic glamor of that simple service lingers unforgettably throughout the years. Its spell descends with the first strains of the trombones — those same trombones whose music is a feature of the world-renowned Bach Festival. It grows more potent as the clear soprano voice of a child soloist soars upward in the words of the beloved old Moravian hymn, "Morning Star, O Cheering Sight!" It reaches a soul-stirring climax as at last the church's lights are dimmed and men and women bearing trays of glowing beeswax candles pass the tapers reverently to every member of the congregation — symbols of the Light that came into the world on Christmas Eve so many years ago.

And when the candle service finally has ended and each family starts for home and its own private celebration, then at last the long-awaited *Putz* and presents come into their own. Then, too, the heaping tins and trays and plates of Christmas cakes and cookies that have been accumulated through the weeks preceding are brought forth and passed about the circle. Every family has its special recipes and favorites, and a list comprising all of them would be enough to fill a modest cookbook in itself.

What to choose and record within the following pages from out of this amazing register of foods has offered somewhat of a problem, a recurrent problem cropping up anew in each department of the book. With such a wealth of old-time Pennsylvania German recipes from which to choose, the only course remaining to the authors was to pick out those most typical and most delicious, with the hope that somewhere in their number everyone may find the dishes best adapted to his individual taste.

ANN HARK

The author expresses her thanks to THE CONDE NAST PUBLICATIONS, and to GOURMET, INC., for permission to reprint here parts of her articles "Who Are the Pennsylvania Dutch?" in *House and Garden*, June, 1941, and "Common — But Good!" in *Gourmet*, December, 1943.

A. H.

 # Herbs and Greens

*Jocund and fragrant was the old-time rural kitchen*
*With wholesome garden-herbs and spices then —*
*Sweet marjoram, coriander, garlic, thyme —*
*And others, which perhaps would hardly rhyme.*

From "The Winter Carnival" in H. L. Fisher's
OLDEN TIMES. York, Pa. 1888.

## HERBS

HERBS have stirred the memory and stimulated the fancy of man since earliest times. Although cabbages and turnips and other vegetables have been cultivated for thousands of years, it is not of them, but of basil, thyme, bdellium, of spikenard and rue, of hyssop, balm and saffron, that sages and bards have written and sung. The literature of ancient and modern civilization, our own Anglo-Saxon and Germanic folklore and legendry abound in allusions to herbs and their uses.

Our pioneer German forefathers came to Pennsylvania with all the rich culinary and medicinal herb lore of their homeland. In their newly established gardens they cultivated the old-world herbs and introduced other native ones. In the course of time some fell into disuse, but it is one of the pleasant aspects of present-day gardening that herbs are once more taking their rightful place in our gardens.

It must be stated at the outset that kitchen herbs never had the same importance in Pennsylvania German cookery they have in the French cuisine. No distinction is made between *les fines herbes* and those of a sturdier character. Our cookery is simple and straightforward. The sophisticated blending of herbs in salads, for example, is foreign to it. It is not imaginable that the head of a Pennsylvania German household ever prepared a salad before his table-guests, at the same time with pleasant chitchat diverting their attention from his subtle secrets, while performing the ritual of mixing oil and vinegar with his own various nuances of estragon, borage, thyme, sweet basil and burnet. Cooking and the seasoning of the dishes he left to his undaunted *Hausfraa,* upon whom also rested the honors of achievement. She drew upon her own stock of herbs, gathered freshly from the garden or carefully dried during the summer months and stored away in sundry caddies or herb chests.

Let us follow our Pennsylvania German *Hausfraa* into her kitchen garden, a part of her very own domain. It lies within easy reach of her summer kitchen and often adjoining it, confined in part by a low stone wall, or by a pale fence, freshly whitewashed and gleaming in the early springtime sunshine. Within these confines are the neatly laid-out vegetable beds. There is no formal herb garden. Here a simple plant democracy prevails. Against the sheltering wall of kitchen or bakeoven clusters of daffodils, narcissus and early primroses announce themselves as the cheering harbingers of spring, while only a few feet away the less glamorous pieplant generously lifts its luxuriant leaves and supplies the housewife with her first pie material. Nothing so convinces her family of the reality of spring as a fresh rhubarb pie. In close proximity a few square feet of earliest seed lettuce will soon be ready for the first cutting. It matters not that an impertinent *Dischtelfink*, sitting on the nearby apricot tree and biding his favorable moment, darts down, like a flash of gold, amid a shower of white petals, and snatches a morsel from the edge of a crisp green lettuce leaf. Along the edge of the lettuce bed, always among the first to heed the summons of spring, clumps of chives, gentlest of the mighty onion family, are sending forth their slender, grass-like leaves, ever ready to add their mild flavor to soups, salads, fried potatoes and *Schmierkaes*.

The old parsley bed also shows signs of life. Last fall our *Hausfraa* was tempted to pot a few of the strongest plants for winter use, but she remembered the dire tradition that a member of the family will die if parsley is transplanted into pots. She will let the old plants in the bed go to seed. In the meanwhile she sowed a new bed, even casting the seed upon the snow, for she knows how slow parsley is in germinating. The bed is again just within the garden gate, for there is no spot in her garden to which she has such frequent recourse. Somewhere in that garden there is a small plot of saffron, which also shows its slender leaves in early spring; later they will disappear, leaving a bare spot but for the sheathes of garlic, that most belligerent of the onion family, planted there among the saffron bulbs to ward off the destructive mice. In late summer, after a long dry spell followed by refreshing rains, the crocus-like lavender blossoms appear. The three golden stigmata that each blossom bears are carefully gathered, dried and put away in the saffron caddy, to be used for flavoring and coloring noodles, dumplings, chicken soup and potpie, and sundry breads and cakes. The garlic, standing guard among the saffron, renders twofold service, for some of its cloves will find their way into our *Hausfraa's* much vaunted *Gnowwlochwarscht*, her garlic sausage.

In sharp contrast with the deep green shadows of an ancient boxwood, stands a gnarled sagebrush, drooping its silvery-gray branches into the garden path. Our Pennsylvania German housewife dries its leaves for winter use. She is less given to the use of sage in fowl stuffing than her Anglo-Saxon sisters, but a strong decoction of sage leaves is so good for gargling a sore throat. Hard by the old boxwood the crown imperial will soon be lifting its haughty brow and the peony *materna* display its crimson splendor.

Somewhere along wall or fence horseradish stalks will be twirling their awkward foliage in rank disorder. In late winter and early spring their roots, ground and mixed with vinegar, salt and sugar, will furnish a pungent condiment which her family likes to eat with pork, and hard-boiled eggs, and especially with boiled ham and parsnips.

Not too far away, where they are least in the way of the usual garden vegetables and where they can grow unmolested, stand other favorite perennial herbs. Some of them are little used but have always been there and somehow seem to belong to the other intimates of the family. Our housewife could hardly do without her clumps of thyme, her *Kwendeltee*, which she uses not only to flavor meats, soups and fried potatoes, but from which she brews a "tea" in spring to thin out the blood of her family after the sluggish winter time. She is particularly fond of her *Maranstock*, the sweet marjoram, so good for seasoning heavy meats such as pork, but also delicious in potato soup, in coleslaw, and sprinkled over the tender first turnips. Her forefathers had called it *Warschtgraut*. It added a delicious flavor to their sausages. She loves its fragrance and thinks of it with gratitude, for a "tea" of it had hurried forth her children's stubborn measles. In the shelter of the old boxwood grows her little patch of *Buhnegreidel,* her summer savory, that retiring little annual that seeds itself. Its tender leaves add a delicate flavor to the early spring beans. Over there are a few stalks of lovage, the charming *Lieb-schteckel,* the seeds of which can be used for flavoring meats and soups, but which are kept rather for their association, although somewhat dimmed by time. Her Palatinate forefathers had sucked milk and honey through the hollow stems to alleviate a sore throat. This sweet-scented herb is a long way from home. From ancient Rome it made its way across the Alps with the establishment of monastic gardens. Among the peasantry of Europe it was considered especially potent as a love charm. — Some of the ancestral herbs never became firmly established in our Pennsylvania German gardens. Little known, if at all, are tarragon, sweet basil, burnet and winter savory.

Our Pennsylvania German *Hausfraa* likes the seed-producing herbs and grows such annuals as dill for cucumber preserves; coriander for seasoning her pork sausage — that coriander, to which the children of Israel had likened their manna: "and it was like coriander seed, white" (Exodus 16:31); caraway, or *Kimmel,* seeds she strews upon her bread and Christmas cookies and sprinkles over pickled beets and sauerkraut; fennel seed may take the place of caraway; and aniseed she needs for certain cakes and cookies.

Some few herbs are given a place in the garden solely for their sweet fragrance and beauty. There is *Rosmarein,* or rosemary, an ancient herb, like myrtle, sacred to *Venus*. It seems to have made its way from the Mediterranean basin, where it grew wild, to northern Europe in the early centuries of the Christian era. It was used upon life's most lofty occasions, at christenings, weddings and funerals, perhaps in the belief that its sweet odors kept sinister spirits away. The old folks used to lay a sprig of *Rosmarein* in their hymnbooks, wherewith to refresh their lagging spirits during the long sermons. So too bergamot, with its lemon scent, and garden balm and lavender adorn the garden and lend their fragrance to rooms, chests and drawers.

Various members of the mint family are garden favorites. The young leaves of garden mint and of the downy mint, or *Wollicher Balsem,* our Pennsylvania German housewife gathers and dries. She prefers the meadow balsam and the peppermint, both of which like "wet feet" and thrive best hard by the meadow springhouse and bordering the rill that flows from it. To increase her variety of "teas" she sends her men folks forth of a Sunday afternoon to gather dittany, her favored *Buschtee,* and the sweet goldenrod, the *Blobarricktee,* most highly prized of all. Perhaps she learned from her grandmother that such herbs are best gathered on the calendar day of John Huss (July 6) or on the day of the Assumption of the Virgin (August 15), for then their fragrant leaves will yield doubly strong those delightful effusions that grace her supper table during the winter months.

More valuable to the Pennsylvania German housewife than the culinary and sweet-scented herbs were those having medicinal properties. No people in America possesses so extensive a folk medicine as that of the Pennsylvania Germans. There was a time when no garden was without its horehound, or *Eedann,* bush, from which a decoction was made against cold, or a brew to be used in the making of horehound candy, delicious even without a cold; or the gray-leaved southernwood, *Alder Mann,* that herb of constancy; catnip, or *Katzegraut,* so good for baby's colic; chamomile, *Kamilletee,* an excellent tonic; feverfew, or *Meederle,* a good stomachic as well as a sudorific in fevers; valerian, or *Marienwarzel,* St. Mary's root, effective against dysentery; rue, lovely with its bluish-green foliage and rich in poetic associations, when steeped in whiskey furnishes the household with the familiar *Raudebidders* for stomach disorders; the root of the rhubarb provides a ready family laxative; and the dried panicles of the elder bush, leaning over the garden fence, steeped in boiling water, yield an excellent winter sudorific.

But the zealous housewife, reared in plant lore, goes beyond the confines of her garden. Meadow, field and forest give forth their precious medicinal herbs. Her winter store contains pennyroyal, or *Groddebalsem,* that king of medicinal herbs; mountain mint, with its charming German name *Wohlgemut* (of good cheer); boneset, or *Darrichwachs,* whose stem grows right through its coupled leaves, a good emetic and purgative; speedwell, or *Ehrenpreis* (praise and honor) useful in preparing a throat gargle; and cinquefoil, or *Fimffingergraut,* believed by some to prevent forgetfulness, and efficacious in staying severe cases of dysentery. These are but a few of the many herbs whose very names convey their charm and rich association to the ears of those reared in the Pennsylvania German counties. A more detailed consideration of them lies beyong the scope of this chapter.*

# GREENS

STRANGERS journeying through the German-populated counties of eastern and southeastern Pennsylvania on late February days or in March behold a strange spectacle. Everywhere along roadsides and in open fields, even though snowdrifts may be lingering here and there, they will see men and women and children with baskets or bags bending over and cutting young dandelion plants. At this time of the year all true Pennsylvania Germans yearn for a "mess" of dandelion salad. While it is true that dandelion is eaten in other parts of the country, boiled after the manner of spinach, it is only here that it is served as a salad with the famed Pennsylvania German hot bacon dressing and adorned with sliced hard-boiled eggs. Dandelion, with its aristocratic Norman-French name, grew over wide areas of Europe, followed the early settlers to America, and is today one of our most common weeds. Both the English *dandelion* and the German *Löwenzahn* denote "lion's tooth," because of its deeply indented leaves. In our dialect it is sometimes called *Pissebett* (French pissenlit) referring to its diuretic properties, but it is perhaps best known and characterized among the Pennsylvania Germans as *bidderer Selaat* (bitter salad).

This lowly weed attains its full glory on Maundy Thursday. Serving a dish of greens on *Griener Dunnerschdaag*, or "Green Thursday" of Holy Week, is one of our most cherished and deeply-fixed traditions. Why this day should be called "Green Thursday" (the term occurs as early as the 12th century) is still controversial among folklorists, although it is likely that green is a pre-Christian symbol of the advent of spring. Of the various German customs associated with this day only this one remains here in Pennsylvania: the custom of eating something green in order to remain well throughout the year. Dandelion was of course not the only springtime green used on this day, but it has remained the most favored one through the years. In some parts of Germany it was the custom of serving on this day a dish containing seven different greens, or a seven-herb soup. Here, as so often in folklore, we have the appearance of the sacred number seven.*

---

*We refer our readers to the very excellent work Plant Names and Plant Lore among the Pennsylvania Germans by David E. Lick and the Rev. Thomas R. Brendle. The Pennsylvania German Society. Volume XXXIII, 1922.

*We have only once come upon an instance of this custom here in Pennsylvania. Our informant, Lillie Mary Angelina Himmelreich (name not fictitious!) of Sinking Springs, Berks County, tells of serving a dish in their household on *Griener Dunnerschdaag* consisting of a mixture of dandelion, beet tops, cabbage, onion tops, water cress, chives and *Krischble* (presumably wild lettuce) as a protection throughout the ensuing year against pneumonia. It is quite likely that this custom prevailed more extensively in earlier times and that the set-up of seven greens contained more of sorrel, dock, nettles or plantains.

Most of the wild plants eaten as greens in early spring were not unknown to the Pennsylvania Germans in their fatherland. They seem to have followed the early settlers to America. Some of them had been cultivated in old-world gardens, but here they got out of bounds and spread over the countryside as common weeds. Some few were native American plants which the early Pennsylvanians learned to know through their Indian friends.

Edible wild plants seem to have been in special favor and use among the Pennsylvania Germans. There were various reasons for this. Gathering greens along fence rows, in pasture lands and meadows appealed to the innate thriftiness of the Pennsylvania German housewife. After all, she was getting something for nothing, but for the slight effort of gathering them. But she also took pride in adding variety to her cookery. Some of the wild plants, so firmly established in Nature's habitat, responded more rapidly to spring growth than those in her own gardens and thus provided a welcome transition from the monotonous cooking of the latter winter months to her own first garden products. Then too there was the age-old folk tradition of the mystic use of green things in early spring, faint echo of the pagan celebration of the resurrection of Nature. Then again our Pennsylvania German housewife was steeped in the lore of folk medicine, and certain greens were considered effective as blood purifiers and antiscorbutics. To be sure, our forefathers knew nothing of vitamins, of thiamine and riboflavin, nor of the relative mineral contents of vegetables, but they sought to satisfy a certain "hidden hunger," an instinctive craving for fresh, growing things after the lack of them during the winter months. Research in our laboratories today indicates that wild plants growing in soil enriched only by Nature's own composting are rich in vitamin and mineral content and that the beautiful fresh vegetables now so readily accessible throughout the entire winter, having been forced by chemical fertilizers, are often lacking in that which we hope they contain.*

We believe it proper to include a consideration of greens in this cookbook, not only because they were once prominent in Pennsylvania German cookery, but also in the belief that we do well to resort once more to the use of wild plants as greens because of their rich vitamin and mineral contents. Some of the greens were preferably used as salads, others again were best adapted to use as potherbs.

The following are to be recommended for salads:

Water Cress (Nasturtium officinale), *Brunnegresse,* was known to our ancestors in the Palatinate. It was introduced from Europe and formerly cultivated. It now grows profusely in wet places, around springhouses and along the borders of springs and creeks. Used chiefly as a garnish it deserves to be used in larger quantities. It is delicious when served with a dandelion or endive dressing (see Index).

*We refer our readers to U. S. Department of Agriculture Miscellaneous Publication No. 572 which contains a Table listing 37 plants and which indicates that the common dandelion contains more Vitamin A than any other, with 13,650 international units, whereas spinach contains only 9,420 and our much-used head lettuce only 540!

Wild Lettuce (Lactuca canadensis), *Millichgraut,* is native to our fields and fence rows. It must be gathered early in spring and is best served like dandelion.

Corn Salad (Valerianella), *Ritscherli,* was known in the Palatinate and formerly was cultivated in our gardens. This too is best served with a bacon dressing or one of the cream dressings (see Index).

Catchfly (Silene inflata), *Dauwekreppche Selaat,* Pigeon Crop Salad, was also in earlier days cultivated in our gardens. It is best served like the Corn Salad above.

The modern housewife will of course not hesitate to deviate from the old-time preparation of the above salads. These greens can be used singly or in combination, and tossed in a French dressing. And all of them can be used as potherbs, boiled with ham or bacon and potatoes. But these tender leaves with their delicate flavor hardly deserve this act of violence.

Of the following potherbs once used by the Pennsylvania Germans, some few are still prepared, but most of them have fallen into disuse — more's the pity!

Sorrel (Rumex acetosa), our familiar *Sauerambel,* whose tart leaves children roaming the fields still love to chew in spring, was extensively used. Various forms of it are cultivated in European gardens and used for salads, potherbs, in soups and in the making of fish and meat sauces. This very useful perennial should once more find a place in our gardens (listed in Burpee's seed catalog). Our Pennsylvania German forefathers knew it only in its wild form, but used it for salads, cooked greens and even in pies (see Index).

Dock (Rumex crispus), known in the vernacular as *Schpitzicher Halwer Gaul* (pointed half-horse!) was perhaps the most favored of all the wild potherbs. The leaves must be gathered when still very tender and are good boiled with ham or bacon and potatoes. Mrs. William J. Kressler offers this recipe: boil the young leaves in salt water for 3 minutes, drain and serve with hot bacon salad dressing (see Index).

Both sorrel and dock were close seconds to dandelion as salad greens. When used as such there is a special dressing for them in the chapter of Salads and Salad Dressings (see Index).

Shepherd's Purse (Capsella bursa pastoris), *Deschelgraut,* came from Europe, but now grows far and wide as a weed. Its young leaves offer a good potherb.

Winter Cress (Barbarea vulgaris), known in the dialect as *Leffelgraut* because of its spoon-like leaves, came from Europe, but has spread over our cultivated fields as a weed. Some may find this member of the mustard family somewhat bitter and prefer to combine it with some other spring green as a potherb.

Purslane (Portulaca aleracea), the familiar *Seibarzel,* which grows so profusely in our gardens as a low, spreading weed with thick, reddish, succulent stems and small leaves, is popular in many lands and was formerly used here as a potherb. We suggest that this be boiled with some other potherb like Shepherd's Purse.

Common Plantain (Plantago major), familiar to every Pennsylvania German by the name of *Seiohrebledder*, pigs' ears, can well be used as a potherb if the leaves are taken when quite young. One informant, Mrs. Stanley Arthur, writes: "Scald and drain the leaves twice before adding to the ham or bacon. They ask for a dash of vinegar."

Stinging Nettle (Urtica dioica), *Brennessel*, was used for "greens" when taken young. It was considered a preventive against scurvy. The leaves possess a delicate flavor and are good in soups.

Pokeweed (Phytolacca decandra), *Dindebeere*, or ink bush, is one of the most desirable of our edible wild plants. Our forefathers used to cover the roots with leaves or corn stalks in late fall. In early spring, thus protected, the thick succulent shoots would appear like bleached asparagus and were cut when four or five inches high. These shoots can be used as potherbs and are then best mixed with other herbs like dock or sorrel. But it is better to serve them like asparagus. Put them into boiling water for a minute, drain them, boil until tender, drain again and serve either with browned butter and seasoning or a white sauce.

Burdock (Arctium minus), the common *Gledde* of our dialect, with its large rhubarb-like leaves, whose seeds and roots were considered excellent blood purifiers, was also used as greens. Its tender leaf stems are gathered in early spring, peeled and boiled, but since they are rather strong in flavor they are best used with other potherbs such as plantain, dock, purslane or sorrel. — There is one other way of preparing them, so interesting that we give it here as it came from our aged informant, Mrs. William J. Kressler, who writes: "And did you ever eat the justly despised burdock? If you have not, you will agree with Emerson's definition of a weed as a plant whose virtues have not been discovered. Take the thick stalks of the burdock, and cut them, after peeling them as you do rhubarb, in four-inch lengths. Boil them in salted water until tender. Drain and when cool, take three stalks at a time, tie them together with thread, dip in beaten egg, roll in bread crumbs and fry. I got this recipe from a friend who got it from an old German woman who lived on Morgan's Hill." —

A few concluding remarks about the preparation of the above-mentioned wild edible greens may be in order. In gathering them, do not pull the leaves or stems, but cut them. A few of the above — water cress, dandelion, sorrel, early dock, wild lettuce and corn salad, are good served raw with one or the other of the hot bacon or sour cream dressings (see Index).

But the others are best used as potherbs; that is, when boiled with a piece of ham, bacon or salt pork, seasoning and diced potatoes. The meat liquor should be reduced to a minimum before the potherbs are added and boiled but a few minutes, thus losing none of the mineral values of the greens. Dock and sorrel can each be cooked alone, but the rest, with more decided flavors, some housewives will prefer to cook together with others. Any one or a combination of plantain, poke shoots, purslane and burdock, are, for example, better mixed with dock, sorrel or nettles. Some may prefer simply to boil these greens in salt water and serve them chopped, seasoned and dressed with butter, like spinach. In that case we advise that plantain, burdock, purslane, poke shoots and nettle be parboiled about five minutes, drained, then steamed in very little salted water until tender. Of course some of the mineral values will thus be lost.

We conclude with the hope that some of our readers will be induced to go forth and gather the wild edible plants that grow so abundantly along our highways and in the open fields and meadows. Some few will be found mild and gentle; others are more forceful in character and the eating of them will be a matter of taste, and of course — *de gustibus non est disputandum* — yet, on the other hand,

> *Better is little, with the fear of Jehovah,*
> *Than great treasure and trouble therewith.*
> *Better is a dinner of herbs, where love is,*
> *Than a stalled ox and hatred therewith.*
>
> Proverbs 15:16, 17.

SAFFRON BOXES

ELEANOR BARBA.

Springhouse and hakeoven on the farm formerly owned by Maria Jung, better known in
Pennsylvania colonial history and legend as *Die Baerrick Maria*, or "Mountain Mary."
Pike Township, Berks County, Pa.

# Breads, Rolls Biscuits, Muffins

*En halwer Leeb Brot iss besser ass gaar ken Brot*

Half a loaf or half a ton —
Each is better far than none!

What unsung housewife ages ago, Prometheus-like, snatched from the gods the precious possession of the yeast plant and bestowed it upon her mortal kin? Or was she some caveman's slatternly mate who gossiped over the back fence while her batch of dough was slowly fermenting? Was leavened bread an accident like the roast pig in Charles Lamb's delightful essay? Or was it a miracle that of the 200 and more sorts of yeast plants that float about in the air about us the right sort attached itself to the rudely ground grain of ancient days and man ate aërated bread for the first time in history? Be that as it may, provided with fire and with yeast man challenged the gods and started upon his slow upward journey.

Ferments became the kindly agents of the tiller of the soil, with whose aid he preserved what the good earth provided. Through them the vintage was converted into the wines that gladdened the heart of man. Fermented cabbage, known to the world as sauerkraut, preserved him from the attacks of scurvy through the long northern winters. Ferments converted the abundant harvests of wheat, rye and barley, into potable beers and digestible starches in the form of leavened bread.

What a pity that modern housewives are so little given to the use of yeast. Indeed many fear to work with it. Yeast-baking still provides one of the great kitchen adventures. Here as nowhere else in cookery art dominates over science. In this domain the Pennsylvania German housewife excels. Where else does one find so many delightful creations of yeast dough? (See Chapter XI.) Yeast-baking is a deep-seated tradition among us. The outdoor bakeoven of the Rhineland and of the Palatinate became firmly established in the new world. Our Pennsylvania landscape is dotted with these old ovens, some attached to the kitchen and approached from within, others standing in the open a short distance from the kitchen, a quaint bit of old-world architecture with their low projecting roofs and side shelves to receive the rows of loaves and pies that came forth from their capacious interiors. Friday was the traditional baking-day. Baking was indeed a major operation, not only in the preparation of the breads, begun the day before, but of the many pies and

11

cakes that had to be done when the big bake oven was put into weekly action. The housewife knew by long experience just when the interior glowed with the right temperature.   Then she hurried to scrape out the wood coals with her *Offekitsch,* swab the oven-floor of ashes with her long-handled broom of slivered hickory saplings or her rag *Huddelwisch,* plunged into a bucket of cold water.   Only then was she ready nimbly to toss the loaves from the straw baskets on to the long peel (*der Backoffeschiesser*) and slide them to the rear of the oven, in order to leave space in front for the pies which baked more quickly and were the first to be removed.   Most of these great old ovens are inactive today, but the art of baking with yeast is still practiced among us.   In the following recipes we have endeavored to adapt the processes to the modern kitchen.

### POTATO YEAST
#### (Liquid Yeast)

| | |
|---|---|
| 1½ quarts water | 1 tablespoon sugar |
| 6 medium-sized potatoes, grated raw | 1 tablespoon salt |

1 yeast cake or 1 cup potato yeast

Bring water to boiling and add potatoes, sugar and salt.  Boil 5 minutes, stirring constantly.  Pour into some receptacle previously scalded.  Allow to cool until lukewarm.  Add yeast cake or cup of potato yeast and set aside in a warm place for 24 hours.  When light and foamy store the vessel, tightly covered, in a cool place and use as needed for baking.  Be sure to reserve 1 cup as a "starter" for next mixture.  One cup of liquid yeast may be used in place of yeast cake in bread recipes, taking that much less of liquid called for in recipe.  This yeast should not be kept longer than 2 weeks without starting a fresh supply.

*Adapted from the Bethlehem Cook Book, 1900.*

Do you remember the days when your mother or perhaps your grand-mother sent you with a tiny tin pail to the cross little old woman around the corner for a penny's worth of yeast?   And the crosser she was the better the yeast! — You may even recall that picturesque piece of kitchen furniture, the doughtrough (*die Backmol),* in which the large mass of bread dough was mixed.  After it had been removed into the straw bread baskets for its last rising, the frugal housewife or her daughter used a little iron scraper (*die Deegkitsch*) with which she carefully scraped together the bits of dough, which was then used as leaven or "starter" for the next yeast. — There is an old doughtrough story that used to be told the daughters of the household as a lesson in frugal housekeeping.   A canny young Pennsylvania German farmer sent word throughout the community that he had a sick horse that required frequent dosages of doughtrough scrapings.   A number of girls responded promptly with generous amounts of scrapings.   But one replied saucily that she never had any scrapings left over. She was just the sort he was looking for. They were happily married and prospered.

*When starting yeast do not forget to put in the names of three shrews.*

## HOMEMADE BREAD

*Backkarb Leeb, gebacke drauss*
*Im grosse alde Backoffe,*
*Mit de siesse Holsesch Gruscht,*
*Hot alles iwwerdroffe.**

| | |
|---|---|
| 1 cup potato yeast | 2 teaspoons salt |
| (or 1 yeast cake) | 1 tablespoon sugar |
| 1 cup lukewarm scalded milk | 1 tablespoon shortening |
| (2 cups with yeast cake) | 6 to 7 cups sifted flour |
| 1 cup mashed potato | |

Combine yeast, milk, potato, salt, sugar and shortening. (If yeast cake is used add two cups of milk instead of one.) Measure 6 cups of sifted flour into bowl and gradually blend liquid mixture with it. If necessary, add more flour. Knead until it is elastic and no longer sticks to the hand. Place in bowl, cover and set in a uniformly warm place (about 85°). Let rise until double its original bulk. Cut it down from the sides of the bowl and knead once more until free from gas bubbles. It may be necessary to add more flour at this time. Mold into 2 loaves and place into 2 lightly greased breadpans. Cover and set in warm place. When doubled in bulk bake in hot oven, 425° F., for 15 minutes, then reduce to 350° and bake 40 to 50 minutes longer. Bread is done when crust is brown and shrinks from sides of pan. — In bread recipes it is not possible to give the exact amount of flour required. If hard-wheat flour is used the dough should be left to rise 3 times its original bulk. If soft-wheat flour, then only twice the original bulk. In Pennsylvania an all-round flour blended of hard and soft wheat is commonly used.

## OATMEAL LOAF

| | |
|---|---|
| 1 cup oatmeal | 1 teaspoon sugar |
| ½ cup hot milk | ½ teaspoon salt |
| 1 cup white-bread dough | 2 cups sifted flour (scant) |
| 1 teaspoon butter, melted | |

Since this recipe calls for 1 cup of white-bread dough, it is most conveniently used when baking wheaten bread, thus adding variety to your batch of loaves.

Mix the oatmeal and milk and cool to lukewarm. Add the dough (which has risen overnight) and the dry ingredients. Knead a few minutes, cover

*Loaves raised in straw baskets and baked in the big old out-door ovens, with crust sweet with fragrant woodashes, surpassed all else.—From Joseph P. Delbert's *Der Mudder Ihre Disch.*

closely and set in a warm place to rise for about 1 hour, or until double in bulk. Punch down, knead and form into a loaf. Place in a greased bread pan and brush with the melted butter. Let rise again for 1 hour, or until double in bulk. Bake in a moderate oven, 350° F., for 40 to 45 minutes. Raisins may be added, if desired.

## OSCHDER BROD
### (Easter Bread)

A favorite recipe contributed by Mary J. Barber, Food Consultant of the U. S. War Department, from the cookbook of her sister, Edith Barber. The Barbers' interest in food traces back to their Pennsylvania German ancestry. Their great-great-grandfather came to Lancaster County from Germany.

| | |
|---|---|
| 1 yeast cake | ½ cup sugar |
| 1 cup scalded milk, lukewarm | 4 egg yolks, well beaten |
| 1 teaspoon salt | ½ cup melted shortening |
| 4½ cups sifted flour | |

Crumble the yeast cake into the milk and stir until dissolved. Add the salt, sugar, and egg yolks, reserving a small amount, and half the shortening and flour. Beat until smooth. Add the remaining flour and mix well, then the remaining shortening and mix well. Knead on a floured board until the dough is smooth, then place in a greased bowl, cover, and let stand in a warm place to rise until double in bulk. Divide the dough into 2 parts and place in greased bread pans. Brush the tops with melted butter and let rise again until double in bulk. Brush with the remaining egg yolk, diluted with water. Bake in a moderate oven, 350° F., for 35 to 40 minutes.

## BRAN BREAD

| | |
|---|---|
| 2 cups white flour | 4 cups bran |
| 4 teaspoons baking powder | 1 tablespoon melted butter |
| 1 teaspoon salt | 2 cups milk |
| ½ cup molasses | |

Sift together the flour, baking powder and salt, and add bran. Add the melted butter and mix in the milk to form a soft batter. Add the molasses. Pour into 2 greased 8-inch square pans. Bake in a hot oven, 400° F., for about 25 minutes. Cut into small squares.

## RAISIN BREAD

| | |
|---|---|
| 1 medium-sized potato, pared | 1 cup sugar |
| 3 cups water | 1 tablespoon butter |
| 9 cups sifted flour (about) | 1 pound seedless raisins |
| 1 yeast cake | 2 teaspoons cinnamon |
| 1 cup warm water | ½ teaspoon cloves |

Boil the potato in the quart of water, remove, and mash. Mix enough flour with the potato water to make a smooth batter. Dissolve the yeast cake in the warm water. Add to the batter and set aside in a warm place to rise for 4 hours. Then add the remaining ingredients and knead well on a lightly floured board. Add more flour if necessary, but be careful not to let dough get too stiff. Let rise for 2 hours more, then form into 3 loaves. Place in greased bread pans and let rise until light. Bake in a hot oven, 400° F., for 10 minutes, then reduce to 350° F. and bake for about 25 minutes.

### NUT AND RAISIN BREAD

| | |
|---|---|
| 1 cup sifted white flour | 2 cups sour milk (or |
| 1 teaspoon baking powder | buttermilk) |
| 2 cups graham flour | ½ cup brown sugar |
| 1 teaspoon soda | 1 cup seeded raisins |
| | ¼ cup ground peanuts |

¼ cup chopped walnuts

Sift together the white flour and baking powder, add the graham flour and mix well. Add the soda, which has been dissolved in the milk, and the brown sugar. Mix thoroughly, and add the raisins and nuts. Pour into a greased loaf pan. Bake in a moderate oven, 350° F., for about 1 hour.

### NUT BREAD

| | |
|---|---|
| ¾ cup sugar | 2½ cups sifted flour |
| 1 egg, well beaten | 5 teaspoons baking powder |
| 1 cup milk | 2 cups English walnuts, |
| | chopped |

Gradually add the sugar to the egg, then stir in the milk. Sift together the flour and baking powder and stir into the egg mixture. Add the nuts last. Pour into a buttered bread pan and let rise 20 minutes, or until nearly double in bulk. Bake in a slow oven, 300° F., for about 60 minutes. Cut in thin slices, butter and place 2 pieces together. Serve as sandwiches.

### DUNKER COMMUNION BREAD

Among the earliest sectarians to come to Pennsylvania were the Dunkards, known also as Dunkers and "Tunker," so called because they baptized by adult immersion or dipping (Ger. *tunken*, to dip). Under their capable leaders, Alexander Mack and Peter Becker, they established flourishing congregations in Lancaster, Berks, Dauphin and Lebanon Counties. Most influential among them was Christopher Sauer the Elder, who gave the Pennsylvania Germans their first German almanac (1739) and their first newspaper in German type (1739), and who printed the first Bible in the American colonies (1743).

Their communion bread is unleavened, therefore the absence of any leavening agent in this recipe. This bread is served, together with wine, at all Dunker love-feasts. Their service is divided into three parts: First the feet-washing, then the love-feast meal, and then the communion.

| | |
|---|---|
| 1 pound butter | 3 cups milk |
| 3 cups light cream | 4 teaspoons salt |

20 cups sifted flour, approximately

Cream the butter, add the cream, milk and salt. Then gradually stir into this mixture the flour in quantity to form a soft dough. Knead for 1 hour. Spread the dough about ¾ inch thick in large, shallow, greased pans. Then perforate into 2½-inch squares. Mark each square with 5 nail prints, to symbolize the 5 wounds of Jesus. Bake in a moderate oven, 350° F., for 1 hour, until a light golden brown. Cover with a damp cloth and let stand overnight, or until ready to serve. Cut in long slabs of several squares each and set aside for the communion service.

*Mrs. Wayne Keller*

### MORAVIAN LOVE-FEAST BUNS

These buns are served with mugs of steaming coffee at Moravian love-feasts, when members of the congregation eat and drink together in the fellowship of the Lord.

| | |
|---|---|
| 1½ cups light brown sugar | 14 cups sifted winter flour |
| 1½ cups butter and lard | 14 cups sifted spring flour |
| 4 eggs, well beaten | ¼ cup salt |
| ¼ cup malt | ¼ pound yeast |

4 cups water

Cream the sugar and butter together, and add the eggs. Mix together the malt and both types of flour. Add the salt. Dissolve the yeast in the water and add, alternately with the flour, to the first mixture. Let rise to half again its former bulk, then shape the dough into balls. Press them flat about ¾ inch thick and about 2 inches in diameter and place on greased baking sheets. Let rise again until double in bulk. Bake in a moderate oven, 350° F., for about 30 to 40 minutes.

This large recipe, devised for Moravian communal feasts, can readily be reduced to ¼ the amount. We also suggest that cake flour be substituted for winter flour.

### RAISED ROLLS

| | |
|---|---|
| 3 eggs, well beaten | 1 teaspoon salt |
| ½ cup sugar | 2 yeast cakes |
| 1 cup melted shortening | 3 tablespoons warm water |
| 1 cup warm water | 2 tablespoons sugar |

6½ cups sifted flour (about)

Mix together in a large bowl the eggs, sugar, shortening, water, and salt. Dissolve the yeast cakes in the warm water and 2 tablespoons of sugar, and

add to the egg mixture.  Add enough flour to make a soft dough and beat
well for 5 minutes.  Add the remainder of the flour to make a stiff dough and
let rise until double in bulk.  Divide the dough into sections, roll each section
into a disc ¼ inch thick and brush with melted butter.  Cut each disc into 8
pie-shaped wedges or triangles, and roll each triangle, beginning at the point.
Place on greased baking sheets and let rise again until double in bulk.  Bake
in a very hot oven, 450° F., for 15 minutes.  Makes about 3 dozen rolls.

*Mrs. William Engel*

## VIENNA ROLLS

| | |
|---|---|
| 1 tablespoon butter | 2 teaspoons baking powder |
| 4 cups sifted flour | ½ teaspoon salt |

1½ cups milk (about)

Place the butter in a bowl and soften it with a spoon.  Sift together the
flour and baking powder, and add to butter.  Add salt to milk and stir in
enough of the milk to make a fairly stiff dough.  Turn out on a well-floured
board and knead until smooth.  Roll out ½ inch thick and cut into 4-inch
rounds.  Wet each round slightly with water so it will not stick together and
fold over into half-moon shape.  Place on well-greased baking sheets, brush
with milk and bake in a hot oven, 400° F., for about 20 minutes.  Makes about
16 rolls.

## RAISED BISCUITS

| | |
|---|---|
| 1 yeast cake | 6 cups sifted flour (about) |
| 2 cups scalded milk, lukewarm | ½ cup butter and lard |
| ¼ cup sugar | 1 egg, separated |
| ½ teaspoon salt | 1 teaspoon sugar |

Dissolve the yeast in a little of the milk, add half of the sugar, the salt,
and stir into the remaining milk.  Add 2 cups of the flour, beat well, cover and
set in a warm place for 1 hour, until light and foamy.  Cream the butter and
remaining sugar, add the egg white, beaten stiff, and the remaining flour.
Combine with the first mixture.  Knead on a well-floured board for about 5
minutes, then place in a bowl and let rise again until double in bulk.  Pat out
about ½ inch thick, cut in 2-inch rounds, and brush the tops with a mixture
of the egg yolk, sugar, and a little milk.  Place on greased baking sheets and
let rise until double in bulk.  Bake in a moderately hot oven, 375° F., for 15
to 20 minutes.  Makes about 3½ dozen biscuits.

## POTATO BISCUITS

| | |
|---|---|
| ½ yeast cake | 1 cup mashed potatoes |
| 1 cup potato water | 1 egg |
| 1 teaspoon sugar | 2 tablespoons butter |
| 3 cups sifted flour | ½ teaspoon salt |

Melted butter

Dissolve the yeast in 1 cup of the water in which potatoes were boiled. Add the sugar and 1 cup of the flour. Add the potatoes, cooled to lukewarm. Stand in a warm place and let rise for 1 hour or more, until light and foamy. Beat together the egg, butter, and salt, and add. Stir in the remaining flour and let rise for 1 hour. Pat out 1-inch thick, cut into small rounds and dip each round in melted butter. Place on baking sheet, fairly close together, and let rise for 1 hour. Bake in a moderately hot oven, 375° F., about 25 minutes. Makes about 2 dozen biscuits.

### CREAM BISCUITS

| | |
|---|---|
| ¼ pound butter | 1 tablespoon cream |
| 1 cup powdered sugar (about) | 2 cups sifted flour |
| 1 egg | 2 teaspoons baking powder |
| ½ teaspoon salt | |

Cream together the butter and sugar, add the flour, egg, and cream. Beat well. Roll out very thin, and cut with a floured 2-inch biscuit cutter. Place on ungreased baking sheet. Bake in a hot oven, 400° F., about 10 minutes, or until a light golden brown. Makes about 1 dozen biscuits.

### "TANTE" BETTY'S BUTTERMILK BISCUITS

| | |
|---|---|
| ½ teaspoon soda | 4 cups sifted flour |
| 1 teaspoon salt | 1 tablespoon lard |
| 1 cup buttermilk | |

Sift together the soda, salt, and flour, and rub in the lard. Make a hole in the center of the mixture and pour in the milk, a little at a time, mixing thoroughly each time. Toss onto a well-floured board and knead the dough until perfectly smooth. Then roll out ½ inch thick, cut in 2-inch rounds, and place on a greased baking sheet. Bake in a hot oven, 400° F., for about 10 minutes. Makes about 24 biscuits.

### PEANUT MUFFINS

| | |
|---|---|
| 1 egg, separated | 3 teaspoons baking powder |
| ½ cup sugar | ½ teaspoon salt |
| ½ cup milk | 1 tablespoon melted butter |
| 2 cups sifted flour | ½ cup peanuts and pecans, ground |

Beat together the egg yolk and sugar. Add the milk alternately with the sifted dry ingredients. Then add the butter. Fold in egg white, beaten stiff and the ground nuts. Pour batter into well-greased gem pans. Let stand for ½ hour. Then bake in a moderate oven, 350° F., for 30 minutes. Makes 8 biscuits.

## RAISED BREAKFAST MUFFINS

| | |
|---|---|
| 3 cups sifted flour | ¼ cup warm water |
| 1 teaspoon sugar | 1 tablespoon butter |
| 1 teaspoon salt | 2 eggs, well beaten |
| 1 yeast cake | 2 cups boiled milk, lukewarm |

Sift together the flour, sugar, and salt. Add the yeast which has been dissolved in the warm water. Add the butter and mix well. Then add the eggs and milk, and set aside in a warm place. Cover and let rise overnight. In the morning, without stirring, drop dough from tablespoon into warm, well-greased gem pans and let stand a short time until quite light. Bake in a hot oven, 400° F., about 15 minutes. Makes 12 muffins.

## RICE MUFFINS

| | |
|---|---|
| 1 cup cold boiled rice | 2 teaspoons baking powder |
| 1 egg, separated | 2 cups sifted flour |
| ½ teaspoon salt | 1 cup milk |
| 1 teaspoon sugar | 1 tablespoon melted butter |

Combine the rice, egg yolk, salt, and sugar and beat well. Sift the dry ingredients and add alternately with the milk. Beat the egg white until stiff, and add. Pour into greased muffin pans and bake in a hot oven, 400° F., for 20 to 25 minutes. Makes about 15 muffins.

## BIG VALLEY BRAN MUFFINS
### (An Amish recipe)

| | |
|---|---|
| 1 cup sifted flour | ¼ teaspoon salt |
| 1½ cups bran | 1 egg |
| ½ cup brown sugar | 1 cup milk |
| 3 teaspoons baking powder | 1 tablespoon melted butter |

Mix together the dry ingredients. Beat the egg and milk together and add. Then add the butter. Pour batter into greased muffin tins. Bake in a moderate oven, 350° F., for about 35 minutes, according to size of muffins. Makes 8 large muffins.

## CORN MUFFINS

| | |
|---|---|
| 1½ tablespoons sugar | 2 cups sifted flour |
| 2 eggs | Pinch of salt |
| 1½ cups milk | 3 teaspoons baking powder |
| 1 cup corn meal | 1 tablespoon melted butter |

Beat together the sugar and eggs, add the milk and corn meal. Sift the dry ingredients together and add to first mixture. Add the butter and mix well. Pour into greased gem pans. Make in a hot oven, 400° F., for 30 minutes, according to size of muffins. Makes 12 large muffins.

### STEAMED CORN BREAD

| | |
|---|---|
| 4 cups corn meal | 4 teaspoons soda |
| 2 cups sifted flour | 2 tablespoons warm water |
| 4 cups buttermilk | ¾ cup sugar, or molasses |
| 4 teaspoons salt | |

Mix the corn meal and flour, and stir in the buttermilk. Dissolve the soda in the warm water and add with the sugar and salt. Pour batter into a large greased mold, filling ⅔ full. Cover tightly, and place in pan of hot water. Steam for 3 hours.

### WELSCHKORNKUCHE
### (Corn Cake)
#### (From an old Pennsylvania German almanac)

| | |
|---|---|
| 4 cups corn meal | Salt |
| Warm water | 2 eggs, well beaten |
| ½ yeast cake | 1 teaspoon soda |

Mix the corn meal with enough water to form a mash. Add the yeast dissolved in a little warm water and salt to taste. Cover and let stand overnight. In the morning, stir well and add the eggs and soda. Beat thoroughly with a large spoon. Pour into a buttered loaf pan. Bake in a moderate oven, 350° F., for 1 hour. — This is not "cake," but corn bread in loaf form.

### JOHNNYCAKE

| | |
|---|---|
| 1 teaspoon soda | 2 cups corn meal |
| 2 teaspoons warm water | 1 cup sifted flour |
| Pinch of salt | 1½ cups sour milk |
| 1½ tablespoons sugar | ⅓ cup butter and lard |
| 1 egg, separated | |

Dissolve the soda in the hot water. Mix together all the ingredients except the egg white. Beat egg white until stiff and add last. Pour mixture into a greased loaf pan. Bake in a hot oven, 400° F., about 45 minutes.

### SALLY LUNN

| | |
|---|---|
| 1 cup milk | 3 cups sifted flour (scant) |
| 2 eggs, well beaten | 3 tablespoons sugar |
| 1 teaspoon butter, melted | 3 teaspoons baking powder (scant) |

Mix together the milk and eggs. Add the butter. Sift together the dry ingredients and add to first mixture. Turn into a greased 9-inch square pan. Bake in a moderate oven, 350° F., for about 30 minutes.

## RAISED SWEET BUNS

| | |
|---|---|
| 2 cups mashed potatoes | 2½ cups water |
| 2 cups sugar | ½ cup lard |
| ¾ teaspoon salt | 1 yeast cake |

9 cups sifted flour

Mix together the potatoes, sugar, salt and lard. Dissolve the yeast cake in the water and add to potato mixture. Turn out on floured board and knead. Place in covered vessel and let rise until double its bulk. Put once more on floured board, work down and pat out 1 inch thick. Cut in 1-inch rounds. Let rise until light. Sprinkle the tops with granulated sugar and place on well-greased baking sheet. Bake in a moderate oven, 350° F., for about 20 minutes.

## HOT CROSS BUNS

| | |
|---|---|
| 2 cups sugar | ½ yeast cake |
| ½ cup butter | ¼ cup warm water |
| 2 eggs, well beaten | ½ teaspoon salt |
| 2 cups scalded milk, lukewarm | ⅛ teaspoon nutmeg |

6 cups sifted flour (about)

Mix the sugar, butter, eggs, and milk. Add the yeast which has been dissolved in the warm water. Sift the salt and nutmeg into the flour and add enough to make a fairly stiff dough. Let rise overnight. In the morning, toss onto a floured board, pat out ½ inch thick, cut in rounds and place close together on a well-greased baking sheet. Top each bun with a cross made of narrow strips of the dough. Let rise until light. Bake in a moderate oven, 350° F., for about 15 minutes. Makes about 36 buns.

## RUSKS

### (From an old Lancaster County almanac)

| | |
|---|---|
| 4 cups sifted flour | 3 egg yolks |
| 7 teaspoons baking powder | ½ cup butter |
| 1 teaspoon salt | 1 cup sugar |

Sift together the flour, baking powder, and salt. Beat the egg yolks thoroughly and add to them the butter and sugar. Stir enough water into the flour mixture to make a dough of the proper consistency for bread. Add the egg mixture and blend thoroughly. Form into small cakes and brush the top of each with sugar and water mixed. Then sprinkle with sugar. Place on greased baking sheet. Bake immediately in a moderately slow oven, 300°-325° F., for about 45 minutes, or until evenly browned and dry. Makes about 15 rusks.

## KIPFELS

(Probably a corruption of the German word **Gipfel**, meaning peak.)

| | |
|---|---|
| 1 yeast cake | 4 cups sifted flour |
| ¼ cup warm water | Pinch of salt |
| ¾ pound butter | 1 egg, beaten |
| 3 cups scalded milk, lukewarm | Coarse salt |

Caraway seeds

Dissolve the yeast cake in the warm water. Combine with the butter, milk, flour and salt. Let rise until light. Turn onto floured board and pat out 1 inch thick. Form into crescent shapes. Brush the tops with beaten eggs and sprinkle with a half-and-half mixture of coarse salt and caraway seeds. Place on a greased baking sheet. Bake in a hot oven, 400° F., for about 25 minutes.

*Annere Leit ihr Brot schmackt immer besser.*
Other people's bread always tastes better.

PAINTED BREAD TRAY

# Soups

*Was butt die Supp, wammer ken Leffel hot?*
What good is soup in dish or cup
Without a spoon to dip it up?

Pennsylvania German fare has always found generous expression in soups. They are a deep-seated tradition among us. Our pioneer forefathers remembered the wide-bellied *Suppehaffe* which stood constantly on the hearth in their Rhenish and Palatine homes ready to receive what the day afforded in the way of flesh, fowl, vegetables and herbs. There were soups for all seasons of the year. In early spring there were soups of herbs and "greens"; summer yielded young vegetables for milk and stock soups; on hotter days there were cold soups of fruits and berries such as currants and gooseberries; fall and winter called for sturdier soups of potatoes and dried legumes, of meats and sausages. In the New World increasing prosperity brought a greater plenty of meats, milk, butter and eggs. Soups of new vegetables such as corn, certain bean varieties, and in time the tomato, supplanted humbler soups. But herb, cider, apple, *Riwwel* and browned flour soups contained in this chapter are reminiscent of earlier times. — The soups prepared in the Pennsylvania German kitchen are for the most part thick soups. In many a household they often constitute the major portion of an evening meal. Except for the few clear soups with their unusual garnishes (see Index), only a few would serve as introductory to a more pretentious course dinner.

## APPLE SOUP

| | |
|---|---|
| 4 large apples | Lemon rind |
| 1 stick cinnamon | 2 tablespoons cornstarch |
| Juice of ½ lemon | ¼ cup currants |
| 1 cup red or white wine | |

23

Core and cut apples in small pieces, but do not pare them. Cover with water, add the cinnamon, the lemon juice, and the piece of rind. Boil the apples until almost soft. Mix the cornstarch with a small amount of water, add to apples and cook until fruit is done. Strain, add the currants and wine, and return to heat. Boil about 5 minutes longer. Serve either hot or cold. If desired, other fresh or dried fruits or berries may be used instead of apples. Serves 4. — Fruit soups, served cold in summer, are a German culinary tradition.

### ASPARAGUS SOUP

| | |
|---|---|
| 2 pounds fresh asparagus | 3 tablespoons flour |
| 4 cups chicken or beef broth | 2 egg yolks |
| 3 tablespoons butter | 2 tablespoons cream |

Clean and remove scales from asparagus stalks. Break off tender tips and boil them until tender, about 10 minutes. Break up tough ends of stalks and boil in broth until soft. Force through strainer. Blend butter and flour, and add asparagus pulp and broth, stirring until smooth and creamy. Beat egg yolks with cream and add to soup. Just before serving add the cooked asparagus tips. Serves 6.

### BEAN SOUP

| | |
|---|---|
| 1 pound navy beans | ½ cup diced potatoes |
| 1½ pounds ham (butt end) | ½ cup chopped onion |
| 2 cups tomatoes, strained | 2 cups diced celery |
| 2 teaspoons minced parsley | Salt and pepper |

Cover the beans with water and soak overnight. Drain, place the beans in a large amount of fresh water and cook until almost soft. Wash the ham thoroughly, cover with cold water, and boil until tender. Then skim off the fat, add the beans and other vegetables and season to taste with salt and pepper. Cook until vegetables are soft. Serve at once. Serves 8.

### BRAUNI WASSER SUPP
#### (Browned Flour Soup with Water)

| | |
|---|---|
| 1 ounce butter | Salt and pepper |
| 2 tablespoons flour | 2 eggs, beaten |
| 6 cups water | Buttered croutons |

Place butter in a saucepan, add the flour and brown it in the butter. Gradually add the water and let mixture boil for ½ hour, adding salt and pepper for seasoning. Stir in the beaten eggs and serve with croutons. Serves 6.

## BRAUNI MEHL SUPP
### (Browned Flour Soup with Stock)

| | |
|---|---|
| ⅔ cup flour | 5 cups hot soup stock |
| ¼ cup butter, melted | Salt and pepper |

Grated cheese

Stir the flour into the butter. Add the stock very slowly, stirring constantly to prevent lumps. Blend well and season to taste with salt and pepper. Cover the pot and simmer for ½ hour. Pour into individual bowls and sprinkle with grated cheese. Serve with croutons, if desired. Serves 4.

## CALF'S HEAD SOUP

| | |
|---|---|
| 1 calf's head | 1 teaspoon sweet marjoram |
| 3 tablespoons flour | ½ teaspoon cloves |
| 5 hard-cooked eggs, finely chopped | Butter Balls (see Index) |

Forcemeat Balls (see Index)

Remove the brains from the calf's head and soak head in salted water for ½ hour. Then boil until the meat is tender. Strain the broth, cut the meat fine, and return it to the broth. Brown the flour and add to the broth with the eggs and the seasonings. Add the Butter Balls and simmer for 10 minutes. Then add the Forcemeat Balls and serve. Serves 6.

## CALF'S HEAD SOUP

After removing the brain cook calf's head in water until meat is tender enough to remove from bone. Strain broth into another kettle. You need about 2 quarts of broth adding water if not enough is obtained from straining. Add 2 diced raw medium sized potatoes, 2 stems diced celery and one large diced onion. Remove meat from calf's head, let cool, cut it up, removing all fat and add to the broth. Add 1 tablespoon minced parsley and cook until vegetables are tender.

Crack an egg in a small bowl and add 1 tablespoon flour (or enough so that mixture can be dropped into soup). Drop with a fork over the top, let simmer 5 minutes, add salt and pepper to taste and 1 teaspoon nutmeg.

If desired, add sherry when served.

*Mrs Kensie N. Yoder*

## CHESTNUT SOUP

| | |
|---|---|
| 4 cups chestnuts | 2 cups rich cream |
| 4 teaspoons cooking oil | 1 teaspoon sugar |
| ¼ pound butter, melted | Pinch of cayenne |
| 8 cups rich veal stock | Salt |

Place chestnuts in pan, mix with oil and bake in hot oven, 450° F., for 20 minutes. When cool enough to handle, remove shells and skins with sharp knife. Toss into the butter, stirring constantly to avoid burning. Add the veal stock and boil for 20 minutes, or until chestnuts are tender. Remove chestnuts and mash them through a fine sieve. Return them to the broth, let it boil again, and add the remaining ingredients. Bring to a boil and serve. Serves 8.

## CHICKEN–CORN SOUP

Lowell Thomas, who claims Pennsylvania German descent through his mother, designates this soup as one of his favorites.

| | |
|---|---|
| 1 4-pound stewing chicken, | Parsley, chopped |
| cut in pieces | 12 ears corn, grated |
| Celery, diced | Salt and pepper |

Butter Balls (see Index)

Wash the chicken and place in kettle with water to cover. Boil until tender. Remove chicken from broth and cut meat from bones. Return meat to broth. Add, to taste, the celery, parsley, the corn and seasonings. Cook for 5 to 8 minutes. Add the Butter Balls and simmer for 10 minutes longer. Serves 6 to 8.

## CHICKEN–NOODLE SOUP

| | |
|---|---|
| 1 4-pound stewing chicken, | 1 carrot, sliced |
| cut in pieces | 1 teaspoon minced parsley |
| 3 quarts cold water | 1 bay leaf |
| 1 onion, sliced | Noodles (see Index) |

Wash the chicken, place in kettle with cold water and add the onion, carrot, and seasonings. Simmer for 3 hours or until the chicken is tender. Skim off the fat, remove the chicken, and add the noodles. Cook for 15 minutes. Return some of chicken meat to broth, if desired. Serves 6.

## CIDER SOUP

This soup is served in Pennsylvania German homes as part of the evening meal on cider-making day.

| | |
|---|---|
| 2 quarts cider | 2 cups milk |
| ¾ cup sugar | Allspice or nutmeg |
| 3 eggs, beaten | 3 cups diced bread |
| 3 tablespoons flour | Butter |

Boil the cider, skim, and add ½ cup of the sugar. Mix the eggs with the flour and add the milk, the remaining sugar and the desired spice. Pour into the boiling cider. Brown the diced bread in a little butter and add. Serves 6.

## CORN CHOWDER

| | |
|---|---|
| 1 ounce salt pork | 6 large soda crackers |
| 1 large onion, sliced | 1 cup milk |
| 4 large potatoes, sliced | 2 cups cooked corn |
| 2 cups water | 1 teaspoon salt |

¼ teaspoon paprika

Cube the salt pork and brown with the onion in a pan. Add the potatoes and water. Cook until the potatoes are soft. Soak the crackers in the milk and stir into the potatoes with the corn, salt, and paprika. Bring to a boil, remove from the heat, and serve. Serves 4 to 6.

## DUNKER LOVE-FEAST SOUP

This soup is served at Dunker, or Church of the Brethren, Love-feasts. On these occasions the back of every third pew in the church is turned over to make a table, which is set with knives, forks, tablespoons, and plates. As in all "Plain" churches, the men sit on one side and the women on the other side of the church. The love-feast meal, preceded by feet-washing, consists of bread and butter, hot sliced roast beef, and soup. The love-feast is followed by communion. (See Communion Bread, p. 15).

Boil until tender as much beef as is desired. Then remove from the broth, and grind. Wash rice, add to the broth and boil until tender. Then add the ground beef and reheat. Place dry bread crumbs 1 inch deep in the bottom of each serving bowl and pour soup on top.

*Mrs. Wayne Keller*

## GENERAL WASHINGTON'S SOUP

This recipe was handed down in the family of John Potts, whose home at Valley Forge was used by General Washington as headquarters during the Revolution. The soup is believed to have been a favorite with the Commander-in-Chief.

| | |
|---|---|
| 12 hard-shelled crabs | 2 tablespoons butter, melted |
| ⅛ pound lean bacon, diced | 2 tablespoons flour |
| 2 quarts water | 1 quart rich milk |

Salt and pepper

Boil the crabs in rapidly boiling salted water for 20 minutes. Plunge them in cold water and when cool enough to handle pick meat from the shell. Combine the crab meat, bacon, and water in a pan. Boil until only half of the liquid remains. Mix together the butter and flour. Gradually stir in the milk and cook for a few minutes until blended. Add to the crab-meat mixture, season to taste, and serve. Serves 6 to 8.

*Mrs. Albert T. von Trott*

## HERB SOUP

### (Kreidersupp)

| | |
|---|---|
| 1 cup young sorrel leaves | 2 tablespoons butter |
| 1 cup chervil | 2 egg yolks, beaten |
| 1 cup spinach | 4 cups beef broth or consommé |
| ¼ cup chopped parsley | ¼ cup bread crumbs |

Wash the greens. Place butter in saucepan and add the greens with water clinging to leaves. Steam until cooked. Force greens through strainer and add egg yolks to the pulp. Bring broth to a boil and add bread crumbs, made from grated bread crust. Add pulp, and serve at once. Serves 6.

## LENTIL SOUP

| | |
|---|---|
| 1 cup lentils | 4 cups ham or beef stock |
| 3 cups water | Small potatoes (optional) |

Wash and pick over lentils, rejecting imperfect ones. Cover with water and soak overnight. Drain, add water, and boil with meat for 3 hours, or until the lentils are soft. Toward the end of cooking time diced potatoes may be added, if desired, and boiled until tender. Serves 6 to 8.

## LENTIL SOUP

| | |
|---|---|
| 1 lb. smoked sausage cut in 1 inch pieces | 1 large onion, diced |
| 2 medium potatoes, diced | 1 cup lentils (do not soak) |
| 2 stems celery, diced | 2-3 quarts water |

Cook above ingredients until vegetables are soft (about 1 hour). Add 2 heaping tablespoons browned flour and simmer about 5 minutes. Salt and pepper to taste.

*Mrs. Kensie N. Yoder*

## OYSTER STEW

| | |
|---|---|
| 2 dozen oysters | 3 cups milk, scalded |
| 1 cup hot water (scant) | Salt and pepper |
| 3 tablespoons butter | Oyster crackers |

Remove the oysters from the liquor and add the hot water. Season to taste and allow to boil up once, then add the oysters, and bring to a boil. Simmer until the oysters start to ruffle at the edges. Add the butter, and when melted, add the heated milk and season to taste. Serve with oyster crackers. Serves 4 to 6.

## PANCAKE SOUP
### (Pannekuche Supp)

| | |
|---|---|
| 1 egg | Pinch of salt |
| 1 tablespoon flour | 1½ tablespoons butter or fat |
| ½ cup milk (about) | 6 cups beef stock or consomme |

Minced parsley (optional)

Beat the egg thoroughly and add gradually to the flour. Add milk to make a thin batter and season with salt. Heat butter or fat in frying pan, pour batter into pan and let it run into a large thin cake. Brown on both sides. Roll and cut into slender threads. Drop pancake slices into hot stock or consommé. Let it boil up once and serve immediately. Minced parsley may be added to the pancake batter, if desired. Serves 6.

## GREEN PEA SOUP

| | |
|---|---|
| 1 quart fresh peas | Sugar |
| 1 bunch parsley | White pepper |
| 1 carrot, sliced | 2 egg yolks, beaten |
| 1 ounce butter | 3 tablespoons cream |
| 6 cups soup stock | Diced bread |

Shell the peas and combine with parsley, carrot, butter and soup stock. Simmer together until the peas are tender. Force vegetables through a fine sieve and return to soup stock. Season with a little sugar, white pepper. Combine egg yolks and cream. Add to soup stock and serve piping hot. Top with bread which has been browned in butter. Serves 6.

## PEA POTAGE
### (A springtime soup)

| | |
|---|---|
| 3 small onions | 1 pint shelled peas |
| 1 small head lettuce, shredded | 2 cups water |
| 1 tablespoon flour | 1 egg, beaten |
| 3 tablespoons butter | ½ cup cream |

Chopped parsley

Chop onions, including green tops, and combine with lettuce. Melt 1 tablespoon of the butter in saucepan, add flour and mix well. Add onions and lettuce, and steam for a few minutes. Boil peas in the water until tender. Add to onion and lettuce. Add eggs and cream, the remaining butter, and parsley as desired. Serve at once. Serves 6.

*A Palatine recipe.*

## SPLIT PEA SOUP

| | |
|---|---|
| 1 cup split peas | 3 tablespoons flour |
| 3 quarts water | 3 tablespoons melted butter |
| 1 ham bone | 1 teaspoon salt |
| 1 tablespoon minced onion | 1/8 teaspoon pepper |
| | 2 cups milk |

Wash the peas, cover with water and soak overnight. Drain, place in pan with the fresh water, add the ham bone, onion, and cook until the peas are soft. Remove the bone and purée the peas by rubbing them through a sieve. Stir the flour into the butter and blend well. Add the seasonings and milk and cook until the mixture thickens, stirring constantly. Then combine with the puréed peas and simmer until mixture thickens. Serves 6.

## PEPPER POT

| | |
|---|---|
| 2 pounds honeycomb tripe | 4 medium-sized potatoes, diced |
| 2 pounds plain tripe | 1 bunch pot herbs |
| 1 3-pound veal knuckle | Cayenne pepper |
| 3 quarts cold water | Salt |
| 1 bay leaf | Chopped parsley |
| 1 large onion | Butter Balls (see Index) |

Prepare the tripe a day ahead as follows: Wash tripe thoroughly, cover with water, and boil 4 hours. Remove from water, cool, and cut into small squares.

Wash the veal knuckle, place in kettle with the cold water and simmer 3 hours. Skim broth occasionally while it is cooking. When tender, remove the meat from the bones and cut into small pieces. Strain the broth, return it to the kettle, add the bay leaf, and onion, and simmer for about 1 hour. Add the potatoes, the pot herbs, meat, tripe, and seasonings. When potatoes are almost cooked add the Butter Balls. Cook for 10 minutes, add a little chopped parsley, and serve at once. Serves 8 to 10.

## POTATO SOUPS

*Grumbeere Supp iss gut genunk,*
*Ich saag dir, die iss allfart gsund.*
*Grumbeere Supp iss gut genunk,*
*Wann mer aa noch Brot nei dunkt.**

One wonders whether any other soup has been so continuously a favorite among succeeding generations of Pennsylvania Germans. The *Hausfraa* serves her *Grumbeere Supp* in a number of variations. In offering the following nine recipes we do not claim to have exhausted the list.

---

*From an old dialect song that has come down to us only in fragments.

### POTATO SOUP I

| | |
|---|---|
| 4 cups diced potatoes | 1 cup flour |
| 6 cups water | ½ cup butter |
| 2 teaspoons salt | 3 cups milk or cream, scalded |

2 teaspoons dried parsley

Cook the potatoes in the water, with salt added, until they are soft. Brown the flour in the butter and stir into the potatoes and water. Add the milk or cream and bring to a boil. Add the parsley and serve. Serves 8.

### POTATO SOUP II

| | |
|---|---|
| 4 cups diced potatoes | Pepper |
| 1 medium sized onion, chopped | ¼ cup flour |
| 1 quart milk | 1 tablespoon butter |
| ½ teaspoon salt | 1 egg, well beaten |

Boil potatoes and onion together in small quantity of water until tender. Add milk, salt and pepper, and reheat. Brown flour in the butter and slowly stir into potato mixture. Add a little water or milk to egg and stir into the soup. Boil a few minutes and serve with chopped parsley. Serves 6.

*Variation:* Left over mashed potatoes may be used as a substitute. Then add an equal amount of milk and proceed as above. If flour is omitted, serve soup with croutons.

### POTATO SOUP III
#### (with grated potatoes)

| | |
|---|---|
| 2 cups grated raw potatoes | ¼ teaspoon celery seed |
| 1 onion, minced | 6 cups beef broth |

Salt and pepper

Add potatoes, onion, and celery seed to the beef broth. Simmer for 20 minutes. Season with salt and pepper. Serves 6.

### POTATO SOUP IV
#### (a summer soup)

Prepare the desired amount of new potatoes, add in small quantity diced young carrots, peas, kohl-rabi and asparagus. Simmer gently in chicken broth until vegetables are tender. Add garden herbs (summer savory, thyme, and marjoram) to taste. Bits of chicken meat may be added. Serve piping hot.

### POTATO SOUP V
#### (for late fall)

Prepare the desired amount of potatoes, add leeks and celery, and simmer until vegetables are tender. Force through a sieve. Add butter, salt and pepper to taste, and 1 cup of sour cream. This makes a fine supper soup, served with *gschmelzte* noodles (see Index) and stewed fruit.

### POTATO SOUP VI
#### (for winter days)

Prepare the desired amount of diced potatoes and boil in water until tender. Fry several onions in butter. Add flour to thicken, stirring constantly, and season with salt and pepper. Add a finely chopped clove of garlic. Add onion mixture to cooked potatoes and mix well. Fry small pieces of smoked sausage. Place sausage in soup plates and pour the hot soup over it.

### POTATO SOUP VII
#### (with vinegar)

| | |
|---|---|
| 4 medium-sized potatoes, diced | 3 small onions, diced |
| 5 cups water | 2 tablespoons butter |
| 1 teaspoon salt | 1 tablespoon vinegar |

Cook the potatoes in water, with salt added, until they are tender. One bay leaf and 2 cloves may be added, if desired. Brown the onions in the butter and add to potatoes and water. Add vinegar and serve. Serves 4.

### POTATO SOUP VIII
#### (with herbs)

Prepare the desired amount of onion, leeks and celery and add 2 tablespoons butter. Steam in a large saucepan for a few minutes. Add 1 quart of water. Bring to a boil. Add 3 to 4 medium-sized raw potatoes grated. Add a few sprigs of thyme and marjoram and boil for 10 minutes. Serve very hot. Serves 4.

*A Palatine recipe.*

### POTATO SOUP IX
#### (with tomatoes)

Mathilda Jung's delightful *Eine Landschaft kocht* (Saarbruecken, 1941) devoted to the cuisine of the Palatinate, and the only cookbook we know that is also a literary achievement, contains five variations of *Grumbeeresupp*, one of which the author claims journeyed back from the Pennsylvania Germans to the Palatinate. We have never met it here in Pennsylvania and yet it bespeaks the inventiveness of the Pennsylvania German *Hausfraa*. It deserves to return to Pennsylvania and here it is:

"Take an equal quantity of potatoes and tomatoes and as many garden herbs as you like (marjoram, thyme, summer savory, etc.) and boil until a smooth, thick soup of a delicate red color is formed. Add salt and butter. Serve it with tiny islands of whipped sour cream floating on the surface."

Thereupon the author grows lyrical and terms this a late-summer poem. A noonday meal of this glorious soup, finished off with mirabelle or plum tarts, conjures up from out of the consumer's dream-consciousness the gracious plenitude of the Palatine landscape with all its color, its fragrance, and its sweet fruition! May it do the same for our Pennsylvania landscape.

## PRETZEL SOUP

| | |
|---|---|
| 3 tablespoons butter | 2 cups water |
| 2 tablespoons flour | Salt and pepper |
| 4 cups rich milk | 1 teaspoon minced parsley |

¼ pound pretzels

Melt the butter in a saucepan and add the flour. Combine the milk and water and gradually stir into flour mixture. Bring to a boil over a low heat, stirring until smooth and creamy. Season to taste. Just before serving add the parsley and the pretzels broken into small pieces. Serves 6.

## RIWWELSUPP I
### (Rubbed Crumb Soup)

This old-time homely fare continues to be a favorite. Wherever Palatines have gone, whether to the Banat and the Batschka in the Danubian basin, or across the sea to Pennsylvania, their indigenous *Riwwelsupp* has continued to give them aid and comfort. *Riwwle* (plural) are to the Palatines what *Spätzli* are to the Swabians. The dough is quite the same for both. *Spätzli* is rolled out thin and dexterously scraped from the edge of the board into the boiling water, while the *Riwwle* are rubbed (compare German *reiben*) through the hands into the milk or broth.

| | |
|---|---|
| 4 cups milk | 1 egg, beaten |
| 1 cup flour | 1 teaspoon salt |

Bring the milk to a boil. Beat flour, egg and salt until the dough shows bubbles. Rub through the hands into the boiling milk and boil gently until the *Riwwle* rise to the surface. If desired, the dough can be rubbed through a colander. Serve at once.

## RIWWELSUPP II

| | |
|---|---|
| 4 cups chicken or beef broth | 1 egg, beaten |
| 1 cup flour | ½ teaspoon salt |

Bring the broth to a boil. Combine flour, egg and salt and beat until it shows bubbles. Rub through the hands into the boiling broth and boil until the *Riwwle* rise to surface. Serve at once.

### SORREL SOUP
#### (Sauerambelsupp)

| | |
|---|---|
| 2 tablespoons flour | 4 cups beef broth or bouillon |
| 2 tablespoons butter | 2 egg yolks |
| 2 cups sorrel leaves | 2 tablespoons heavy cream |
| Pinch of nutmeg | |

Brown the flour in the butter. Add the chopped greens, which have been carefully washed. Add beef broth or bouillon and simmer until greens are cooked. Beat egg yolks with the cream, add the nutmeg and stir into the soup. Serves 4 to 6.

### SPINACH SOUP

| | |
|---|---|
| 1 pound spinach | 1 slice dry bread |
| 1 onion, chopped, or ⅔ cup | 3 cups milk (about) |
| chives or onion tops | 1 tablespoon butter |
| 3 medium-sized potatoes | Pinch of marjoram |
| Chopped parsley | |

Wash spinach carefully and chop fine. Combine with onion. Pare and dice potatoes. Place vegetables in saucepan, add bread and just enough water to cover. Simmer until done and force through a sieve. Add milk, butter, marjoram and parsley. Heat thoroughly and serve. Serves 6.

*A Palatine recipe.*

### TOMATO SOUP I

| | |
|---|---|
| 1 tablespoon flour | 1 teaspoon salt |
| 2 tablespoons butter | ¼ teaspoon celery seed |
| 3 cups milk | Dash cayenne pepper |
| 2 cups raw unstrained tomatoes | Pinch of baking soda |

Blend flour and butter in saucepan over fire, add milk and bring to boiling point. In separate saucepan boil tomatoes 10 minutes (if canned tomatoes, take only 1½ cups). Add salt, pepper and celery seed and lastly the soda, stirring constantly. Pour gradually into the milk mixture and bring to boiling point. Do not allow to boil. Serve at once with crackers or pretzels.

### TOMATO SOUP II

| | |
|---|---|
| 4 cups beef stock | 1 teaspoon salt |
| ½ cup finely chopped onion | Pepper |
| ½ cup finely chopped celery | ¼ cup chopped parsley |
| 2 cups strained tomatoes | Croutons |

Add onion, celery and tomatoes to beef stock and boil 10 minutes. Add salt, pepper and parsley and serve with croutons.

### TOMATO SOUP III

| 1 soup bone | 1½ cups chopped celery |
| 4 cups diced tomatoes | 1 cup chopped cabbage |
| 1 onion, diced | Salt and pepper |
| 4 small potatoes, diced | Toast squares |

Cover soup bone with water and boil 2 hours. Add vegetables and seasoning, and continue boiling until vegetables are tender. Strain through a colander and serve with toast squares which have been dipped in browned butter. Serves 6.

### CREAM OF TOMATO SOUP

| 2 tablespoons flour | 2 cups strained tomatoes |
| 2 tablespoons butter | 1 teaspoon salt |
| 1½ cups milk | Dash of cayenne pepper |
| ½ cup water | 1 bay leaf |
| ¼ teaspoon baking soda | |

Blend flour and butter, add milk and water and bring to boiling point. In a separate saucepan pour tomatoes, add seasonings and heat. Add soda and stir well. Pour gradually into milk mixture. Heat again but do not let it boil. Serve with crackers or buttered toast.

### YELLOW TOMATO SOUP

| 2 cups diced yellow tomatoes | 1 tablespoon butter |
| 4 cups water | 1 teaspoon salt |
| 2 cups milk, scalded | ¼ teaspoon black pepper |
| ½ teaspoon soda | |

Boil tomatoes in water until tender. Add soda, stirring well. Heat milk, butter, salt and pepper in separate saucepan, and bring to a boil. Now pour tomatoes gradually into milk mixture and bring only to a boil. Serve with salt crackers.

### VEAL SOUP

| 1 veal knuckle (about 2 pounds) | Diced celery |
| ½ pound pork, diced | Diced carrots |
| 1½ quarts water | 3 sage leaves |
| Chopped onions | 3 whole cloves |
| Salt and pepper | |

Place veal knuckle and pork in large saucepan. Add water and boil for 3 hours, skimming occasionally if necessary. During last hour of cooking, add desired amounts of vegetables, the spices, and season to taste with salt and pepper. Serves 6.

*Die Geschickte Hausfrau, Harrisburg, 1852.*

## VEGETABLE SOUP I

| | |
|---|---|
| Small soup bone | 1 cup chopped onions |
| 2 pounds stewing beef | 1 cup chopped celery |
| 2 quarts water | 2 teaspoons salt |
| 1 cup tomatoes | ¼ teaspoon black pepper |

Other vegetables as indicated below

Can anyone fail in creating a good vegetable soup? There is the greatest latitude in the use of ingredients and the greatest number of combinations.

Put soup bone and beef in 2 quarts of water and boil 2 hours. Remove undesirable amount of fat. Add tomatoes, onions and celery. Consider these as basic; then add in small quantities, chopped or diced, whichever ones of the following are readily accessible: potatoes, cabbage, carrots, turnips, string beans, corn, peas, asparagus, sweet peppers. Boil until vegetables are tender. Add pepper and salt. You may also wish to add a tablespoon of rice or barley or alphabet noodles. If so, boil with meat and bone the last 20 minutes, before adding vegetables.

## VEGETABLE SOUP II

| | |
|---|---|
| 1 cup chopped celery | 4 cups milk, scalded |
| 1 cup grated fresh corn | ¼ pound butter |
| 1 cup diced tomatoes | Salt |

Riwwels (rubbed crumbs)

Simmer vegetables in small amount of water until tender. Add milk, butter and salt, and bring to a boil. Into the boiling mixture drop the Riwwels, made as follows:

### Riwwels

| | |
|---|---|
| 1 cup flour | 1 egg, beaten |

Pinch of salt

Combine ingredients and rub mixture through the hands into the boiling soup. Boil about 5 minutes. Serves 4 to 6.

*Mrs. Walter Erdman*

# SOUP GARNISHES

The following delightful garnishes are to be used in clear soup or consommé. Liver dumplings and forcemeat balls are preferably used in beef stock. All others may be used in beef or chicken stock.

## MOCK PEA SOUP

| | |
|---|---|
| 2 tablespoons flour | 2 tablespoons cream |
| 2 eggs, beaten | ¼ teaspoon salt |
| Hot fat | |

Make a thin batter of the flour, eggs and cream. Add the salt. Pour the batter through a colander into boiling hot fat. As soon as these little drops of batter (the mock peas!) are fried a light brown, remove them from the fat and drain on absorbent paper. Add the mock peas to 6 cups of hot soup stock and serve. Serves 6.

## BUTTER BALLS

| | |
|---|---|
| ½ cup butter | ½ teaspoon salt |
| 1 cup flour | Ice water |

Combine the butter, flour and salt. Moisten with ice water and form into balls. Roll in a little flour to prevent sticking and drop into the soup. Simmer for 10 minutes. Serves 6 to 8.

## EGG DROPS

### (Eilaaf)

| | |
|---|---|
| ½ cup flour | 2 eggs, well beaten |
| ½ cup milk | ½ teaspoon salt |

Combine flour and milk into a smooth paste. Add salt. Add eggs gradually and as much more milk needed to form a thin flowing batter. Drop batter, drop by drop, into 6 or 8 cups of hot broth and boil for 5 minutes. Serves 6 to 8.

## BUTTER DUMPLINGS

| | |
|---|---|
| ⅛ pound butter | ½ cup flour |
| 2 egg yolks, well beaten | ½ teaspoon salt |
| 1 egg white, beaten stiff | Grated nutmeg |
| Chopped parsley | |

Cream the butter and add the egg yolks and egg white. Beat thoroughly until well mixed. Add the flour, salt, nutmeg (to taste) and parsley. With a teaspoon dip out small amounts of dough and drop from spoon into boiling soup. Cover and boil gently for 10 minutes. Serves 6 to 8.

### FORCEMEAT BALLS

| | |
|---|---|
| 1 pound ground veal | 2 tablespoons butter, melted |
| 1 egg, beaten | Salt and pepper |

Mix together all the ingredients and form into small balls. Fry in butter. Drop into 8 cups of broth. Serves 8.

### SMALL POTATO DUMPLINGS

| | |
|---|---|
| 1 tablespoon butter | 1 cup grated boiled potatoes |
| 2 eggs, separated | Grated lemon rind |
| 1 cup bread crumbs | ½ teaspoon salt |

Combine butter with egg yolks, add other ingredients and beat thoroughly. Fold in egg whites, beaten stiff. Form into small dumplings and drop into boiling soup. Cover and steam for 10 minutes. Makes about two dozen small dumplings.

### MARROW DUMPLINGS
#### (Marricksgnepp)

| | |
|---|---|
| ⅛ pound beef marrow | 3 slices white bread |
| 2 eggs, beaten | Salt |
| | Grated nutmeg |

Melt the pure beef marrow and add the eggs. Beat until frothy. Soak the trimmed bread in water, then press out water and add salt and grated nutmeg to taste. Combine with marrow and shape with the hands into 12 small round dumplings the size of hazelnuts. Drop into gently boiling soup, cover, and boil for 15 minutes. Serves 6.

### LIVER DUMPLINGS
#### (Lewwergnepp)

| | |
|---|---|
| ¼ pound calf or goose liver | 3 slices white bread, trimmed |
| 2 ounces butter | ½ teaspoon salt |
| 1 egg white, beaten stiff | Grated nutmeg |
| 2 egg yolks, well beaten | Chopped parsley |

Cook liver until tender, then press through a fine sieve. Soak bread in water, press out water and put through a fine sieve also. Combine bread with other ingredients and add to the liver. Work the mixture thoroughly with a tablespoon and form into small oblong dumplings with spoon. Drop into 6 cups of gently boiling broth, cover tightly and boil for 8 minutes. Makes 12 small dumplings. Serves 6.

# Meat Dishes and Meat Condiments

(For butchering among the Pennsylvania Germans see Introduction)

*En zweebeenichi Sau gleicht niemand*

Don't gormandize when you go to dine;
Nobody likes two-legged swine!

## FLEESCHBOI
### (Meat Pie)

A by-product of Pennsylvania butchering time was the *Fleeschboi* or meat pie, indicative of the thriftiness of an earlier generation. Usually there was a little bone-meat left, in excess of what went into the making of sausage, liverwurst, etc. The meat was for the most part pork. It was cooked on the bone, removed and cut into small pieces. The broth was saved. Instead of pastry a wheaten bread dough was used. Since it was a matter of using up the bits of meat, half a dozen or more such pies were made at the time of the winter butchering and stored away until needed. Before serving they were heated by steaming on a rack in a large boiler. The following recipe will serve those in whose households there is no winter butchering.

## PORK PIE

| | |
|---|---|
| 3 pounds spare ribs | ½ recipe bread dough (see Index) |
| Broth | Shortening |
| Salt and pepper | Sugar |

Boil spare ribs until tender, adding as much salt and pepper as desired. Remove meat from bones and cut into small pieces. Save broth and when cool skim some fat from it. Prepare bread dough, but add some extra shortening and a bit of sugar. Let the dough rise, then roll out thin and line deep pie pan with the rolled dough. Fill with as much meat as it will hold and cover with lid of rolled bread dough. Let dough rise again and bake. —

When serving cut a small rectangular hole into the top of the pie and pour in ½ cup of the broth. Eat while hot, with additional broth if desired.

*Cora I. Hollenbach*

## PICKELFLEESCH
### (Pickled Pork)

This is another recipe associated with butchering time. Take a pork loin (*Rickmeesel*) and cut it into serving pieces. Trim off all fat and pack meat in a stone crock, sprinkling each layer with brown sugar, ground coriander seed, and enough salt to season well. Set in a cold place and freeze.

When ready to use, remove desired amount of meat. Fry in as little fat as possible. Serve hot.

*Cora I. Hollenbach*

## GFILLDER SEIMAAGE
### (Stuffed Pig's Stomach)

This continues to be a favorite winter dish among us. We come honestly by our love of it, for it continues to this day to be an outstanding item in Palatine cuisine. Indeed it is amazing how very similar is the recipe "Pfälzer Saumagen mit Sauerkraut" as published in Bernhard Klaffke's *Seht, das ist Deutschland!* (1936).

| | |
|---|---|
| 1 pig's stomach | 3 cups diced boiled potatoes |
| 2 pounds smoked sausage meat, diced | 3 cups sliced apples |
| | 2 cups chopped celery |
| 2½ cups bread crumbs | Chopped parsley |
| 1 medium-sized onion, chopped | Salt and pepper |
| Pinch of marjoram | |

Thoroughly clean the stomach and soak it in salted water. Combine the remaining ingredients and mix well. Stuff the stomach with mixture, sew up opening, and place in a large kettle with water to cover. Simmer for 2 hours. Place in a roasting pan with some hot fat and brown in a hot oven, 400° F., basting frequently. Serves 6 to 8.

*Variation I:* Instead of sausage take two pounds of spare ribs, 4 cups diced raw potatoes, 1 cup chopped onions, parsley, salt and pepper. Proceed in other respects as in recipe above.

*Variation II:* The recipe from the Palatinate, mentioned above, is similar in essentials. It calls for grated boiled potatoes, raw fatty pork chopped coarsely, salt, pepper, nutmeg and marjoram. Mix ingredients, stuff pig stomach, sew it up and boil in water with carrots and onions for 1 hour. After the water has boiled down, let the pig's stomach simmer in its own fat 2 more hours. Serve with sauerkraut. This is a man's dish, to be concluded with a sturdy draught of plum brandy.

## CIGARMAKERS' DUTCH TURKEY
### Filled Pig's Stomach

| | |
|---|---|
| 1 pig's stomach | 2 stems diced celery |
| 3 diced potatoes | 3 large diced onions |
| 1 lb. loose (without casing) | salt and pepper |
| fresh sausage | |

Mix potatoes, celery, onion, sausage and salt and pepper, and fill stomach with mixture. Sew stomach shut and simmer in water in kettle on top of stove until soft. Then place it in a roasting pan and brown in hot oven.

*Mrs Kensie N. Yoder*

## PIG'S KNUCKLES AND SAUERKRAUT
### (with dumplings)

| | |
|---|---|
| 2½ pounds sauerkraut | ½ cup water |
| 5 to 6 pig's knuckles | 1 cup sifted flour |
| 1 egg, well beaten | ½ teaspoon salt |
| 1½ tablespoons butter, melted | Dash of nutmeg |

Place the sauerkraut in a kettle, and add the pig's knuckles which have been thoroughly cleaned and scraped. Cover with cold water and cook slowly until the knuckles are tender. Mix together the egg, butter, and water. Add the flour sifted with the salt and nutmeg, and beat well. (If necessary, add more flour to make a batter stiff enough to drop from a spoon.) Drop from spoon into the hot sauerkraut mixture, cover tightly and cook for 20 minutes. Serve immediately. Serves 6.

## BAKED SAUERKRAUT AND SPARERIBS
### (with dumplings)

| | |
|---|---|
| 2½ pounds spareribs | 2 cups sifted flour |
| 2 pounds sauerkraut | 1 cup milk |
| 1 egg, well beaten | 1 teaspoon baking powder |

Cut the spareribs into portions for serving and place them in a roasting pan. Cover with the sauerkraut. Bake in a moderate oven 350° F., for 1½ hours.

Make dumplings by combining the other ingredients. Drop from a spoon on top of the hot sauerkraut. Cover the pan tightly and bake for 20 minutes longer. Serves 6.

## SAUERKRAUT UN SCHPECK
### (Sauerkraut and Bacon)

Cook together 2 pounds of lean bacon and 1½ pounds of sauerkraut until tender. Serve with mashed potatoes. Serves 6.

## HOMEMADE SAUSAGE

(General Jacob Loucks Devers, commander of the U. S. armored forces in Europe during World War II, is a Pennsylvania German with an avowed fondness for pork sausage and flannel cakes, a typically Pennsylvania German combination which often was served at his home in York. General Devers is a great-great-great-grandson of John George Loucks who came to this country from the Palatinate in 1710.)

| | |
|---|---|
| 9 pounds fresh pork (both | 4 tablespoons sage |
| 2 tablespoons black pepper | Cloves |
| 3 tablespoons salt | Mace |
| lean and fat) | Nutmeg |

Cut the pork into small pieces and force it through a meat grinder. Add pepper, salt, sage and other spices to taste. Stuff well-cleaned casings with the mixture, or form it into small cakes. Brown on both sides in a hot frying pan, until well done. Serves about 18.

## SAUSAGE CAKES

| | |
|---|---|
| 1 pound pork sausage | 1 small onion, minced |
| 1 teaspoon butter or lard | 1 tablespoon flour |
| 1 cup clear beef broth | |

Form the sausage into small, flat cakes and fry on both sides until brown. Remove from the pan and keep warm. Brown the onion in the hot shortening, blend in the flour, add the beef broth and stir until thick and smooth. Pour over the sausage cakes and serve. Serves 2.

## POTATO PIE WITH SAUSAGE

| | |
|---|---|
| 1 recipe Basic Pastry (see | 6 potatoes, pared and diced |
| Index) | Salt and pepper |
| 1 pound pork sausage | |

Line a pie tin with pastry and add potatoes. Add salt and pepper to taste, and a little water. Place pieces of sausage on top and cover with a top crust. Bake in a moderate oven, 350° F., for about 1 hour. Serve with cold milk poured over each portion. Serves 6.

## SAUSAGE WREATH

| | |
|---|---|
| 1 yeast cake | 4 cups sifted flour |
| ¾ cup scalded milk, lukewarm | 1 pound sausage in casing, |
| 1 egg, beaten | raw or smoked |
| ⅛ pound butter, melted | Sliced ham (optional) |

Dissolve yeast cake in the lukewarm milk. Add egg, butter, and gradually stir in the flour. Set aside to rise. When double in bulk, pat out dough.

Shape sausage meat into long thin pencil-like roll. Place sausage on dough with very thin slices of ham, if desired. Roll up sausage in dough and shape dough into a circle, bringing ends together. Place in a pan and let rise again. Bake in a hot oven, 400° F., for about 35 minutes, or until crust is brown and sausage is done. Serve hot with a cup of bouillon.

*A Palatine Recipe.*

## SCRAPPLE
### or
## PANNHAAS
### (Pan Rabbit!)

*Der Pannhaas yaagt mer net mit Hund;*
*Er hot ken lange Ohre.*
*Un der iss heit noch graad so gsund*
*As wie vor hunnerd Yohre.*
—JOHN BIRMELIN

This ancient dish is unique in our cookery. Formerly the by-product of the winter butchering season, it today enjoys widespread popularity and can be bought the year round in the meatshops throughout eastern Pennsylvania. Its name is mystifying. It has nothing to do with rabbit, not even humorously as in the case of Welsh "rabbit." Although known in English as Philadelphia scrapple, the city of brotherly love had no part in its creation; nor is it scrapple, a term more correctly applied to pot pudding (see Index). It has its roots in Germany, where the word occurs in various forms, *Pannhase, Pannasch* and *Pannharst* (*harst* is Low German for *roast*)*. *Pannhaas* is a result of native thriftiness. In butchering nothing must be wasted. The nourishing liquid that remained in the big iron kettle after scrap meats, liver and other internal organs had been cooked form the base for this delectable dish. If small scraps of meat lingered in the broth so much the better. If too little, the ambitious housewife might add some of the ground meat that had been designated for the pot pudding and the liver "wurst." In Germany buckwheat was used, but in Pennsylvania a mixture of buckwheat and cornmeal is preferred. The recipes for scrapple offered here are attuned to the needs of the modern housewife.

### SCRAPPLE

| | |
|---|---|
| 1½ pounds pork liver | 4 cups buckwheat flour |
| (or heart and liver) | 2 cups cornmeal |
| 1½ pounds pork | ¼ teaspoon sage |
| 2½ quarts water | (or two leaves) |

Salt and pepper

*For a more detailed consideration of *Pannhaas* see *'S Deitsch Eck* (Allentown Morning Call) for Dec. 28, 1935 and April 9, 1938.

Cover liver and pork with water and boil until very tender. Remove meat. Cool broth and skim fat from surface. Grind meat, return to broth, add salt, pepper and sage, and bring to a boil. Let the mixture of buckwheat flour and cornmeal trickle slowly into meat and broth, stirring constantly. Boil about an hour, or until it has a heavy consistency and releases itself from vessel. (Be sure to stir frequently.) Pour into small bread pans. When cold, slice finger thick and fry until light brown and crisp on both sides.

*Variation:* Take two quarts of meat broth, empty a pound of liver pudding into it and bring to a boil. Let about 4 cups of meal trickle slowly into the boiling mixture and proceed as in the recipe above. Some prefer to use only cornmeal. It then more nearly resembles mush. As one quaint character in the Hegins Valley used to say: *"Ich will ken Mush; ich will Pannhaas."*

(Scrapple is a favorite dish of ex-president Herbert Hoover. Mr. Hoover, one of the many famous Americans who trace their ancestry back to Pennsylvania German forebears, is a descendant of Andreas Huber, a native of the Palatinate, who arrived in Pennsylvania in 1738.)

### AUNT ELLIE'S POT PUDDING

On butchering day take the cleaned heads of hogs, hearts, tongues, and trimmings from bones, as well as any leftover scraps of both pork and beef, and boil them for about 3 hours, or until the meat separates from the bones. Skim off the fat, remove the meat and put it through the meat grinder coarsely. Return meat to the broth. Season with salt and pepper and thyme or sage, and cook for 1 hour longer, until the consistency of scrapple. Pack in crocks or jars, pour melted fat over the tops and store in a cool place until ready for use.

### ZITTERLI
#### (Souse)

Another delicious by-product of the butchering season, in the making of which the housewife takes great pride.

Scrape and wash thoroughly 4 pig's feet. Cover with water and boil until the meat is tender. Pick all meat from the bones in small pieces, return to the vessel with the broth, considerably reduced in quantity, season with salt and pepper and add vinegar as desired. Pour into moulds. When cold the jellied form is turned out on a plate when used. A fine supper dish. — Described as "Round, shiny molds of souse that gleamed like jellied jewelry in an errant shaft of sunlight" in Ann Hark's Hex Marks the Spot (J. B. Lippincott Co., 1938).

### KUTTELFLECK
#### (Soused Tripe)

Cleanse tripe thoroughly, boil until tender and keep it in salted water until ready to use, changing water and salt daily. When some is to be used, cut it in 2-inch squares, dip in beaten egg and bread crumbs, and fry in hot fat. Or, you may vary in use by taking some of the tripe, cutting it in squares, boiling it in a small quantity of water with chopped parsley and onion. Serve it with browned butter.

*Die Geschickte Hausfrau, Harrisburg, Pa. 1852*

## SAURER RINDSBRATEN
### (Sour Beef Roast)

| | |
|---|---|
| 4 pounds beef (sirloin or round) | 12 cloves |
| | Ginger root |
| Salt | Juniper berries |
| Cider vinegar | 1 slice bacon |
| 6 bay leaves | 1 crust of bread |

¾ cup flour, browned

Select a piece of beef, without bones, but with some fat. Rub with salt. Place in a crock or bowl, cover with vinegar and add spices. Let meat stand in mixture for 8 to 10 days, turning it several times.

When ready to use, place meat in heavy pot. Place bacon and large crust of bread on top. Over all pour equal parts of liquid (in which meat soaked) and water, adding spices. Cover tightly and steam for 2 to 3 hours. Just before meat is done, add the flour which has been browned in oven. Cook 10 minutes, strain gravy, and continue cooking meat and strained gravy for 10 minutes longer. Serve with noodles and stewed fruit. Serves 8.

*Die Geschickte Hausfrau, Harrisburg, Pa. 1852*

## ROLITSCHES

This unusual dish, little known in our generation, probably came into Pennsylvania by way of New Amsterdam. In Dutch it is known as *Rolletje*, in English as Rollichies.

| | |
|---|---|
| 1 beef tripe | 1 small bay leaf |
| 12 pounds beef (round or chuck) | Piece of dried red pepper |
| Salt and pepper | ½ cup vinegar |
| Thyme | Cider vinegar |
| Sweet marjoram | Salt and pepper |
| Rosemary | Sugar |
| 1 onion | ¼ cup pickle spices |

Clean and thoroughly scrape the beef tripe. Remove fat, bones and gristle from beef. Cut the tripe into 14-inch squares. Cut beef in strips (12x2x2 inches) and place 5 to 6 strips of beef on square of tripe. Season carefully with salt and pepper, and equal amounts of thyme, sweet marjoram, and rosemary, used sparingly. Roll lengthwise as tight as possible, and sew both ends and down the side. This quantity will make about 5 rollichies.

Place rollichies in a large pot, cover with about 5 inches of water, add the onion, bay leaf, piece of red pepper and ½ cup of vinegar. Quickly bring to a boil and simmer for about 3 hours. When done, remove and place in a large crock.

Next morning prepare a pickling solution of cider vinegar, salt, pepper, sugar to taste, and mixed pickle spices (tied in a muslin bag). Boil mixture for 5 minutes, remove spice bag and let liquid cool to room temperature. Pour over rollichies, weight them down with a plate on which a heavy stone is placed. Store in a cool place for 8 weeks.

When ready to use, cut rollichies in ½-inch slices. Roll in flour, and brown in butter. Use ½ cup of the pickling mixture for gravy.

*Mrs. William J. Kressler*

### BEEF LOAF

| | |
|---|---|
| 3½ pounds ground beef | ⅛ teaspoon nutmeg |
| 3 eggs | Salt and pepper |
| 2 tablespoons butter | 20 soda crackers, crushed |
| 1½ cups milk | |

Combine all the ingredients, adding the milk last. Mix well. Place in a greased baking dish and bake in a moderate oven, 350° F., for 1½ hours. Cool and slice. Serves 6 to 8.

### STEAMED CABBAGE and MEAT LOAF

| | |
|---|---|
| 1 medium-sized head cabbage | 3 tablespoons butter |
| ¾ pound ground beef | Salt and pepper |
| ¾ pound ground pork | 5 soda crackers, crumbled |
| 2 eggs | 2 egg yolks, well beaten |

Remove the tough outer leaves and core of the cabbage. Boil the cabbage in salted water until tender, then drain. Mix together the meat, 2 whole eggs, 1 tablespoon of the butter, and season to taste. Place alternate layers of cabbage leaves and meat mixture in a large buttered mold, with layer of cabbage on top. Cover the mold tightly and steam for 2 hours. When ready to serve, drain off broth and make a gravy by adding the remaining butter, cracker crumbs and egg yolks. If too thick, stir in a little water. Pour gravy over the cabbage and meat mixture. Serve hot. Serves 6.

### GFILLDER GRAUTKOPP
#### (Filled Cabbage Head)

| | |
|---|---|
| 1 medium-sized head cabbage | Chopped parsley |
| 4 medium-sized potatoes, diced | Salt and pepper |
| 2 tablespoons shortening | ½ pound ground beef or smoked |
| 1 onion, chopped | sausage (optional) |
| 1 egg, well beaten | Melted butter |

Hot milk

Separate cabbage leaves and lay a circle of leaves on a large napkin. Fry the potatoes in hot fat, add onions, and egg. Add parsley and salt and pepper to taste. If desired, the fried meat may be added also. Place mixture on the cabbage leaves and arrange more cabbage on top. Draw up ends of napkin and tie them together. Place on a rack in kettle, with small amount of water in bottom. Cover, and steam for 15 minutes. Turn out on platter and pour melted butter and hot milk over all. Serves 6.

*Mrs. Birdie M. Reichard*

## MEAT and CABBAGE ROLLS

| | |
|---|---|
| 1 pound ground beef | 1 egg, well beaten |
| Salt and pepper | ⅓ cup uncooked rice |
| 6 cabbage leaves | |

Season the meat with salt and pepper to taste. Add the egg, mix thoroughly, and add the rice. Wash the cabbage leaves and boil them until tender. Then place in each leaf 2 tablespoons of the meat mixture. Roll tightly, fastening each leaf securely with a toothpick, and place in a saucepan. Pour the following sauce over the rolls, cover, and simmer for 3 hours. Serves 6.

**Sauce:**

| | |
|---|---|
| 1 onion, finely sliced | ½ cup chopped celery |
| 2 tablespoons melted butter | 1 teaspoon sugar |
| 1 can (10½ oz.) tomato soup | Juice of 1 lemon |
| 1 teaspoon minced parsley | Salt and pepper |

Add the onion to the melted butter and cook for several minutes. Combine the tomato soup with an equal amount of water, pour into the onion mixture. Then add the other ingredients and season to taste. Cook for 10 minutes.

## MEAT-FILLED PEPPERS

| | |
|---|---|
| 1½ pounds ground beef and pork, mixed | 2 eggs, well beaten |
| | ½ teaspoon salt |
| 3 tablespoons uncooked rice | 6 green peppers |
| 1 can (10½ oz.) tomato soup | |

Mix together the meat, rice, eggs, and salt. Cut the tops off the peppers, scoop out the seeds, and soak peppers in hot water for 5 minutes. Drain and fill peppers with meat mixture. Place in a large baking pan, pour the tomato soup over all. Bake in a slow oven, 300° F., for 1 hour. Serves 6.

## ROULADES

Take desired amount of thinly sliced round steak and cut into strips. Pound and rub with salt, pepper (and cloves if desired). On each piece of beef lay a thin slice of bacon, roll up tightly and secure with a tooth pick. Dip the rolls in flour, brown in hot fat, and cover tightly. Simmer and turn after they have cooked for 5 minutes. Add enough boiling water to barely cover the rolls, cover tightly, and simmer for about 1 hour. If cooked too fast or too long the rolls become dried out. When ready to serve, thicken the liquid and pour over the rolls.

*Henriette Davidis: Praktisches Kochbuch*

### STUFFED BEEF HEART

| | |
|---|---|
| 1 beef heart | 1 cup cracker crumbs |
| 1 cup chopped roasted chestnuts | ½ cup medium white sauce |
| Salt and pepper | |

Remove the muscles and arteries from the beef heart and wash it thoroughly. Stuff cavity with a filling made of the other ingredients and fasten securely. Cover with boiling water and boil for 10 minutes. Then reduce heat and simmer until tender, about 2 to 3 hours. About ½ hour before serving, remove the heart from the water, sprinkle with additional cracker crumbs, salt and pepper, and bake in a moderate oven, 350° F., until brown. Allow about ½ pound of heart per portion.

### BAKED CALF'S HEAD

| | |
|---|---|
| 1 calf's head | Salt and pepper |
| 1 pound veal, cooked and chopped | Herbs (sprigs of thyme and marjoram) |
| 15 to 20 oysters, chopped | Bread crumbs |
| 1 egg, well beaten | |

Remove the brains from calf's head and let head stand in salted water for ½ hour. Drain, place in fresh water, and boil until the meat is tender. Strain the broth, pick the meat from the bones and chop fine, together with the calf's tongue. Add the veal and oysters, season to taste with salt and pepper. Add herbs. Place in a greased baking dish and add enough of the broth to moisten well. Sprinkle bread crumbs on top and brush with egg. Bake in a moderate oven, 350° F., for about 30 minutes. Serves 6.

### GEBRATENE KALBSLEBER
#### (Baked Calf's Liver)

| | |
|---|---|
| 6 slices calf's liver, cut thick | Salt and pepper |
| 2 cups bread crumbs | Pinch of thyme or marjoram |
| 2 tablespoons butter | 1 egg, well beaten |
| 1 medium-sized onion | ¼ pound pork, chopped fine |
| 6 slices bacon | |

Wash and dry the liver. Cut a pocket in each slice and fill cavity with a mixture of the remaining ingredients, except the bacon. Place stuffed slices of liver in a greased casserole. Lay a slice of bacon on top of each slice of liver. Cover and bake in a slow oven, 300° F., for about 45 minutes, or until tender. Make a brown gravy of liquid in pan. Serve with red currant jelly. Serves 6.

*Die Geschickte Hausfrau. Harrisburg, Pa. 1852*

## LIVER CAKES

| | |
|---|---|
| 1 pound ground calf's liver | 1 tablespoon flour |
| 1 egg, well beaten | Salt and pepper |
| 1 small onion, minced | ¼ pound sliced bacon |

Mix together thoroughly the liver, egg, onion, and flour, and season to taste. Form into round cakes, wrap a slice of bacon around each cake and secure with a toothpick. Fry in hot fat until thoroughly cooked. Serves 4.

## WIENER SCHNITZEL
### (Viennese Cutlets)

| | |
|---|---|
| 1 2-pound veal steak, ½-inch thick | Bread crumbs |
| | 1 egg, well beaten |
| Salt and pepper | Lemon juice |

Cut the veal into 6 equal portions. Sprinkle with salt and pepper to taste, dip in bread crumbs, then in beaten egg, then in the crumbs again. Let stand for a few minutes. Then brown in hot fat on both sides, cover, and simmer for 20 minutes. Sprinkle with lemon juice and serve. Serves 6. ("Wiener Schnitzel" is a relatively recent term and not used by the Pennsylvania Germans. But breaded veal cutlet is good by any name!)

## CREAM SCHNITZEL

| | |
|---|---|
| 4 slices bacon, finely diced | 1 teaspoon paprika |
| 1 1½-pound veal steak | Salt |
| 2 tablespoons minced onion | 1 cup sour cream |
| ½ cup tomato sauce | |

Fry the bacon until crisp. Cut the veal into 4 equal portions, add to the bacon, and brown on both sides. Add the onion, season with the paprika and salt to taste. Add the sour cream and tomato sauce, cover, and cook about 20 minutes. Serve at once. Serves 4.

## HAM AND EGG CUTLETS

| | |
|---|---|
| 2 tablespoons butter, melted | 1 onion, minced |
| 2 tablespoons flour | 4 hard-cooked eggs, chopped |
| 1 cup milk | Nutmeg |
| 4 tablespoons chopped, boiled ham | Salt and pepper |
| 5 mushrooms, chopped | 1 egg, beaten |
| | Bread crumbs |

Blend the butter and flour, add the milk gradually and boil mixture for 3 minutes, stirring constantly. Remove from the heat. Add the other ingredients. Turn out onto a plate to cool. Shape into cutlets, brush with egg and roll in bread crumbs. Fry cutlets in deep hot fat. Serves 4 to 6.

## SCHNITZ UN GNEPP
### (with ham)

This, probably the best-known of all Pennsylvania German dishes, is the only one that remains today of a number of similar dishes that characterize South German cooking. Dried tree fruits, known as *Hutzle,* whether of apple, pear or plum, were stewed and served with various forms of dumplings and meats, especially with sour pot roasts and venison. Whether the dumplings took on the form of the North and Central German *Kloesze,* the South German *Knoedel,* or the Rhineland *Knoepp* and Palatine *Knepp,* they are all known in our own dialect as *Gnepp* or *Knepp.* Apples, cut in six or eight sections, were dried in earlier days in the outdoor bake oven, strung in festoons by the open hearth or behind the kitchen stove, or on wooden frames in the sun. In their dried form they are known as *Schnitz* (sing. *Schnutz;* compare the verb *schneiden,* to cut) and were carefully stored in bags suspended from the attic rafters. It must be pointed out that the *Hausfraa* was especially careful in drying the *Schnitz* for this dish. In the first place she used only so-called *Siess Ebbel,* sweet apples. Lacking acidity such apples were not used for general cooking and baking. Old favorites are the Sweet Bough, Golden Sweet, Autumnal Swaar, Paradise and sweet *Hengscht* (stallion!) or Pound apple. These apples were always cut and dried with the skin, so that the *Schnitz* might retain their form after cooking. With the flesh and skin of sweet apple, the starch and protein of dumpling and meat, this dish is not only delicious, but offers a wellnigh perfect food.

| | |
|---|---|
| 1 pint Schnitz (dried apples) | 1 teaspoon salt |
| 3 pounds smoked ham | 4 teaspoons baking powder |
| 2 tablespoons brown sugar | 1 egg, beaten |
| 2 cups sifted flour | 2 tablespoons butter |

½ cup milk (scant)

Wash the dried apples, cover with water and soak overnight. In the morning put ham in a vessel fairly large in diameter, cover the ham with cold water and boil two hours. Then add the apples and the water in which they have been soaked. Boil another hour and add the brown sugar.

To make the *Gnepp,* or dumplings, sift together the flour, salt and baking powder. Stir in the egg, the melted butter and enough milk to make a moist, moderately stiff batter. Drop from spoon into the boiling ham and apples. Cover the vessel tightly and boil for 25 minutes without uncovering. Serve on a large platter with meat in center and the *Schnitz un Gnepp* arranged around it. Serves 6.

Nowadays the housewife finds it convenient to make the dumplings with baking powder, but in the earlier days the dumplings were raised with yeast (see Yeast Dumplings in Index). They are more certain to remain light and spongy!

### HAM AND NOODLES IN CASSEROLE

| | |
|---|---|
| ½ package (8 oz.) noodles | 2 eggs, beaten |
| 1½ cups cooked ham, diced | 1½ cups milk |

Cook noodles in salted boiling water for about 10 minutes. Drain into colander and let cold water run over them. Place alternate layers of noodles and ham in greased casserole to within 1 inch of top. Beat eggs with milk and pour over noodles and ham. Place casserole in shallow pan of hot water. Bake in a moderate oven, 350° F., for 1 hour. Serves 6. — This dish is very good served with spinach or sauerkraut.

*Henriette Davidis: Praktisches Kochbuch.*

### HAM WITH LIMA BEANS

| | |
|---|---|
| 1 2-pound ham butt | 3 tablespoons butter |
| 1 pound dried lima beans | ½ teaspoon cornstarch (optional) |

Soak beans overnight. Cover ham butt with water and cook 1 hour. Add the lima beans and cook slowly 1 more hour, or until ham is tender. If necessary, add more water while cooking so there will be a heavy liquid when finished. Add the butter and if necessary thicken the liquid with cornstarch. Serves 6.

### POTPIE

| | |
|---|---|
| 1 cup flour | ½ teaspoon salt |
| 2 teaspoons baking powder | 1 egg, beaten |
| Milk or cream | |

Sift flour, baking powder and salt into a bowl, form a "well" in the middle, into which pour the beaten egg. Mix thoroughly and if the dough is not soft enough, add some milk or cream. Roll out on floured board to ¼-inch thickness and cut into 1½-inch squares. These squares are dropped into the pot of boiling meat or meat stews, covered tightly and boiled for about 20 minutes.

*Mrs. Paul R. Wieand*

The dough fashioned after the above recipe is a cross between the noodle and biscuit dough. A variation, preferred by some, is obtained by taking the basic noodle recipe and adding a tablespoon of butter to it. — There are some who bake the potpie in the oven. We adhere in the following recipes to the original sense of the word, i.e. pie boiled in the pot.

## SAFFRON CHICKEN POTPIE

| | |
|---|---|
| 1 young chicken | 3 onions |
| 4 large potatoes | Salt and pepper |

½ teaspoon saffron*

Cut up the chicken into serving portions, add salt and pepper, cover with water and cook until tender. Pare and cut potatoes into ¼-inch slices. Slice the onions. Prepare one recipe of potpie dough (see Index). Cover with cloth and let it stand for ½ hour. Roll out thin on floured board and cut into small squares. Have sufficient broth on chicken in pot, and bring to a lively boil. Now spread on it a layer of potato and onion, then a layer of potpie squares, alternating, but with a final layer of potpie, on which sprinkle the saffron. Cover and let simmer about 20 minutes, or until potatoes are tender. Serves 6.

*Mrs. Arthur D. Graeff*

## VEAL POTPIE

| | |
|---|---|
| 2 pounds veal | 2 onions, sliced |
| 6 medium-sized potatoes | ½ teaspoon saffron (see Index) |

Pepper and salt

Cut the veal in small portions, cover with water, add pepper and salt and cook until tender. Pare and slice potatoes ¼ inch thick; slice the onions. Prepare one recipe of potpie dough (see Index). Upon the boiling meat and reduced broth place a layer of potato and onion, then a layer of dough squares, in alternating layers, ending with upper layer of dough squares. Sprinkle saffron between layers, cover tightly, and boil for 20 minutes. Serves 6.

*Variation:* Beef or pork may be used instead of veal, and parsley substituted for saffron. Otherwise proceed as above.

## LAZY POTPIE

| | |
|---|---|
| 1½ pounds spareribs | Salt |
| 6 medium-sized potatoes | Pinch of saffron |

Boil the spareribs, salted to taste, until fairly tender. Pare potatoes, add salt and the saffron and parboil. Place pork and potatoes in a kettle and

---

*Saffron (an Arabic word) is obtained from the dried stigmas (60,000 to the pound!) of the autumn-flowering Crocus Sativus. One of the oldest of flavoring and coloring agents, it was used by the Ancients (Solomon sang of "spikenard and saffron"), by the Chinese, the Persians and the Turks. It later came to Europe, presumably with the returning Crusaders, and was widely disseminated there. It was known in the Rhenish Palatinate and continued to be cultivated in Pennsylvania. Our housewives liked to put a pinch of saffron into their soups and noodles, into their yeast dough for breads and coffee cakes as well as other cakes. Although still extensively used among the "plain people" of Lancaster County, it is in other parts little used today. Ask for it in the apothecary shop.

enough water to almost cover the potatoes and pork. When boiling, drop in dumplings made as follows:

| | |
|---|---|
| 1½ cups sifted flour | 1 teaspoon salt |
| 1 teaspoon baking powder | 1 egg, beaten |

Milk

Sift flour, baking powder and salt. Add the egg and enough milk to make a thin dough. Drop from the spoon into the boiling broth. Cover kettle, and keep it covered about 20 minutes. A little parsley may be added to the dough, if desired. Serves 6.

*Miss Katie Spangler*

### CHICKEN–CORN PIE

| | |
|---|---|
| 1 3-pound chicken | 3 cups fresh corn |
| 1 recipe Basic pastry | Salt and pepper |
| (see Index) | Butter |

Thoroughly wash and clean the chicken and cut into serving portions. Stew the chicken for 1 hour, reducing the broth to a small amount. Line a deep baking dish with pastry, place the chicken in it, and cover with the fresh corn. Add salt and pepper to taste, dot generously with butter and pour chicken broth over all. Cover with a top crust and pierce crust with fork to allow steam to escape. Bake in oven at 450° F. for 20 minutes, reduce to 350° for 40 minutes more. Serves 6.

### CHICKEN CORN–MEAL PIE

| | |
|---|---|
| 2 eggs | ½ recipe Basic Pastry (see Index) |
| ½ cup milk | Salt and pepper |
| 1 cup corn meal | 2 cups sliced cooked chicken |

6 slices bacon

Beat the eggs until light and add the milk. Stir in gradually the corn meal and beat thoroughly. Line a baking dish with pastry, pour in half of the corn-meal batter, and add salt and pepper to taste. Place sliced chicken on top of batter. Top with slices of bacon and cover with another layer of corn-meal batter. Bake in oven of 400° F. for 30 minutes. Serves 6.

### RABBIT PIE

| | |
|---|---|
| 1 rabbit, dressed | 2 tablespoons minced parsley |
| Salt | Flour |
| 3 tablespoons butter | Dash of tabasco |
| 2 tablespoons minced onion | 1 recipe Basic Pastry (see Index) |

Cut the rabbit into several large pieces. Place in a skillet and barely cover with water. Cover, and simmer until tender, adding salt to taste when partly done.

In a separate skillet, heat the butter, add the onion and parsley and cook for about 5 minutes, stirring constantly. Drain the liquid from the rabbit and add to the onion mixture. Stir in 1½ tablespoons of flour for each cup of liquid. When thick, add the tabasco and additional salt, if needed.

Remove meat from bones. Line a greased baking dish with pastry, place meat in dish, pour in sauce, and top with pastry. Bake in a moderate oven, 350° F., for about 35 minutes. Serves 4.

## HAASEKUCHE
### (Rabbit Cake)

| | |
|---|---|
| 1 rabbit, dressed | 2 tablespoons melted butter |
| 2 cups hot mashed potatoes | 1 onion, minced |
| 1 egg, well beaten | 1 teaspoon salt |
| 4 cups stale bread cubes | ½ teaspoon poultry seasoning |
| Cold water | Pinch of pepper |
| 1 tablespoon minced parsley | ½ cup flour |
| ½ cup diced celery | 1 cup rabbit broth |

Cook the rabbit until tender, in water to cover, and separate the meat from the bones. Cut into small pieces. Mix the potatoes and egg. Soak the bread cubes in cold water, squeeze dry, and add to the potato mixture. Stir in the parsley, celery, butter, onion, and seasoning. Mix well. Butter a baking dish and place a layer of filling in the bottom, then a layer of meat. Make a sauce by combining flour and broth, and season to taste. Add 1 tablespoon of sauce to layers in baking dish and repeat process until dish is filled. Bake in a moderate oven, 350° F., for about 25 minutes, or until brown. Serves 6.

## HASENPFEFFER
### (Pickled Rabbit)

| | |
|---|---|
| 1 rabbit, dressed | 2 bay leaves |
| Vinegar | Salt and pepper |
| 1 large onion, sliced | Butter |
| Pinch of ground cloves | 1 cup thick sour cream |

Yes, as in days of old, one first catches the rabbit! Cut the rabbit into serving portions and place in a jar. Cover with equal parts of vinegar and water. Add the onion, cloves, bay leaves, and season with salt and pepper. Let stand in solution for 2 days. Remove the meat and brown it in hot butter, turning often until well browned. Gradually add some of the pickling liquid and simmer meat until tender, about 30 minutes. Just before serving stir in sour cream. Serves 4.

*Henriette Davidis: Praktisches Kochbuch*

### ROAST SQUAB

Pick, singe and dress the squab  Fill it with cooked chestnuts and po-tatoes in equal measure and allow ¼ ounce butter to each bird.  Roast before a good fire.

To serve with this, take a cupful of boiled chestnuts and a cupful of stoned raisins cooked in just enough water to plump them.  Mix and pour over all a pint of wine (I use sherry).  Let stand over night.  Make a sauce of tablespoon butter, tablespoon flour, and the wine drained from the nuts and raisins.  Add 2 ounces fine sugar and a pinch of mace.  Boil up and put in nuts and raisins and boil again when it is ready to serve.  This recipe must be started a day before wanted.

The above ancient recipe was translated from a German cookbook of a Pennsylvania German housewife who kept house in Lancaster from 1767 to 1811.

### ROAST DUCK

Dress a young duck and rub overnight with salt and pepper.

For the filling, take of sour stoned raisins, currants, chopped sour apple and bread crumbs, a small handful of each, and one large cooked mealy potato mixed with an ounce of butter while hot.  Mix all together, fill duck lightly, sew up vents, truss into good shape and bake before a hot, steady fire.  Do not overdo.  Make a gravy by browning a tablespon of flour in the drippings, adding the giblets (which should be cooked and pounded fine in a mortar) with the water they were cooked in.  Boil up and it is done.  Garnish duck with thin slices of lemon.  Serve with it a compote of cherries or currants.

This old recipe is from the same source as that for roast squab.  Both go back to the days when fowl were roasted before an open fire on the hearth.

# STUFFINGS

### STUFFING FOR GOOSE OR DUCK

| | |
|---|---|
| 3 cups browned bread crumbs | 1 onion, minced |
| 1 tablespoon butter | 1 teaspoon ground sage |
| Salt and pepper | 3 potatoes, grated raw |
| 1 egg, beaten | 1 apple, grated |

Salt and pepper

Place the bread crumbs in a large dish, add the butter, salt and pepper to taste, and the egg.  Add the onion and sage and mix well.  Add potatoes and apple.  Mix all ingredients well before stuffing the fowl.

*Vollmer's Vollständiges deutsches Vereinigten Staaten Kochbuch, Philadelphia, 1865.*

## BREAD FILLING FOR FOWL

| | |
|---|---|
| 2 to 3 loaves of bread | 2 to 3 eggs |
| 6 medium-sized onions | Pinch of saffron |
| ½ cup finely chopped celery | ½ cup boiling water |
| Salt and pepper | 3 cups milk (about) |

Remove crusts from bread (may be used for bread crumbs). Dice the bread and let it dry out. Remove any excess fat from the fowl to be stuffed, render it in a skillet, and fry the onions in the fat until light brown. Add the cubed bread, celery, and season to taste with salt and pepper. Mix well over low heat. Beat the eggs, add the saffron which has been mixed with the boiling water, and about 2 cups of the milk. Pour over the bread mixture and mix thoroughly until the bread is moistened, but not soggy. Add more milk, if necessary, but keep the filling light and fluffy. Makes about 14 cups of filling.

This filling may be served as a separate dish with roast pork or beef, if desired. Place mixture in greased casserole and bake in a moderate oven, 350° F., for 15 to 20 minutes.

*Mary Elizabeth Spangler*

## TURKEY FILLING

| | |
|---|---|
| 2 slices bread | 3 eggs, well beaten |
| 4 tablespoons melted butter | ½ cup chopped celery |
| 1 large onion | 1 teaspoon minced parsley |
| 3 cups mashed potatoes | ½ teaspoon sweet marjoram |

Cube the bread and brown in half of the butter. Chop the onion and brown in the remaining butter. Combine all ingredients and mix well. Makes about 4 cups of filling.

Increase amounts according to the size of turkey to be filled.

*Mrs. Mary M. Kutz*

## CHESTNUT STUFFING FOR POULTRY

| | |
|---|---|
| 1 quart chestnuts | 1 teaspoon salt |
| 1 tablespoon butter | 1 egg, well beaten |
| 2 cups bread crumbs | 1 cup chopped celery |
| 2 teaspoons poultry seasoning | ¼ cup butter, lard, or chicken fat |

Place chestnut in iron skillet with the butter and bake in a hot oven, 450° F., for 20 minutes. When cool enough to handle, remove shells and skins with sharp knife. Cover with boiling salted water and cook until tender, about 20 minutes. Drain and put through a potato ricer. Add the remaining ingredients and mix well. Makes about 5 cups of filling.

## GRUMBEERE FILLSEL
### (Potato Stuffing)

| | |
|---|---|
| 2 cups hot mashed potatoes | ¼ cup chopped parsley |
| 1 egg, well beaten | ½ cup chopped onion |
| 4 cups cubed dry bread | 1 teaspoon salt |
| 3 tablespoons butter or fat | ½ teaspoon poultry seasoning |

Pepper

Combine potatoes and egg. Fry the cubed bread in butter, or use fat from the fowl to be stuffed. Add the potato mixture and stir in the remaining ingredients. Season with pepper, and mix well. Makes about 6½ cups filling.

## PIG'S STOMACH FILLING
### (Seimaage Fillsel)

| | |
|---|---|
| ½ pound smoked sausage | 2 slices bread, cubed |
| 6 medium-sized potatoes | 1 egg, beaten |
| 4 tablespoons butter and lard | 3 tablespoons minced parsley |
| 1 large onion, chopped fine | Hot milk |

Boil potatoes in "jackets" until tender, then peel and cube them. Melt butter and lard in a frying pan and add the onion and the bread. Stir constantly until a golden brown. Add mixture to the potatoes. Add the egg and parsley and mix well. Add enough hot milk to lend desired consistency. Cut smoked sausage into half-inch slices and add to the mixture.

## BERKS COUNTY POTATO FILLING
### (Grumbeere Fillsel)

| | |
|---|---|
| 10 medium-sized potatoes | Hot milk |
| 2 cups bread crumbs | 1 tablespoon chopped celery |
| 1 large onion, chopped | 1 tablespoon chopped parsley |
| 2 tablespoons butter | 1 tablespoon flour |
| 2 eggs, well beaten | Butter |

Pare and boil potatoes until they are tender. Combine bread crumbs and onion and fry in the butter until lightly browned. Drain potatoes, mash them and add the eggs. Add the bread crumbs, and onions, and enough hot milk to form a light creamy mixture. Beat well. Add chopped celery, parsley and the flour. Beat all together until well mixed. Turn into a greased baking dish, dot with butter, and place in a hot oven, 400° F., for about 15 minutes, or until well browned. Serves 6 to 8.

*Mrs. Arthur D. Graeff*

# MEAT SAUCES

### BROWN SAUCE

| | |
|---|---|
| 1 tablespoon butter | 1 cup beef stock |
| 1 tablespoon flour | ½ teaspoon salt |

½ teaspoon pepper

Brown the butter in a saucepan. Add the flour and stir until smooth and brown. Add the stock and stir mixture until it thickens. Season with the salt and pepper. Makes 1 cup sauce.

This recipe serves as a foundation for various other sauces, depending upon ingredients added, such as curry, catsup, or Worcestershire sauce.

### HORSERADISH SAUCE I

| | |
|---|---|
| ½ cup grated horseradish | ½ teaspoon paprika |
| 1 teaspoon flour | 1 tablespoon butter |
| ¼ teaspoon salt | ¼ cup cream or rich milk |

1 egg yolk, well beaten

Combine the horseradish, flour, salt, paprika and butter. Add the cream or milk and cook until smooth and thick, stirring constantly. Remove from the heat, and add the egg yolk. Return to heat and cook for 30 seconds longer. Serve either hot or cold with roast beef. Makes ¾ cup sauce.

### HORSERADISH SAUCE II

| | |
|---|---|
| 1 stick horseradish | 1 tablespoon butter |
| 1 cup soup stock | ½ cup bread crumbs |

Grate the horseradish and combine with the other ingredients. Place in saucepan over heat and boil until of proper consistency. Makes about 1 cup sauce.

*Vollmer's Vollständiges deutsches Vereinigten Staaten Kochbuch,*
*Philadelphia, 1865.*

### HORSERADISH SAUCE III

| | |
|---|---|
| 1 tablespoon flour | 1 cup soup stock |
| 1 tablespoon butter | ½ cup grated horseradish |
| Salt | Sour cream |

Brown the flour in the butter and add salt to taste. Stir in the soup stock and horseradish. Boil until slightly thickened. Add some sour cream just before serving. Makes about 1½ cups sauce.

*Vollmer's Vollständiges deutsches Vereinigten Staaten Kochbuch,*
*Philadelphia, 1865.*

## HORSERADISH IN MILK

| | |
|---|---|
| 1 tablespoon butter | Sugar |
| 3 tablespoons grated almonds | ½ cup grated horseradish |
| 1 teaspoon flour | ½ cup milk (about) |

Melt butter in saucepan and add the almonds, flour, sugar to taste, and horseradish. Gradually pour in the milk (the sauce must remain pretty thick). Let it boil up once and serve. Makes about 1 cup sauce.

*Vollmer's Vollständiges deutsches Vereinigten Staaten Kochbuch,*
*Philadelphia, 1865.*

## WARM MUSTARD SAUCE

| | |
|---|---|
| 4 egg yolks | Sugar |
| 1 tablespoon flour | ½ cup butter, melted |
| Juice of 1 lemon | 2 cups bouillon |

### 3 teaspoons dry mustard

Combine egg yolks, flour, lemon juice and mix well. Add sugar to taste, butter, and bouillon. Cook over low heat, stirring constantly. When sauce boils, add mustard and beat it in well. Makes about 2½ cups sauce.

*Vollmer's Vollständiges deutsches Vereinigten Staaten Kochbuch,*
*Philadelphia, 1865.*

## SORREL SAUCE

### (Sauerambel)

| | |
|---|---|
| 1 cup sorrel leaves | 6 peppercorns |
| 2 tablespoons butter | 5 hard-cooked egg yolks |
| 1½ cups bouillon | ½ tablespoon lemon juice |

Wash sorrel leaves and press out as much water as possible. Crush leaves to a pulp. Melt butter in a saucepan, add crushed sorrel and bouillon. Crush peppercorns, and place in muslin bag, and add to bouillon. Simmer about 20 minutes and strain. Mash egg yolks and combine with small amount of hot bouillon to make a paste. Stir into remaining bouillon and mix until smooth. Add lemon juice and serve hot. Makes about 1½ cups sauce.

*Das Neue Leipziger Koch-Buch von Johann Christ. Wolf,*
*Frankfurt u. Leipzig, 1779.*

## TOMATO SAUCE

| | |
|---|---|
| 2 cups strained tomatoes | 2 tablespoons butter |
| 1 onion, chopped | 1 tablespoon flour |
| 1 bay leaf | 1 teaspoon salt |
| 1 tablespoon chopped parsley | Pepper |

Combine the tomatoes, onion, bay leaf, and parsley, and simmer for 10 minutes. Melt the butter, blend in the flour, and stir until smooth. Add to the first mixture and simmer for 3 minutes. Makes 2½ cups sauce. Serve with pork or veal chops.

*Die Gentelleit un ann're Leit*
*Hen all genunk zu esse;*
*Doch hen sie in re Yaahreszeit*
*Siwwe Pund Dreck zu esse.*
                                    —JOHN BIRMELIN

A little grime occasionally
Will no one ever hurt;
Each man must swallow annually
His seven pounds of dirt.

# Cheese and Cheese Dishes

*En hungrich Maul losst sich net neetiche.*

A hungry man need not be pressed
To be a willing table guest.

In the cookery of the Pennsylvania Germans cheese dishes were restricted largely to such that could be made of skimmed milk curds. Although used to commercial cheeses in their homeland, where Limburger and *Mainzer Handkaes* and the neighboring Low German and Holland cheeses were readily accessible, the early German pioneer in Pennsylvania and generations of his descendants, with their inborn sense of thrift and new-world economic independence, looked upon "store" cheese as a luxury. Their mode of farming and their household menage was attuned to dairy cattle. The picturesque, low-roofed stone springhouses, sheltered in the cool shade of a patriarchal sycamore, elm or willow, that dot our Pennsylvania meadows and lend a distinctive note to our landscape, still bear silent testimony to the extensive dairying of an earlier day. Here the rich cream was skimmed from the earthen dishes and crocks, and churned into the saffron-colored butter that found a ready market in the nearby town or more distant city. But what to do with the remaining skimmed milk? The raising of hogs was a necessary concomitant and large quantities of such milk found their way into the *Seifass*, or swill-barrel, to be transmuted into pork and sausage of high quality. But the zealous housewife also knew how to divert enough of the thick, skimmed milk into her kitchen, where she converted the curds into delicious *Schmierkaes* and other domestic cheeses that could be made with the simple kitchen apparatus at hand. The abundance of thick, sour milk and the thriftiness of the Pennsylvania German *Hausfraa* account for its frequent appearance in recipes throughout this book. We have included in this chapter not only recipes for the making of the few domestic cheeses, but also such dishes that required sour milk curds, although some of them might also have found a place under another category.

## SCHMIERKAES
### (Cottage Cheese)

The making of cottage cheese is the simplest of all cheese processes. Heat two quarts of thick, sour milk gently over a low heat until the curds begin

61

to separate from the whey. If exposed to too high a temperature the curds will get too hard and crummy. Pour into a bag of cheese cloth and hang it up to drain thoroughly. Remove the curds, cover and set aside in a cool place. When the curds are to be used, measure a cupful into a bowl, add the desired amount of salt; then add gradually a cup of cream, sweet or sour, stirring and beating until the cheese has the consistency of soft butter.

*Schmierkaes un Lattwaerrick* are almost as inseparable on the Pennsylvania German menu as *Schnitz un Gnepp*. Cottage cheese spread upon a slice of bread and covered with a thick layer of sweet-tart applebutter is a classic. Some have been known to spread a layer of butter, then a layer of *Schmierkaes,* and over that a thick layer of applebutter, but the thrifty housewife looks askance upon such temerity.

### COTTAGE CHEESE AND SALADS

The modern housewife will be able to build pleasant variations upon an old theme, by adding finely chopped parsley, sage, thyme or chives to the cottage cheese when serving it with fresh lettuce, cress or endive. *Schmierkaes* is still a favorite in the Palatinate of our forefathers where we have had it served with chopped onions with our breakfast coffee.

### HAFFEKAES
#### (Pot Cheese)

Pot cheese, often called cup cheese, is a popular commodity in the cheese shops and markets of eastern Pennsylvania. It can easily be made in the kitchen. Place 2 quarts of thick milk in a baking dish and scald it in the oven. The curds should be harder than for cottage cheese. Drain off the whey and place the curds in a crock. Stir in new curds daily until the desired quantity is reached. Then set the crock in a uniform temperature of about 75° F. and leave there to season or ripen. The longer the ripening process is continued the stronger the finished product. But whenever it has become a sticky mass it may be considered ready for the next step. Now pour the mass into a double boiler and allow to simmer, gradually bringing it to the boiling point, but without stirring it. To every 2 pounds of curds thus treated (or proportionately) now add 2 teaspoons of salt, a cup of sweet cream, 4 tablespoons of butter, ½ teaspoon of soda and stir thoroughly. Bring to a boil in the double boiler and boil for 15 minutes. Now add 2 well-beaten eggs. Boil 5 minutes longer, then pour into small dishes or cups to cool, after which it is ready to be served.

*The Pennsylvania German, March, 1907.*

### BALLEKAES
#### (Ball Cheese)

Known also as summer cheese, this is the height of Pennsylvania German cheese-making. Although not impossible elsewhere, its manufacture lends itself best to the rural kitchen, where a daily supply of thick milk is available. Scald thick milk over a low fire, taking care not to scald it too hard. Drain the curds from the whey and store them daily in an earthen crock kept in a cool place. Whenever a sufficient quantity has accumulated, say at the end of the week, remove the curds from the crock into another receptacle, in which, after adding the desired salt, the whole mass is kneaded until it becomes smooth and shows a tendency to cling together. Then pat and press into balls 2½ or 3 inches in diameter. It is necessary that these balls be fashioned solid from the core. They are then placed on thin boards, kept for that purpose, to dry, starting with a cool temperature, gradually raised, so that by the end of a week they are quite dry and solid. If dried too rapidly, cracks form and that is fatal to the later processing. These dried balls are then carefully placed in crocks, well covered and set in a cool place. In due time a heavy mold forms on the surface of each, which is left until the balls are thoroughly ripened, when they are taken out, carefully scraped and washed, after which they are ready to serve. In earlier days the manufacture of these cheese balls was kept up during the entire fall and winter, the balls being intended for use the following spring and summer, hence the name "summer cheese." They were fine eating during harvest time, but after that they were usually found too assertive for quiet, peaceful mortals. — Custom varied with respect to the treatment of the moldy balls. Some washed them weekly and preferred to wrap them in cheese cloth sprinkled with baking soda. It may be mentioned here that the Pennsylvania Germans used moldy cheese on boils, carbuncles and sores long before the scientist came upon penicillin.

*The Pennsylvania German, March, 1907.*

## EGG CHEESE

| | |
|---|---|
| 4 cups full sweet milk | 2 cups thick, sour milk |
| 4 eggs, well beaten | 2 tablespoons sugar |
| 1 teaspoon salt | |

Scald the sweet milk in a double boiler. Combine eggs, sour milk, sugar and salt and stir into the scalded milk. Simmer gently in double boiler for about 15 minutes, stirring now and then until soft curds set in. Remove from heat, cover and set aside to cool for 15 minutes. Pour cheese into a cheese colander or, better still, press into the perforated heart-, tulip- or star-shaped little cheese molds used for this purpose in the olden day. Chill in the refrigerator. When ready to serve, turn out of the molds on to the plates. — Egg cheese is delicious served with a fruit salad, or with fresh rolls and currant or geranium apple jelly.

## CURD DUMPLINGS
### (Gnepp mit Schmierkaes)

| | |
|---|---|
| 1 tablespoon butter | 1 teaspoon sugar |
| 3 eggs, separated | Grated lemon peel (optional) |
| 1 cup cottage cheese | 3 tablespoons flour |
| Pinch of salt | Browned butter |

Cream the butter until soft, add the egg yolks, cheese, salt, sugar and a bit of grated lemon rind, if desired. Beat egg whites until stiff and fold into mixture. Add flour and mix well. A little more flour may be needed to stiffen dough. Drop from spoon into boiling water. Cover, and steam for about 10 minutes. Remove from water, and serve with browned butter poured over them. Dumplings may be boiled in milk, if desired. Serves 4.

## COTTAGE CHEESE CUSTARD PIE I
### (This is the modest Kaeskuche of the olden days)

| | |
|---|---|
| 1 cup cottage cheese | ½ teaspoon salt |
| 2 small eggs | 1⅛ cups milk |
| 2 teaspoons flour | Cinnamon or nutmeg |
| ¼ cup sugar | 1 unbaked pastry shell |

Crumble cheese with fork, add some milk and beat until smooth and creamy. Combine eggs, flour, sugar and salt, and beat well. Add the rest of the milk to the cheese, beat thoroughly and pour into pastry shell. Sprinkle with cinnamon or nutmeg, if desired. Bake in oven at 450° F., for 15 minutes, than at 325° F. for 30 minutes.

*Mrs. Ellwood Case*

## COTTAGE CHEESE CUSTARD PIE II

| | |
|---|---|
| 1 cup cottage cheese | 2 tablespoons flour |
| 2 tablespoons cream | 1 cup milk |
| 2 tablespoons melted butter | Juice and grated rind of |
| 1 egg, well beaten | ½ lemon |
| ¾ cup sugar | ½ teaspoon salt |
| 1 unbaked pastry shell | |

Mash the cheese with a fork, add cream and beat until smooth and creamy. Combine butter, egg and sugar, beat well and add to the cheese and cream. Add the flour, milk, lemon juice and grated rind, and salt. Pour mixture into an unbaked pastry shell. Bake in hot oven, 450° F., for 15 minutes, reduce to 325° F. and bake for 30 more minutes.

## SWEET CHEESE CAKE
### (From an old Pennsylvania German Almanac)

| | |
|---|---|
| Yeast dough | ½ cup currants |
| 1 cup cottage cheese | ¼ cup sugar |
| 1 tablespoon butter | 1 cup sweet cream |
| 1 tablespoon flour | 2 eggs |

Line a pie tin with a sweet yeast dough (see Moravian Cake or Dough-nuts). Crumble the cottage cheese and sprinkle ½ cup over bottom. Dot with butter. Spread a layer of currants, sprinkle with other half of crumbled cheese and sprinkle lightly with flour. Beat sugar, cream and eggs and pour this mixture over all. Bake in a hot oven, 400° F., for about 30 minutes.

## PEACH and COTTAGE CHEESE PIE

| | |
|---|---|
| 2 cups cottage cheese | ¼ teaspoon salt |
| 2 eggs, well beaten | 1 cup cream |
| ½ cup molasses | 1 cup milk |
| ½ cup brown sugar | 1 unbaked pastry shell |
| 2 tablespoons flour | 7 peach halves |

Mash the cottage cheese with a fork until smooth and creamy, and add the eggs. Mix well. Blend in thoroughly the molasses, sugar, flour, salt, and then add the cream and milk. Mix well. Pour mixture into unbaked pastry shell and arrange the peach halves on top. Bake in a hot oven, 400° F., for about 35 minutes.

From H. L. Fischer's 'S Alt Marik-Haus Mittes in d'r Schtadt, York, Pa. 1879.

Without his beans and bacon, could the Yankee live?
Then could his "wurst" the German long survive?

# Vegetable Dishes

*Wer net kummt zu rechter Zeit,*
*Der muss esse was iwwrich bleibt.*

Come get your dinner while it's good,
Or be content with warmed-up food.

From the terraces of the majestic ruins of Heidelberg Castle, once the proud seat of the mighty electoral princes of the Palatinate, one looks westward over the fertile plain of the Rhine hemmed in the distance by the vine-clad hills of the Haardt. It is the garden spot of Germany. Here winter yields first to the gentle winds of the South. Chestnuts, peaches, apricots, even the semi-tropical figs, almonds and lemons flourish here as nowhere else throughout the German lands. The Rhenish Palatinate has been famed for its orchards, vineyards and gardens since early times. Little wonder then that this ancient soil was drenched with the blood of Celts, Romans, Alemanni, Burgundians and Franks, who in turn through the early centuries fought and died for possession of this fair land; little wonder that the Emperors of the Holy Roman Empire loved to sojourn in their Pfalz and that the French with greedy lust repeatedly invaded this desired land. Here living was good when the fertile soil was tilled. But the despairing populace, who could not enjoy in peace the fruits of its labors, finally sought surcease from its hardships across the sea where they turned Penn's primeval forests into productive gardens not unlike those they knew in their homeland. In their new homes in Pennsylvania the kitchen garden became an important part of their menage. Here they cultivated the vegetables they had known at home and soon acquired additional ones native to their adopted land.

Today we are once more sensitive to the charm of old Pennsylvania German gardens. Unlike the manorial gardens of the South they are in the first place utility gardens and yet not without their distinctive atmosphere. In the intimacy of her garden, just off from the summer kitchen and outdoor bakeoven, enclosed by low stone walls roofed with shingles or red tiles, or at a later time by white-washed pale fences, the Pennsylvania German housewife cultivated her kitchen vegetables. Her men folks turned the rich earth for her

67

in early spring and with her own hands she sowed the seeds and set plants at their proper time and in accordance with ancient tradition. Her German almanac, published by Sauer, of Germantown, or Baer, of Lancaster, had a place of easy access in her kitchen and revealed to her the movements of the moon, whether on the increase or decrease, in apogee or perigee. She studied carefully the signs of the zodiac. She did not forget to sprinkle wood ashes over her garden on Ash Wednesday, to prevent later attacks of aphids. She sowed cabbage seed on Good Friday, but did not work in her garden between Good Friday and Easter, in order not to disturb the repose of Christ in the tomb. She knew that lettuce sowed in Cancer developed good roots. She did not sow radishes in Sagittarius, lest they shoot (go to seed). She sowed beets in Leo, then they would remain red; her cucumbers in Pisces, then they would grow smooth; her beans under an upturned moon, else they would not take to the poles, and preferably in Gemini, so that they would bear twin forms on the stem. She planted potatoes on the 100th day of the year. Turnip seed was sowed either on the day of Peter in Chains (Aug. 1) or on the day of St. Lawrence (Aug. 10). She did not forget to turn over the onion tops on Seven-Sleepers Day (June 27), thus increasing their growth. She would not hoe the cabbage during the Dog Days and thus prevent the attack of aphids. She would not make sauerkraut in Pisces, lest it get slimy, nor in the week of St. Gallus (Oct. 16), lest it become bitter. And thus with zeal and diligence and with a mystic faith in the unknowable processes of nature she furnished her family with garden produce beginning with the tender leaf lettuce, onions and radishes, in early spring, through the summer and fall with cabbage varieties, early and late legumes, tomatoes, corn and peppers, ending only with late celery and endive and her winter supply of root vegetables and late cabbages stored in the earth cellar or in the cave underneath the Switzer barn bridge.

## BEAN SCHNITZEL
### (Bean Cuts)

| | |
|---|---|
| 1 cup diced smoked bacon | 6 cups string beans, cut into |
| 4 medium-sized onions, | 1-inch lengths |
| sliced thin | 1 teaspoon of salt |
| 4 tomatoes, chopped | 1 cup hot water |

Dash of red pepper

Fry the bacon and pour into stew pan containing onions, tomatoes and string beans. Season with salt and red pepper and simmer for 2 hours. Add hot water after vegetables have cooked for 1 hour. Stir occasionally to prevent scorching, adding more water if necessary. When beans are tender there should be a small amount of sauce to serve with them. Serves 6.

## BEAN STEW

| | |
|---|---|
| 2 cups salted water | 4 potatoes, diced |
| 1 teaspoon butter | 1 teaspoon flour |
| 1 pound string beans | 1 tablespoon vinegar |

Salt and pepper

Place water in a saucepan, add the butter and bring to a boil. String the beans, cut them in short pieces, and boil in the salted water. After beans have cooked for 15 minutes, add potatoes and cook until vegetables are tender. Allow about ½ hour for entire cooking time. Sift in the flour, add the vinegar and season to taste with salt and pepper. Cook a few minutes more and serve hot. Serves 6.

## BEAN KRAUT

Prepare the desired amount of string beans and a little salt. Place small amount of beans in a crock, press with a wooden mallet to free the juice, and then add more beans until all are pressed. Cover crock and place a weight on top. Let stand in a warm place to ferment. Cook and serve like sauerkraut.

## GREEN BEANS WITH BACON

| | |
|---|---|
| ¾ cup finely diced bacon | 2 tablespoons flour |
| 1 small onion, minced | 1 cup hot water |

1 quart fresh or canned string beans

Fry the bacon and onion together until light brown. Sprinkle with flour and mix well. Add hot water and beans, cut in 1-inch lengths. Simmer until beans are tender. (Canned beans will take less time.) Add more water while cooking, if needed. Serves 6.

*Mary Elizabeth Spangler*

## HOME BAKED BEANS

| | |
|---|---|
| 2 cups navy beans | 1½ tablespoons sugar |
| ¼ pound salt pork | 1 teaspoon dry mustard |
| 1 tablespoon molasses | 1½ teaspoons salt |

½ cup boiling water

Wash the beans, cover with cold water, and let soak overnight. In the morning, drain, add fresh water and simmer beans until the skins break. To test them, take up a few beans on a spoon and blow on them. If skins break, the beans are sufficiently cooked. Drain beans, add salt pork, cut in strips, and place in an earthen bean pot with several pork strips on top. Mix together the molasses, sugar, mustard, salt and boiling water. Pour over the beans. Cover the pot and bake in a slow oven, 250° F. to 300° F. for about 6 hours. Uncover the pot for the last hour of baking. Serves 6.

## SOUR CABBAGE

| | |
|---|---|
| 4 tablespoons bacon fat | 1 teaspoon brown sugar |
| ½ cup flour | ½ teaspoon salt |
| ½ cup water | 6 cups shredded cabbage |
| 1 tablespoon butter | 3 tablespoons vinegar |

1 egg yolk

Heat bacon fat in a pan. Mix the flour with the water to make a smooth paste, add the butter, sugar, and salt. Blend into the hot fat. Add the cabbage, cover, and simmer for 20 minutes. Remove from heat. Add the vinegar, stir in the egg yolk, cover, and let stand for 1 hour before serving. Serves 6.

## RED CABBAGE I

| | |
|---|---|
| 1 2-pound head red cabbage | 2 sour apples, pared and |
| 4 tablespoons butter | chopped |
| | 6 cloves |

1 glass red wine (optional)

Remove outer, wilted leaves and chop cabbage as for coleslaw. Add butter, apples, and cloves. Cook for about 15 minutes, or until tender. The wine may be added after cabbage is cooked, if desired. Serves 6.

*Henriette Davidis: Praktisches Kochbuch*

## RED CABBAGE II

| | |
|---|---|
| 1 medium-sized head red | Salt and pepper |
| cabbage | 1 onion, sliced |
| 2 tablespoons vinegar | 2 tablespoons butter |
| 2 cups soup stock | 2 tablespoons flour |

1 glass red wine

Wash cabbage and cut as for sauerkraut. Place in saucepan and add vinegar, soup stock, and season with salt and pepper. Boil until tender. One-half hour before serving, stir in onion, which has been fried in butter and flour until browned. Before serving pour wine over all. If a sweeter flavor is desired, add a small amount of sugar. Serves 6.

*Vollmer's Vollständiges deutsches Vereinigten Staaten Kochbuch,*
*Philadelphia, 1865.*

## WEISS KRAUT

### (White cabbage boiled with ham)

Why we call ordinary boiled cabbage *Weiss Kraut*, or white cabbage, is today forgotten. The curly Savoy cabbage, which when prepared approaches the color of spinach, is not popular among us. Boiled red cabbage too is little used. Both were and continue to be popular in Germany. The firm white cabbage was largely used in the making of sauerkraut, but when boiled it was called *Weiss Kraut*, to distinguish from the green Savoy and the red cabbage.

2 pounds of smoked ham  
1 medium-sized head of white  
   cabbage, cut coarsely  
6 medium-sized potatoes,  
   cut in large slices  
Pepper and salt  
4 cups of water

Cover ham with water, bring to a boil and simmer for 2 hours. Add cabbage, potatoes, salt and pepper and boil until potatoes and cabbage are tender. Serve with the ham. Serves 4.

## DRIED CORN

1 cup dried corn  
1 teaspoon salt  
1 teaspoon sugar  
1 tablespoon butter  
1 teaspoon flour  
1/4 cup milk or cream  
1/4 teaspoon pepper

Wash the corn, cover with lukewarm water, and let soak overnight. In the morning, add the salt, sugar, butter and flour. Simmer for 30 minutes, or until tender. Add milk or cream and sprinkle with pepper. Serves 4.

## CORN PIE

2 medium-sized potatoes  
6 ears corn (or 1 No. 2 can)  
1 teaspoon chopped parsley  
3 hard-cooked eggs, diced  
Milk  
1 recipe Basic Pastry  
   (see Index)

Boil the potatoes until half cooked. Peel and dice them. Cut corn from the cobs and mix with potatoes and parsley. Place in a deep greased baking dish, cover with milk and arrange pastry crust on top. Bake in a moderate oven, 350° F., for 45 minutes. Serves 6.

*Mrs. Wm. Engel*

## CORN PUDDING I

2 cups fresh corn (or 1 No. 2  
   can whole-kernel corn)  
2 tablespoons sugar  
1 tablespoon cornstarch  
1 tablespoon butter  
2 eggs  
1 1/2 cups milk and corn liquid  
Salt

Force corn through food chopper, using coarse blade. (This will prevent corn from settling to the bottom of the pudding.) Reserve any liquid from corn to use with milk. Add the sugar, cornstarch, butter, eggs, and salt. Beat well. Add the milk and liquid from corn. Pour mixture into greased baking dish. Bake in a moderate oven, 350: F., for 45 minutes. Serves 6.

*Mrs. Mollie Gable*

## CORN PUDDING II

2 eggs, separated    4 tablespoons milk
6 ears corn, grated    ¼ teaspoon salt
⅛ teaspoon pepper

Beat the egg yolks, add to corn and mix thoroughly. Add the milk and seasonings. Beat egg whites until stiff and fold into corn mixture. Pour into a buttered baking dish, and place dish in pan of hot water. Bake in a moderate oven, 350° F., for about 30 minutes. Serves 4 to 6.

*Mrs. Wm. Engel*

## STEWED CUCUMBERS

4 medium-sized cucumbers  1 tablespoon sugar
1 tablespoon salt     ¼ teaspoon pepper
6 slices bacon, diced    2 tablespoons vinegar
1 tablespoon flour

Pare and slice the cucumbers. Place in saucepan with small amount of water and sprinkle with the salt. Fry bacon until crisp and brown, and pour it with the fat over the cucumbers. Add the sugar, pepper, and vinegar. Cover and simmer for 25 minutes. Then sift the flour over the cucumbers, stir until smooth, and simmer 3 minutes longer. Serve while hot. Serves 6 to 8. Chopped parsley or chives may be sprinkled over cucumbers, if desired.

## FRIED EGGPLANT WITH APPLESAUCE

1 medium-sized eggplant  Salt and pepper
1 egg, beaten      Hot fat
Applesauce

Pare the eggplant and cut it crosswise into ¼-inch slices. Dip each slice into the egg, seasoned with salt and pepper. Fry on both sides in hot fat. Serve with applesauce which is spread on top of eggplant. Serves 6.

## EGGPLANT PATTIES

1 medium-sized eggplant  1 cup bread crumbs
1 onion, minced     1 cup milk
2 eggs, well beaten    2 teaspoons melted butter
Hot fat

Pare and dice the eggplant. Force through food chopper, using a coarse blade. Add the other ingredients and mix well. Drop mixture from a spoon into deep hot fat, 380° F., and fry for 2 to 4 minutes, or until brown. Drain on absorbent paper and serve while hot. Serves 6.

## BAKED LIMA BEANS

1 pound dried Lima beans      ½ cup molasses or brown sugar
Salt and pepper      ½ cup diced bacon

Wash the Lima beans, cover with water, and soak overnight. In the morning, drain, cover with fresh water and boil for 3 hours, or until soft. Drain, season to taste with salt and pepper. Add the molasses or sugar, and the bacon. Mix well. Place in a greased baking dish. Bake in a moderate oven, 350° F., about 30 minutes, or until brown. Serves 6.

## ONION PIE I
### (Zwiwwelkuche)

8 large onions, sliced      Caraway seeds
¼ pound butter      Salt
4 eggs, well beaten      Pepper
4 cups full milk      ¼ pound bacon, diced
1 recipe Basic Pastry (see Index)

Simmer onions in butter until soft and golden brown. Set aside to cool. Line two 9-inch pie pans with pastry. Fry bacon until crisp and remove from fat. Mix eggs, milk, caraway seeds, salt and pepper. Add the onions and divide equally into the two pastry shells. Spread the crisp bacon on top. Bake at 450° F. for 15 minutes, then reduce to 350° and bake for 30 minutes more. Serves 6. This is a main dish and with coleslaw or a crisp green salad, constitutes a meal.

Variation I: Line pie pan with pastry and sprinkle with flour. Fill with thinly sliced onion. Add salt, pepper, butter and a cup of sweet cream. Bake at 400° F. for 40 minutes.

*Mrs. Irwin Maurer*

Variation II: Fill an unbaked pie crust with sliced onion. Sprinkle with salt, pepper and a little flour. Dot with pieces of thinly sliced bacon and bake until brown.

*Carrie Haas Troutman*

## ONION PIE II

½ recipe Basic Pastry      Butter
  (see Index)      Salt and pepper
6 to 8 large onions, sliced thin      1 teaspoon sugar
2 cups cubed stale bread      ¾ cup milk (more or less)

Line a two-inch deep pan with pastry. Sprinkle with a little flour. Place a layer of onions in bottom of pan, then a layer of bread cubes. Sprinkle with salt and pepper and dot with butter. Repeat process, ending with layer of bread cubes. Sprinkle with sugar and pour in enough milk to cover. Let stand 3 minutes, or until milk is absorbed. Add a little more milk. Bake in a hot oven, 450° F., for 10 minutes, then reduce heat to 350° F. and bake 35 minutes more until onions are done and bread is light brown. Serves 6.

*Mrs. Stanley Arthur*

### ONION CUSTARD PIE

| | |
|---|---|
| 1 unbaked pastry shell | 1 tablespoon flour |
| 6 to 8 large onions, sliced thin | 1 tablespoon butter |
| 1 egg, well beaten | 1 cup scalded milk, lukewarm |

Salt and pepper

Arrange sliced onions in unbaked pastry shell. Prepare a custard by combining the egg, flour, butter, and gradually adding the lukewarm milk. Season with salt and pepper to taste. Pour custard over the onions. Bake in a hot oven, 450° F., for 10 minutes, then reduce heat to 350° F. and bake for 35 to 40 minutes longer, until inserted knife comes out clean.

*Mrs. Jesse Renninger*

### PARSNIPS

| | |
|---|---|
| 12 medium-sized parsnips | 1 egg, slightly beaten |
| 1 cup flour | 1 cup milk |
| ¼ teaspoon salt | 1 tablespoon melted butter |

Hot fat

Wash and scrape parsnips, and cook in boiling water for about 30 minutes, or until almost tender. Drain, cut into desired lengths. If core is fibrous, cut out and discard it. Make a batter of the remaining ingredients. Dip parsnips into batter and fry in hot fat for 3 to 5 minutes, until golden brown. Drain, sprinkle with salt, and serve at once. Serves 6.

*Henriette Davidis: Praktisches Kochbuch*

### SUGAR PEAS

#### (Zucker Aerbse)

For many Americans sugar peas are a stepchild among vegetables. We Pennsylvania Germans come naturally by our love for sugar peas. They continue to be a preferred vegetable in the Palatinate to this day.

Sugar peas demand the earliest new potatoes, smaller than a walnut. The ambitious *Hausfraa* in our rural parts even plants seed potatoes in pots or boxes in the house, to be set out in her garden upon the earliest premonition of spring, so they may be ready for early sugar peas.

String the tender pods, add to the early potatoes when half-cooked, and add salt, butter, and cream. Some people prefer to boil the pods and potatoes with ham or bacon, in which case the meat should be almost cooked before vegetables are added.

But why not try the *Pelser* (Palatine) way? Boil the pods in salted water, add a sour cream dressing, and serve with pancakes, or as in the southern Palatinate with *G'schmelzte Nudle*.

| 2 pounds young sugar peas | 1 teaspoon sugar |
|---|---|
| (In the pod) | 1 teaspoon salt |
| 1 tablespoon butter | 1½ cups beef stock |

Chopped parsley

So-called sugar peas are not shelled, but cooked in the pod. Remove strings from pod and place pods in saucepan. Add other ingredients, except parsley, and simmer until tender. When cooked, sprinkle with parsley and serve. Serves 6.

Variations: Diced new potatoes may be added to pods and cooked until both are tender. Serve with cream sauce.

Sugar peas may be cooked with ham or bacon instead of beef stock, if desired.

*Henriette Davidis: Praktisches Kochbuch*

## POTATOES

The potato was a long time in making its way from Spain and Italy into the countries north of the Alps. It was at first unpopular among the Germans who feared that it caused leprosy. Frederick the Great, recognizing their food value, compelled the peasants of eastern Germany to raise them, but they obstinately refused to eat potatoes until His Majesty himself convinced them that potatoes were harmless by appearing on a balcony in Breslau and eating of them in public. In the course of the 18th century they became the indispensable food of the common people, among whom they were at first known as *Erdäpfel* (earth apples) and *Grundbirnen* (ground pears). The latter word gave way in the Palatinate dialect to *Grumbeere* and *Grumbiere*, both of which forms are in use in Pennsylvania today. The form *Tartuffeln*, borrowed from the Italian *tartufolli* (truffles), was corrupted in Switzerland to *Kartoffeln*, which, strange to relate, found a permanent place in the High German. It is possible that the earliest German settlers in Pennsylvania were not acquainted with the potato, but in the course of time this nourishing tuber became a staple food for their descendants. The Pennsylvania German housewife, like her cousin in the Palatinate, learned to serve the potato in many forms: boiled with or without their "jackets," stuffed, mashed, baked and fried; in salads, soups, pancakes and dumplings (see Index). In many families they are served three times a day, the week through, not without jests and jibes. *Werkdaags esse mer Grumbeere un Sunndaags Kardoffle!*

## GERMAN FRIED POTATOES

| 8 medium-sized potatoes | 2 tablespoons bacon drippings |
|---|---|
| 4 onions | (or 1 of butter and 1 of lard) |
| | Pepper and salt |

Boil potatoes in skins. When cooled, peel and slice. Slice onions. Heat fat in frying-pan, add onions and potatoes and fry 5 minutes. Stir, then cover pan and fry slowly for 10 minutes. Uncover, add seasoning and fry over increased heat for 10 more minutes until they turn brown. Sprinkle with chopped chives, thyme or caraway seeds. Serve at once. Serves 6.

### BAKED POTATOES IN HALF SHELL

| | |
|---|---|
| 6 medium-sized potatoes | 2 tablespoons butter |
| ½ cup milk | ½ cup grated cooking cheese |
| Salt and paprika | |

Bake unpared washed potatoes in hot oven until soft. Remove and cut at once in halves. Scoop out, taking care not to break skins. Mash pulp, add butter, milk and salt. Beat well and replace in skins. Sprinkle tops with cheese and paprika. Return to hot oven and bake about 5 minutes or until cheese turns brown. Serves 6.

### ESCALLOPED POTATOES

| | |
|---|---|
| 6 medium-sized potatoes | Bread crumbs |
| 1½ cups milk (about) | ½ cup grated cooking cheese |
| Butter | 1 tablespoon flour |
| Salt and pepper | |

Pare and slice potatoes. Parboil potatoes. Mix cheese, flour, salt and pepper. Place potatoes in buttered casserole, sprinkling layer for layer with cheese mixture. Melt butter in heated milk and pour over potatoes until it shows through top layer. Sprinkle top with fine bread crumbs and bake in moderate oven, 375° F., for 1¼ hours. Serves 6.

### GRUMBEERE BALLE

#### (Potato Balls)

| | |
|---|---|
| 6 large potatoes | 1½ tablespoons minced parsley |
| 2 tablespoons butter | 1½ teaspoons salt |

Peel potatoes, cut them into small balls with a French cutter or melon scoop. Soak in cold water for 15 minutes. Drain, cover with fresh water, and cook about 12 minutes, or until tender. Drain, add butter, minced parsley, and salt to taste. Serve at once. Allow about 8 potato balls per serving.

### BROWNED POTATO BALLS

| | |
|---|---|
| 4 potatoes | Flour |
| 2 eggs | ½ cup fine bread crumbs |
| 1 teaspoon salt | 1 tablespoon butter |

Boil potatoes until done, peel, and force through a food chopper, using a coarse blade. Add the eggs, salt, and enough flour to make a stiff mixture. Form into balls about 1 inch in diameter. Boil in salted water for 2 minutes. Drain, roll in bread crumbs and brown in butter. Serves 4.

## POTATO PUDDING

| | |
|---|---|
| 8 to 10 medium-sized potatoes | 8 eggs, separated |
| 1 cup flour | Salt |
| ½ cup cream | 2 onions, sliced |
| 2 tablespoons butter, melted | 1 cup coarse bread crumbs |
| | Butter |

Cook potatoes in boiling water for 20 to 30 minutes, until done. Peel and grate. Mix flour and cream to form a smooth paste, and add butter. Place over a low heat and gradually stir in beaten egg yolks. Add potatoes and salt to taste. Fold in egg whites, beaten stiff. Turn mixture into greased mold, cover, and steam in boiling water for 1 hour. Fry onions and bread crumbs in butter until golden brown. Pour over unmolded pudding and serve immediately. Serves 8.

*Das Neue Gothaische Kochbuch, Gotha, 1804.*

## POTATO CAKES

| | |
|---|---|
| 1 onion | 1 tablespoon flour |
| 8 medium-sized potatoes | 1 teaspoon baking powder |
| 2 eggs, well beaten | Salt and pepper |
| | 3 tablespoons hot fat |

Peel the onion and potatoes and grate them. Combine with the eggs, flour, baking powder, and season to taste with salt and pepper. Heat fat in frying pan or griddle and drop mixture from spoon into hot fat. Fry until brown. Serves 8.

*Mrs. E. H. Richards*

## SOUR POTATOES

| | |
|---|---|
| 8 medium-sized potatoes | ¾ cup vinegar |
| ½ cup bacon fat (about) | 2 eggs, well beaten |

Pare the potatoes and slice thin. Boil them in salted water for 15 minutes, or until soft. Drain. Heat bacon fat, add vinegar and eggs and simmer for about 10 minutes, stirring constantly. Pour dressing over the potatoes and serve while hot. Serves 8.

*Maryets Grumbeere in aller Frieh,*
*Middaags Grumbeere in Fleeschbrieh,*
*Owets Grumbeere mit de Heit —*
*Des waehrt bis in die Ewichkeit!*

## BAKED SWEET POTATOES

| | |
|---|---|
| 6 medium-sized sweet potatoes | ½ teaspoon salt |
| 6 tart apples | 1 teaspoon mace or cinnamon |
| ¾ cup brown sugar | 4 tablespoons butter |

Wash the sweet potatoes, cover with boiling salted water and cook 20 to 30 minutes, or until tender. Drain, peel, and slice in half lengthwise. Peel, core, and slice the apples. Place a layer of sweet potatoes in a buttered baking dish, add a layer of apples and sprinkle with sugar, salt, and mace or cinnamon. Repeat process until the dish is filled, ending with layer of apples. Dot with butter. Bake in a moderate oven, 350° F., for about 45 minutes. Serves 6.

### SAUERKRAUT

Sauerkraut is another Pennsylvania German gift to the American people. Today its use is nation-wide. Its very name has become a part of the English language. We do not kuow who first thought of fermenting finely cut cabbage as a means of preservation, nor when. It has been popular for centuries in the northern countries of Europe, in whose cooler summers the cabbage family thrives especially well. Cabbage is one of the oldest of our domestic vegetables. The ancients ate it raw to prevent intoxication. Perhaps they also made sauerkraut, for we know that they preserved turnips by process of fermentation.

Despite the high standardization of commercial sauerkraut, we Pennsylvania Germans throughout the villages and rural parts still like in late summer and early fall to stomp finely-cut cabbage in big stone crocks or wooden vats *(Schtenner)*, cover it with grape leaves and a round board or slate and weight it down with the large ancestral *Wacke* (cobble-stone). — Yes,

> *Cut it on the cabbage cutter,*
> *Slip and slice and flip and flutter,*
> *Tender shreds in barrel dumping;*
> *Nimbly then in barrel jumping,*
> *One of us with naked feet —*
> *That's what makes it good and sweet —*
> *Ever treading, ever spreading,*
> *Salty brine between the toes,*
> *Layer over layer it grows,*
> *Till it reaches to the top,*
> *Then we know it's time to stop.*
> *Sauerkraut, oh Sauerkraut!*
> *See vonce! Now ve find id oudt!*
> —JOHN BIRMELIN

### SAUERKRAUT

Place a 2- to 3-inch layer of thinly sliced cabbage in the bottom of a large stone or earthen crock and sprinkle lightly with salt. Pound well with a heavy wooden "stomper" or potato masher to release the juice. Repeat this process until the crock is almost full. (The salty juice should rise above the cabbage.) Cover with a clean cloth, place a round board on top, weigh it down heavily

Un dichtig g'schtampelt mit die Füss
Sel macht's a' nort so zaart un Süss.

From H. L. Fischer's *'S Alt Marik-Haus Mittes in d'r Schtadt*, York, Pa. 1879

and set it in a warm place to ferment. In about 6 days remove the scum which has formed on the top. Wash the cloth in cold water, replace it and move the crock to a cool place. In about 2 weeks the sauerkraut will be ready for use.

## COOKED SAUERKRAUT

| | |
|---|---|
| 2 pounds fresh pork | 1 quart sauerkraut |

Boil pork until tender and with minimum broth. Add sauerkraut and boil 45 minutes. Serve with mashed potatoes. Serves 6.

Although fresh pork is the preferred meat, the Pennsylvania German housewife will know how to vary the above simple basic recipe. Now and then she will dice a tart apple into the boiling sauerkraut, lending it a wine flavor; or she may add half a dozen juniper berries, or sprinkle it with caraway seed. Instead of the above meat she may substitute frankfurters or pig's knuckles. — A more sophisticated variation is that of boiling it in the same pot with stewed chicken and steaming dumplings (see Index) on top.

## BROWNED SAUERKRAUT

| | |
|---|---|
| 1 onion, chopped | 1 quart sauerkraut |
| 2 tablespoons shortening, melted | 1 potato, grated |
| | 1 teaspoon caraway seeds |

Brown the onion in the shortening, add the sauerkraut, and cook for 8 minutes. Add the potato and caraway seeds, cover with boiling water, and simmer for 1 hour or longer. Cook uncovered for first ½ hour, then cover for remainder of cooking period. Serves 6.

## FRIED GREEN TOMATOES

| | |
|---|---|
| 6 large green tomatoes | 1 teaspoon salt |
| 1 tablespoon sugar | 1 egg, well beaten |
| ½ teaspoon pepper | ½ cup bread crumbs |
| Hot fat | |

Wash the tomatoes and cut into ½-inch slices. Soak for 1 hour in cold, salted water. Add the sugar, pepper, and salt to the egg. Dip each tomato slice in mixture and then in the bread crumbs. Fry on both sides in hot fat until brown. Serves 6.

## BAKED STUFFED TOMATOES

| | |
|---|---|
| 6 large tomatoes | 2 tablespoons melted butter |
| 1 tablespoon minced onion | 1 teaspoon minced parsley |
| 1 egg, well beaten | ½ teaspoon salt |
| 1 cup bread crumbs | ⅛ teaspoon pepper |

Wash tomatoes, remove stem ends, and scoop out center pulp. Chop pulp and mix with other ingredients. Fill the tomatoes with mixture and place them in a greased baking dish. Bake in a moderate oven, 350° F., for 30 minutes. Serves 6.

## TURNIP KRAUT

Peel the desired amount of turnips and slice thin. Add a little salt, and place in a crock. Cover and place weight on top. Let stand in a warm place to ferment. Cook and serve like sauerkraut.

*Mrs. E. H. Richards*

*Deel Leit blanse ihr Gaardesache im rechte Zeeche un annere blanse 's in der Grund.*

Some people plant their vegetables in the right sign of the zodiac and others plant them in the ground.

# Salads and Salad Dressings

*Der Hunger iss der bescht Koch*
Hunger is the best sauce

Long culinary customs and traditions have left the Pennsylvania Germans ill-disposed toward the use of olive oil. The crisp herb salads of lettuce and other greens, favored in the olive-producing Mediterranean countries, are not indigenous to Pennsylvania German cookery. Beechnut and other vegetable oils used in northern Europe were probably not known to our early 18th century German settlers. In Pennsylvania they soon had a greater abundance of animal and dairy fats than they had ever known before and these more nearly satisfied the requirements of hard-working settlers in a more rugged climate. Hot bacon and sour cream dressings came into general use and have remained a distinctive note in the Pennsylvania German cuisine. The outsider is at first shocked when he finds that the Pennsylvania German housewife pours hot dressing over her salads, but whoever eats for the first time young dandelions, uncooked spinach, early leaf lettuce, cabbage or endive, with one or the other of the following dressings, experiences an unforgettable gastronomic delight that dispels all further apprehensions.

## COLESLAW I
### (with Gritzel-Grotzel)

| | |
|---|---|
| 1 small head cabbage | 1 cup sugar |
| 2 eggs, beaten | 1 cup milk |
| ⅔ cup vinegar | ⅛ pound bacon |

Salt

Slice the cabbage very fine. Combine the eggs, vinegar, sugar and salt. Place over heat, stirring constantly. When mixture comes to a boil remove from heat. Cool, and add the milk. Pour over the sliced cabbage. Cut the bacon into ¼-inch squares. Fry until crisp and add with the fat to cabbage mixture. Serve immediately. Serves 6.

*Mrs. J. Max. Hark*

## COLESLAW II

| | |
|---|---|
| 1 small head cabbage | 2 cups sugar |
| 1 teaspoon salt | ⅓ cup cream, sweet or sour |
| 1 onion, grated | ⅓ cup vinegar |

Chopped celery or cucumber (optional)

Slice the cabbage very fine  Add the salt, onion and 1 cup of the sugar. Mix with the hands, squeezing slightly to release the juice.  Blend together the cream, vinegar, remaining sugar, and pour over the cabbage.  Mix well. Chopped celery or cucumber may be added, if desired. Serves 6. — Coleslaw is a Holland Dutch word for cabbage salad.

*Mrs. E. H. Richards*

## HOT CABBAGE SLAW I

| | |
|---|---|
| 1 medium-sized head cabbage | 1 egg, beaten |
| 5 tablespoons shortening | 2 cups grated cheese |
| 1 teaspoon dry mustard | 3 cups milk |
| 1½ tablespoons flour | ⅔ cup vinegar |

Salt and pepper

Slice the cabbage very fine.  Brown it in the shortening.  Place cabbage in top of double boiler, over boiling water.  Combine the other ingredients, and pour mixture over the cabbage.  Mix well.  Cook until thickened.  Serve hot. Serves 6 to 8.

*Mrs. E. H. Richards*

## HOT CABBAGE SLAW II

| | |
|---|---|
| ⅛ pound bacon, diced | 2 tablespoons flour |
| 1½ cups milk | ½ teaspoon salt |
| 2 cups finely cut cabbage | Dash of pepper |
| 1 egg, well beaten | 1½ tablespoons prepared |
| ⅓ cup sugar | mustard |

2 teaspoons vinegar

Fry the bacon until crisp and remove from pan.  To the fat, add the milk and cabbage.  In another pan mix together the egg, sugar, flour, salt and pepper, and cook until thick and smooth.  Pour over the cabbage mixture. Remove from heat.  Add the mustard and vinegar.  Sprinkle diced bacon over the top and serve hot.  Serves 4.

*Mrs. Anna F. Williams*

## CARROT SALAD

| | |
|---|---|
| 1½ cups carrots, cut in strips | Lettuce or parsley |
| 2 tablespoons vinegar | 2 hard-cooked eggs, sliced |

Boil the carrots in salted water for 15 minutes, or until tender.  Drain, add the vinegar, and chill.  Then drain off the vinegar.  Line a salad bowl with crisp lettuce leaves or parsley and place a border of sliced eggs around edge. Mix carrots lightly with either Dutch Dressing or Sour Cream Dressing (see Index), and place on lettuce. Serves 2 to 4.

## CUCUMBER SALAD

| | |
|---|---|
| 2 cucumbers | 2 tablespoons vinegar |
| 1 onion (optional) | 2 cups thick sour cream |
| 1 teaspoon salt | ½ teaspoon pepper |

Peel and slice the cucumbers and onion. Sprinkle with salt and add the vinegar. Pour sour cream over all, mix well, and sprinkle with pepper. Serves 4.

## DANDELION SALAD

This is the favorite salad of Elsie Singmaster, famous Pennsylvania German author.

| | |
|---|---|
| 1 pound young dandelion greens | 1 teaspoon salt |
| ½ cup cream | ½ teaspoon paprika |
| 2 tablespoons butter | 1 tablespoon sugar |
| 2 eggs | 4 tablespoons vinegar |
| ½ teaspoon pepper | ¼ pound bacon |

Wash and pick over the dandelion greens. Dry and place in a salad bowl and set aside in a warm place. Blend the cream and butter. Beat eggs, add the pepper, salt, paprika, sugar, and vinegar. Combine with the cream mixture. Place over heat and stir until it thickens to the consistency of a soft custard. Then pour mixture, while hot, over the dandelion greens. Toss until greens are thoroughly coated. Cut bacon into small squares, fry until crisp. Pour bacon, with the fat, over top of salad. Serves 4.

## MIXED SALAD

| | |
|---|---|
| Lettuce | Chopped celery |
| Boiled potatoes, diced | Tomatoes, sliced |
| Minced onion | Hard-cooked eggs, sliced |

Line a salad bowl with desired amount of crisp lettuce leaves. Cover with a layer of cold potatoes, sprinkle with a little finely minced onion. Add a layer of chopped celery, another layer of potatoes, then sliced tomatoes. Top with thinly sliced hard-cooked egg. Serve with Dutch Dressing (see Index).

## POTATO SALAD I

| | |
|---|---|
| 10 medium-sized potatoes | 2 eggs, beaten |
| 5 hard-cooked eggs | 3 tablespoons sugar |
| ½ stalk celery, chopped fine | ½ cup vinegar |
| 2 teaspoons celery seed | ½ cup milk |
| Salt and pepper | ½ pound bacon, diced |

Boil potatoes until tender, peel, and slice. Chop egg whites and add with the celery to potatoes. Sprinkle with celery seed and season to taste with salt and pepper. Combine beaten eggs, sugar and vinegar. Mix well, place over heat, and bring to a boil. Stir mixture constantly to avoid scorching. Remove from heat, cool, and stir in milk. Pour dressing over salad, mixing well. Arrange salad on a bed of lettuce leaves. Sprinkle with hard-cooked egg yolks which have been pressed through a sieve. Fry bacon until crisp and pour, with fat, over the salad. Chill and serve immediately. Serves 6 to 8.

*Mrs. J. Max. Hark*

## POTATO SALAD II

| | |
|---|---|
| 10 medium-sized potatoes | 1/8 teaspoon dry mustard |
| 4 hard-cooked eggs, sliced | 1/2 cup cream |
| 1/4 cup vinegar | 3 stalks celery, chopped |
| 1/4 cup sugar | Minced onion (optional) |
| 1 teaspoon salt | Paprika |

### Parsley

Pare potatoes, cut into cubes, and cook for about 10 minutes. Drain and add hard-cooked eggs while potatoes are hot. Mix together the vinegar, sugar, salt, mustard, and cream, and pour over the hot potato mixture, stirring until well mixed. Cool. Add chopped celery, and onion if desired. Sprinkle with paprika and garnish with parsley. Chill and serve. Serves 6 to 8.

*Mrs. Walter Sechrist*

## SPINACH SALAD

| | |
|---|---|
| 1 pound spinach | 1 recipe Hot Salad Dressing II |
| | (See Index) |
| 2 hard-boiled eggs | |

Wash spinach and cut. Pour hot dressing over the raw spinach and mix well. Garnish top with sliced eggs.

## TURNIP-TOP SALAD

A favorite salad in late winter, when stored turnips send forth delicate white sprouts. Wash about a pound of turnip tops. Prepare Hot Salad Dressing II (see Index) and pour over sprouts. Garnish with hard-boiled eggs.

## GRANDMOM GABLE'S TOMATO SALAD

| | |
|---|---|
| 6 large tomatoes | 3/4 cup sugar |
| Salt | 2 stalks celery, chopped fine |
| 1/2 cup vinegar | Cinnamon |

Cut tomatoes into thin slices, sprinkle with salt and let stand for 10 to 15 minutes. Drain off juice, add the vinegar, sugar, and celery. Sprinkle lightly with cinnamon. Serves 6.

### RAW VEGETABLE SALAD

Combine equal amounts of raw grated cauliflower, chopped Bermuda onion, and chopped celery. Serve with Sour Cream Dressing (see Index).

*Mrs. Walter Erdman*

### CHICKEN SALAD

| | |
|---|---|
| 6 cups cooked chicken, diced | 1 cup cider vinegar |
| 3 cups diced celery | ½ cup water |
| 3 small boiled potatoes, cubed | 1 tablespoon dry mustard |
| 3 eggs, separated | 1 tablespoon salt |

2 tablespoons olive oil

Combine chicken, celery, and potatoes. Drop egg whites into small amount of hot water. When hard-cooked, chop fine, and add to chicken mixture. Bring vinegar and water to a boil, pour it over egg yolks, mix thoroughly and let stand near heat to thicken. Mix remaining ingredients thoroughly, add to thickened vinegar and beat until creamy. Cool. Pour dressing over salad and chill before serving. Serves 10.

### MEAT AND FISH SALAD

| | |
|---|---|
| ½ cup dried beef, shredded | 2 cloves garlic, minced |
| ½ cup boiled smoked tongue, chopped | 1 small onion, minced |
| | 1 pickled red pepper, chopped |
| ½ cup smoked halibut, chopped | ⅔ cup salad oil |
| 1 cup diced celery | ⅓ cup vinegar |
| 2 cooked potatoes, diced | 6 hard-boiled eggs |

Combine all ingredients, except the vinegar, oil, and eggs. Place in a salad bowl and add desired amount of salad oil. Toss salad until well coated. Add the vinegar and mix gently. Serve on bed of lettuce and garnish with egg yolks, mashed through a sieve, and egg whites cut in strips. Serves 6.

## SALAD DRESSINGS

Any of the following dressings, whether bacon or sour-cream, can be used on dandelions, leaf or head lettuce, cabbage and endive. But Sour-cream Dressing I is preferred on cucumbers.

### HOT SALAD DRESSING I

| | |
|---|---|
| 1 tablespoon bacon fat, or butter | ½ teaspoon dry mustard |
| | ½ teaspoon salt |
| 1 teaspoon flour | ⅛ teaspoon pepper |
| ½ cup vinegar | 2 teaspoons sugar |

1 egg yolk

Melt the shortening and blend in the flour. Add the vinegar and stir until thick. Mix the mustard, salt, pepper and sugar, and add to first mixture. Cook for 4 minutes. Pour over the beaten egg yolk and stir thoroughly. Return to the heat and cook 1 minute longer. Makes about ¾ cup dressing.

## HOT SALAD DRESSING II

| | |
|---|---|
| 3 slices bacon, cubed | 3 tablespoons sugar |
| 1 egg, beaten | ½ teaspoon salt |
| 1 teaspoon flour | 3 teaspoons milk or cream |
| Vinegar | |

Fry bacon until brown and crisp. Mix egg, flour, sugar, salt, and milk or cream. Add to bacon in pan and mix well. Add vinegar to taste. Boil until creamy and thick. Pour over salad. If desired, garnish with sliced hard-boiled eggs. Makes about ½ cup dressing.

*Mrs. Norman H. Hoffman*

## DANDELION DRESSING

| | |
|---|---|
| 3 slices bacon | 5 tablespoons sugar |
| ½ cup milk or cream | 1 tablespoon flour |
| ¼ cup vinegar | Pinch of salt |
| 1 hard-cooked egg, chopped | |

Fry the bacon slowly until crisp. Remove from pan and crush into small bits. Mix cream, vinegar, sugar, flour and salt, and add to the fat. Bring mixture to a boil, stirring constantly. Pour over dandelion greens. Garnish with chopped egg and bacon. Makes about ¾ cup dressing.

## DUTCH DRESSING

| | |
|---|---|
| 2 tablespoons bacon fat | ¼ cup vinegar |
| 1 tablespoon flour | ¼ cup water |
| 2 egg yolks, well beaten | Salt and pepper |
| Paprika | |

Heat the bacon fat and blend with the flour. Add the egg yolks, vinegar, and water. Stir over low heat for a few minutes, until smooth and creamy. Add seasonings to taste. Makes about ¾ cup dressing.

## HOT ENDIVE DRESSING

| | |
|---|---|
| 4 slices bacon, cut in small pieces | 1 tablespoon sugar |
| | ¾ teaspoon dry mustard |
| 2 egg yolks | ½ teaspoon salt |
| 1 tablespoon flour | ¾ cup water |
| 2 tablespoons and 1 teaspoon vinegar | |

Fry bacon until brown and crisp. Mix egg yolks, flour, sugar, mustard and salt. Add water and vinegar. Pour mixture into pan with bacon and fat. Place over heat and stir constantly until it thickens to consistency of soft custard. Pour hot over cut endive.

*Elsie Singmaster*

### MUSTARD DRESSING

| | |
|---|---|
| 1 tablespoon dry mustard | 2 egg yolks, well beaten |
| 1 tablespoon flour | 1 tablespoon sugar |
| ½ cup cream | 1 tablespoon salt |

½ cup vinegar

Mix the mustard and flour with a small quantity of the cream to form a smooth paste. Add remaining ingredients and blend thoroughly. Place over low heat and bring to a boil, stirring constantly. Remove from heat when thick and creamy. Makes about 1¼ cups dressing.

### SALAD DRESSING
#### for Sorrel, Dock or Wild Lettuce

| | |
|---|---|
| 4 slices bacon | 1 egg, beaten |
| ½ cup sour milk | 1 tablespoon flour |
| or buttermilk | 2 teaspoons sugar |
| ¼ cup vinegar | Pinch of salt |

Fry bacon until crisp. Remove from pan and break into bits. Mix milk, vinegar, egg, flour, sugar and salt, and add to bacon fat. Boil until thick, then add bits of bacon. Cool and pour over raw, washed "greens" just before serving.

*Mrs. Stanley Arthur*

For Sorrel, Dock and Wild Lettuce, see Chapter on Herbs and Greens.

### SOUR CREAM DRESSING I

| | |
|---|---|
| 1 cup thick sour cream | 2 tablespoons sugar |
| 2 tablespoons white vinegar | Salt and pepper |

Mix thoroughly the cream and vinegar. Add sugar, and salt and pepper to taste. Serve on sliced cucumbers or cabbage. Makes about 1 cup dressing.

### SOUR CREAM DRESSING II

| | |
|---|---|
| 2 tablespoons sugar | ¼ cup vinegar |
| 1 tablespoon flour | ¼ cup water |
| 1 teaspoon dry mustard | 1 egg, beaten |
| ¼ teaspoon salt | 1 tablespoon butter or bacon fat |

1 cup sour cream, whipped

Mix ingredients and add vinegar, water, and egg. Beat until thoroughly mixed. Place in top of double boiler over hot water and cook for 5 minutes, or until smooth and thick, stirring constantly. Cool. Fold in the whipped sour cream. Makes about 1¾ cups dressing.

### SWEET–SOUR DRESSING

| | |
|---|---|
| 2 eggs | 1 cup sugar |
| ⅔ cup vinegar | 1½ cups milk (about) |

Beat eggs, add vinegar and sugar. Place over heat and bring to boiling point. Remove from heat. Cool. Add the milk, enough to form desired consistency. Makes about 2½ cups dressing.

*Mrs. H. Bingham Hark*

### SALAD DRESSING WITHOUT CREAM

| | |
|---|---|
| 1 tablespoon flour | 2 teaspoons dry mustard |
| 3 tablespoons sugar | ⅓ cup vinegar |
| 1 teaspoon salt | ½ cup water |
| 1 egg, beaten | |

Combine dry ingredients, add vinegar, water, and egg. Beat thoroughly until well mixed. Place over heat and bring to a boil. Cook for 2 minutes, or until smooth and thickened. Serve either hot or cold. Makes about 1 cup dressing.

# Noodles, Dumplings and the Like

*Es kumme meh Leit am Disch um als im Grieg*

There are more table casualties than war casualties

We Pennsylvania Germans have been charged with eating too much starchy food. Our cuisine is rich in boiled dough dishes. We come naturally by our predilection for this form of starch food. Our forebears lived on old-world soil ill adapted for the cultivation of wheat. Rye was the large grain crop, therefore most of the bread consumed was the so-called black bread. There were areas in which, in crop rotation, wheat was grown only every seventh year. For many people lovely white wheaten flour was a luxury, to be used only in smaller quantities in such forms as noodles and dumplings (with their many German provincial names) and their kin. After the potato had made its way north of the Alps the poor man found in it an easy and palatable form of starch. Even though our Pennsylvania farmers in the course of time grew large crops of potatoes, wheat was also grown in large quantity and there was no need to restrain their love of dough dishes. To be sure, with both potatoes and wheat in abundance, the calories do pile up, but we are a happy people and few of us bear a strained and hungry look.

## NOODLES

2 eggs, beaten          ½ teaspoon salt
1 cup sifted flour (scant)

To the eggs, add the salt and as much flour as can be worked in. Knead thoroughly, cover, and let stand for ½ hour. Then roll out very thin, spread on a cloth, and allow to dry before cutting into narrow strips. Serves 6. Place in boiling salted water, cover, and cook for 15 minutes. Drain and serve. — This recipe is basic for various noodle dishes.

## GSCHMELZTE NUDLE

### (Buttered Noodles)

This is still a very popular dish. The word, often misunderstood, comes from *schmälzen*, to pour drippings of butter or fat into (compare the noun *Schmalz*, fat or lard).

Use the basic noodle recipe above. Boil noodles in salted water until soft. Drain, spread on a platter. Fry a cup of bread crumbs in butter until golden brown. Pour over the noodles. Brown some more butter and pour over all. Serve hot.

### WASSERSCHPATZE

(This noodle form is of a larger dimension than the famous Swabian *Spätzle*, but the process is a similar one)

| | |
|---|---|
| 3 tablespoons butter | ½ teaspoon salt |
| 3 egg yolks, beaten | 2 onions cut fine |
| 2 cups sifted flour | 1 cup bread crumbs |
| Milk | Butter |

Cream the 3 tablespoons of butter until soft and add egg yolks. Add flour and enough milk to form a rather stiff dough. Add salt and knead thoroughly on a slightly floured board. Roll out very thin. Cut dough into long ½-inch strips. As the strips are cut scrape them quickly and with a regular motion from the edge of the board into the bubbling boiling water. You may not succeed the first time. Boil until the noodles rise to top, drain and keep hot, ready to serve. Fry onions and bread crumbs in butter and serve over hot noodles. Serve with a crisp lettuce salad. Serves 6.

*Das Neue Gothaische Kochbuch, Gotha, 1804*

### MAULTASCHEN I

The above interesting word is usually very badly mutilated in our cookbooks, since for many of us its significance has become obscured. *Maultaschen* (sing. *Maultasche*) are filled enclosures of various shapes and sizes and made of a noodle or a potpie dough. The name itself means literally "mouth pocket," a vulgar German name for malformed or swollen lips and here applied to the pursed and ruffled overlapped dough when steamed.*

| | |
|---|---|
| Double the noodle recipe | 3 slices white bread, trimmed |
| (see Index) | ½ cup chopped celery |
| 1 pound ground meat | ½ cup chopped onion |
| 1 egg, beaten | 2 tablespoons chopped parsley |
| Salt and pepper | |

Double the basic noodle recipe. After the dough has been kneaded, wrap in cloth and set aside for half an hour. The dough must be softer than for cut noodles. For filling take the raw ground meat (preferably of veal, pork

*The name is familiar to students of Austrian history. Because of her unsightly lips the fourteenth century Duchess Margareta, who, childless, ceded her Tyrolese counties to her Austrian cousin Duke Rudolf IV of Hapsburg, was known as Margareta Maultasche. The American reading public knows her through Lion Feuchtwanger's novel "The Ugly Duchess."

and beef), add beaten egg, bread (previously soaked in water and pressed out), celery, onion, salt and pepper, and mix thoroughly. Roll out the dough into large circular form, spread filling over one half of it, fold over it the other half. Take a small, sharp-edged plate or saucer and press firmly down upon the dough in long parallel lines, then crosswise, thus cutting it into small 1½-inch squares. These squares are then dropped into rapidly boiling salted water. When they come to the top they are done. Dip them out with slotted or perforated spoon upon a large platter, turning them to dry on both sides. Set aside in refrigerator until they are to be used. Then fry them in butter and serve at once.

*Mrs. Robert R. Fritsch*

### MAULTASCHEN II

| | |
|---|---|
| Double the noodle recipe (see Index) | 1 pound spinach |
| ¾ pound ground pork | 1 onion |
| 4 eggs, beaten | 1 cup bread crumbs |
| 5 slices white bread, trimmed | Salt and pepper |
| | Nutmeg |

**Butter**

Soak bread in water. Fry the ground pork. Boil the spinach and drain. Press water from soaked bread. Mix pork, spinach, bread and eggs; add onion, salt and pepper, and a pinch of nutmeg. Stir thoroughly and set aside. Roll out noodle dough in large, circular form, spread filling on one half of the dough and lap over the other half. Then proceed exactly as in recipe for Maultaschen I above. Arrange boiled *Maultaschen* on a platter, sprinkle with parsley and chives. Pour over them the bread crumbs browned in butter and some additional browned butter. Serve with early lettuce from the garden. This is a preferred Eastertide dish.

*Adapted from Mathilde Jung's "Eine Landschaft kocht."*

### BUWESCHENKEL
#### ("Boys' Thighs")

| | |
|---|---|
| 2 pounds beef | 1 tablespoon chopped parsley |
| 6 potatoes | Pepper |
| 3 teaspoons salt | 2 cups flour |
| 2 tablespoons butter | 2 teaspoons baking powder |
| ½ cup chopped onion | 2 eggs, beaten |

**½ cup milk**

Cover two pounds of lean beef with water, add 1 teaspoon of salt and some pepper, and boil until tender. Pare and boil the potatoes. Mash potatoes and add 1 teaspoon of salt, 1 tablespoon of the butter, the onion and parsley. Sift together the flour, baking powder, and remaining salt. Stir in the eggs and milk to make a soft dough. Divide the dough into small equal parts, so that each part when rolled out forms a small circle about 6 inches in diameter. Place filling mixture on one half of the round and lap over the other half, moistening the edges and pressing tightly together. Drop these semi-circular *Buweschenkel* upon the boiling meat and broth, cover tightly and boil about 25 minutes. Remove the meat on a platter, place the *Buweschenkel* around it, and pour the broth (boiled down if necessary) over the whole.

### GFILLDE NUDLE
#### (Filled Noodles)

| | |
|---|---|
| 5 eggs | 1 pound sausage meat |
| 1 teaspoon salt | ½ cup chopped onion |
| 2 cups sifted flour | 1 teaspoon chopped parsley |
| 1 cup bread crumbs | 2 tablespoons butter |

Beat 4 of the eggs, add salt and flour. Knead dough on a lightly floured board. Roll out thin and circular. Fry sausage meat and cool; mix the fried sausage meat, remaining egg, onion and parsley. Spread mixture over one half of the dough and fold over the other half. Cut with sharp-edged plate or saucer as in *Maultaschen I.* Drop into boiling salted water or meat broth. Cover and steam for about 25 minutes. Brown bread crumbs in butter and pour over the filled noodles. Serve with a mixed salad. Serves 6.

The above dishes, whether *Maultaschen, Buweschenkel* or filled noodles, are all kin to the Italian raviolis.

### STEAMED DUMPLINGS
#### (Dampgnepp)

The German *Kloesze* and *Knoedel,* and their kindred forms, were generally known in the Rhenish Palatinate as *Knepp,* hence also in Pennsylvania *Knepp* or *Gnepp.*

| | |
|---|---|
| 2 cups sifted flour | ½ cup milk (about) |
| 4 teaspoons baking powder | 2 tablespoons butter, melted |
| 1 teaspoon salt | 1 egg, well beaten |

Mix flour, baking powder and salt. Add milk, butter and egg, and beat until batter is moderately stiff. Drop from spoon into boiling soup or meat stews, or into boiling salted water. Cover and steam for 20 minutes without removing lid. This is a basic dumpling recipe. These dumplings can be served with stewed chicken, with sauerkraut, and with Schnitz un Gnepp (see Index). For many they are a favorite dessert when served with rich sweetened milk. Our dialect poet, John Birmelin, in playful mood, wrote:

> Der Dampgnopp waerd net aagenaeht
> An Hemmer un an Hosse;
> Er waerd mit Zucker iwwerschdreet
> Un dann mit Millich begosse.

## GREEN DUMPLINGS I

½ cup parsley                     Butter
½ cup spinach                     1 cup bread crumbs
¼ cup chervil                     2 eggs, beaten
¼ cup chives                      Salt and pepper

Wash the greens and chop them fine. Steam in a small amount of butter for about 5 minutes. Add bread crumbs and eggs, season to taste with salt and pepper, and mix thoroughly. Shape into small dumplings and drop into boiling soup. When dumplings rise to the surface they are ready to serve. If cooked too long they will fall apart. Serves 6.

*Henriette Davidis: Praktisches Kochbuch*

## GREEN DUMPLINGS II

1 pound spinach                   2 eggs, beaten
1 onion, chopped fine             1 teaspoon chopped parsley
2 tablespoons butter              Nutmeg
½ pound fine bread crumbs         1 tablespoon flour
                    Salt

Wash the spinach and chop it fine. Combine with onion and place in saucepan with 1 tablespoon of the butter. Steam for 5 minutes. Remove from heat and stir in the bread crumbs, eggs, parsley, nutmeg to taste, and the remaining butter. Add the flour and salt to taste. Mix thoroughly and set aside for ½ hour. Shape into medium-sized dumplings and drop into salted boiling water. Cover, and cook for 10 minutes. Serve with a parsley sauce in the springtime, and in summer serve with Tomato Sauce (see Index). Serves 6.

*A Palatine Recipe.*

## HOORICHE GNEPP
### (Hairy Dumplings)

2 cups grated raw potato          1 cup grated dry bread
1 cup grated boiled potato        3 eggs, beaten
               3 tablespoons flour

Press as much moisture from raw potatoes as possible. Combine with boiled potato, dry bread, eggs, and flour. Knead well and shape into dumplings a little larger than a walnut. Drop into salted boiling water. Cover, and cook for about 10 minutes. Serve with a sauce made of browned butter and thick cream. Serves 6.

*A Palatine Recipe.*

## LIVER DUMPLINGS

| | |
|---|---|
| 1 large onion, diced | 1½ pounds liver |
| 1 tablespoon shortening | 2 eggs, well beaten |
| 8 cups bread crumbs | Salt and pepper |
| Flour | |

Fry the onion in the shortening and add the bread crumbs. Force the liver through a food chopper. Mix liver with the eggs, and the onion, and bread crumbs, and season to taste with salt and pepper. Stir in enough flour to make a fairly stiff batter. Drop batter from a spoon into boiling salted water, soup, or broth. Cover and cook for 30 minutes. Serves 6 to 8.

## POTATO DUMPLING I
### (Grumbeere Gnepp)

| | |
|---|---|
| 6 medium-sized potatoes | 2 tablespoons flour |
| ½ pound sliced bacon | Salt |
| 1 cup coarse bread crumbs | ½ teaspoon mace |
| 6 eggs, beaten | Croutons, buttered |

Boil potatoes, peel, and cut them into small cubes. Put through food chopper, using coarse blade. Fry bacon until crisp, crumble, and combine with bread. Add eggs, flour, mace, and salt to taste. Combine with potatoes, form into balls, and roll in flour. Drop into boiling salted water, or bouillon, cover, and steam for 12 minutes. Serve with croutons, browned in butter. Serves 6.

## POTATO DUMPLING II
### (Grumbeere Gnepp)

| | |
|---|---|
| 8 to 10 medium-sized potatoes | ¼ teaspoon thyme |
| ¼ pound butter, melted | ½ cup flour |
| 4 eggs | 5 slices bread |
| Salt | Milk |
| ¼ teaspoon nutmeg | Chopped parsley |
| ¼ teaspoon marjoram | Butter |

Boil the potatoes and peel them. Cool, and grate them. Stir together the butter, eggs, salt, and add nutmeg, marjoram, and thyme. Beat until frothy. Add grated potatoes and flour. Dice 2 slices of the bread, and soak in milk. Squeeze excess milk from bread, and add bread. Add some chopped parsley and beat mixture thoroughly. Dice remaining slices of bread and brown in butter. Form dumplings with the hands, placing a few croutons in center of each dumpling. Drop into boiling salted water and steam for 15 minutes. Remove from water, place dumplings in a deep dish and scatter bread crumbs, browned in butter, over them. Serves 8.

## SCHNEEBALLE
### (Snow Balls)

| | |
|---|---|
| 10 medium-sized potatoes | 1 teaspoon salt |
| 1 onion, chopped fine | ¼ teaspoon marjoram |
| 2 tablespoons butter | ¼ teaspoon nutmeg |
| 2 eggs, well beaten | 3 tablespoons flour |

Boil the potatoes until tender. Peel them and let stand overnight. In the morning, grate the potatoes. Fry the onion in the butter and add to the potatoes, together with the eggs, salt, marjoram, nutmeg, and flour. Knead until the dough no longer clings to sides of bowl. Dip hands in flour and shape dough into small dumplings. Drop into salted boiling water, cover, and steam for about 10 minutes. Serve with browned butter poured over them. Serves 6 to 8.

*A Palatine Recipe.*

## SCHWOWE GNEPP
### (Swabian Dumplings)

| | |
|---|---|
| ½ recipe bread dough | Butter |
| (see Index) | 1 tablespoon sugar |
| 1 cup cubed bread | 1 cup hot boiled milk |

Shape bread dough into 24 dumplings the size of a small egg. Let them rise. When feathery light, drop gently into boiling salted water. Cover and steam for 15 minutes. Remove and place on a platter. Brown bread in butter, scatter over dumplings, sprinkle with sugar and pour milk over all. Serves 6 to 8.

This old recipe was a favorite in the Yoder and Reiner families of the Mahantango Valley. It is reminiscent of the Swabian traditions in Wuerttemberg.

*Don Yoder*

## SPONGE DUMPLING

| | |
|---|---|
| ¼ cup butter | ½ cup milk |
| ½ cup flour | 2 eggs, separated |
| | Dash of mace |

Melt half of the butter, stir into it the flour and the milk. Beat mixture until it no longer sticks to side of saucepan. Melt the remaining butter, add the egg yolks and mace. Combine with first mixture. Beat egg whites until stiff and fold into batter. Drop from spoon into boiling salted water. Cover, and steam for about 10 minutes. When they come to the surface, the dumplings are cooked. Serves 4.

*Henriette Davidis: Praktisches Kochbuch*

### YEAST DUMPLINGS

| | |
|---|---|
| 2¼ cups sifted flour | ½ yeast cake |
| 3 tablespoons butter, melted | 2 eggs, beaten |
| ½ cup lukewarm milk | ½ teaspoon salt |

Combine flour and butter. Mix milk and yeast together and add to flour with eggs and salt. Beat well and let rise for 1 hour. Punch down and let dough rise again. Roll out in a thick layer, cut with small round cutter and let rise again. Drop into salted boiling water, cover, and steam for about 15 minutes. Serves 6.

This recipe may be used with *Schnitz un Gnepp* (see Index) or dumplings may be served with stewed fruit.

# Pancakes, Waffles Fritters etc.

*Saag mer was du esscht un ich saag der wer du bischt.*

What you eat supplies the key
To what kind of a man you be.

Batter cakes, whether baked over the fire in pans, on griddles, or in deep fat, occupy a major place in Pennsylvania German cookery. In the dialect they are known as *Pannekuche* and *Bladdekuche* (pancakes and griddle cakes). But the word *Pannekuche* also originally denoted cakes fried in deep fat. There is no dialect word for "fritters". All these batter cakes are eaten hot. Doughnuts and crullers, though fried in deep fat, are not batter cakes and have therefore been placed elsewhere. Some of the fritter recipes might also have found a place under "Desserts", but since they usually constitute the main portion of the meal, whether breakfast or supper, they have been placed under this general category.

## PANCAKE BATTER

The German pancake is baked as one large cake instead of a nnmber of small cakes such as the common griddle cake of wheat, buckwheat, or corn meal. Usually a heavy iron pan is kept just for pancakes. If the pan has been used to fry other foods it should be scoured with salt and rubbed, although this frequently causes the pancake to stick to the bottom of the pan.

Always mix the flour with a small amount of warm milk, beat thoroughly and then add the remaining milk. Beat the egg whites separately and fold in last to make a light batter. If crisp pancakes are desired, whole eggs are beaten into the batter.

Use a generous amount of shortening but do not let it get too hot. Spread the batter evenly in the warm pan and bake on top of stove at an even temperature. To brown the top, place pan under a moderate flame of the broiler.

| | |
|---|---|
| 3 tablespoons sifted pastry flour | 4 eggs |
| | Salt |
| 1 cup warm milk | Pinch of mace (optional) |

Hand-carved buttermold with heart and tree-of-life motifs
*Courtesy,* Landis Valley Museum, Landis Valley, Pa.

Beat flour with small amount of milk. Beat eggs with remaining milk
and add to the flour. Add salt, and if this batter is to be used for a small
fruit pancake, add a pinch of mace and 1 tablespoon flour. Makes 2 large
pancakes.

*Henriette Davidis: Praktisches Kochbuch*

Variation: In earlier days the Pennsylvania German housewife would
add 1 cup of pitted sweet cherries and 1 tablespoon sugar to this recipe. Then
it was served as a supper dessert. In season other berries — currants, blue-
berries, raspberries, blackberries — are used in the same way.

In the summer chopped chives may be added to the batter instead of the
fruit and sugar.

### APPLE PANCAKES

| | |
|---|---|
| 1 recipe Pancake Batter | 1¼ cups diced apples |
| (see Index) | Sugar |
| 2 tablespoons butter | Cinnamon |

Prepare Pancake Batter according to recipe. Heat butter in pan, add
apples, sugar and cinnamon to taste, and spread ingredients evently in pan.
Cover and steam apples for about 10 minutes. Add batter and bake as directed
in Pancake Batter recipe. Makes 2 large pancakes.

*Henriette Davidis: Praktisches Kochbuch*

### PLUM PANCAKES

| | |
|---|---|
| 1 recipe Pancake Batter | 6 plums (about) |
| (see Index) | Sugar |

Make Pancake Batter as directed. Pour a thin layer of batter into warm
pan. When batter begins to bake, place halved plums on it, cut side down,
and pour a thin layer of batter on top of plums. Continue baking as directed.
When done, sprinkle pancake with sugar. Makes 2 large pancakes.

*Henriette Davidis: Praktisches Kochbuch*

### EGG PANCAKES I

| | |
|---|---|
| 5 eggs, separated | ½ cup milk |
| 1 cup sifted flour | |

Beat the egg yolks until light and foamy. Gradually add the milk and
flour, and mix until smooth. Fold in the egg whites, beaten stiff. Drop from
a tablespoon onto a hot greased griddle. Makes about 12 pancakes.

### EGG PANCAKES II

| | |
|---|---|
| 6 eggs, separated | 1 cup sour cream |
| 5 tablespoons flour | 1 cup milk |
| Pinch of salt | |

Combine egg yolks, beaten until foamy, with flour, and sour cream. Add salt and the milk. Just before baking add egg whites, beaten stiff. Fry in butter until golden brown. Makes 3 large pancakes.

*Henriette Davidis: Praktisches Kochbuch*

## BREAD CAKES

| | |
|---|---|
| 1 pound dry bread | 2 eggs, well beaten |
| Hot water | 4 tablespoons flour |
| 1½ teaspoons baking powder | Salt |
| Milk | |

Scald the bread with hot water, and mash it smooth. Add other ingredients and salt to taste. Stir until well mixed. Add enough milk to make a thin batter. Bake on a hot greased griddle.

## BUCKWHEAT CAKES I

| | |
|---|---|
| ½ yeast cake | 3 cups lukewarm potato water |
| 1 cup warm water | 1 teaspoon salt |
| 2 teaspoons wheat flour | ½ teaspoon soda |
| 2 teaspoons corn meal | 2 teaspoons molasses |
| 1¾ cups buckwheat flour | ½ cup scalded milk, |
| (about) | lukewarm |

Dissolve the yeast cake in the warm water. Add the wheat flour, corn meal, and enough buckwheat flour to make a thin batter. Set in a warm place to rise for 6 to 7 hours. Add the potato water, salt, and enough additional buckwheat flour to make a stiff batter. Beat hard and set aside to rise again for about 8 hours. Add the soda, dissolved in a small amount of warm water, the molasses, and milk. The final batter should be thin enough to pour easily. Let stand for ½ hour, then bake to a golden brown on a hot griddle. Serve with honey, maple syrup, or molasses. Makes about 18 cakes.

## BUCKWHEAT CAKES II

| | |
|---|---|
| 1 cup potato yeast (or 1 | 1 quart buttermilk |
| yeast cake) | 1 teaspoon salt |
| Buckwheat flour | |

Mix yeast with buttermilk, and add salt. Add enough buckwheat flour to make fairly thin batter. Set in a warm place to rise for 3 hours. Bake on a hot griddle and serve with *Frische Brodwarscht* (fresh pork sausage)— enough said!

*Mrs. Norman H. Hoffman*

## GREAT-GRANDMOTHER STUMP'S CORN CAKES

| | |
|---|---|
| 2 cups corn meal | Pinch of salt |
| ½ cup flour | 1 egg |
| 1 teaspoon soda | 1 tablespoon melted butter |

2 cups buttermilk

Mix together the corn meal, flour, soda, and salt. Break the egg into the mixture, add the melted butter, and blend thoroughly. Add the buttermilk and mix well. Bake on a hot griddle. Delicious served with sausage. Makes 24 cakes.

## BREAD-CRUMB CORN CAKES

| | |
|---|---|
| 2 cups coarse bread crumbs | ½ teaspoon salt |
| (stale but not too dry) | ⅔ teaspoon soda |
| 2 cups sour milk | ¾ cup corn meal |
| 1 tablespoon butter | 2 tablespoons flour |

2 eggs, separated

Combine bread crumbs and sour milk, and let stand overnight. In the morning, add the butter, salt, soda, corn meal, flour and egg yolks. Mix well, then fold in the egg whites, beaten stiff. Drop from a tablespoon onto a hot griddle. Makes about 24 small cakes.

## FLANNEL CAKE I

| | |
|---|---|
| 2 cups sour cream | ½ teaspoon salt |
| 1½ cups sifted flour | 1 teaspoon brown sugar |
| 2 eggs, well beaten | 1 teaspoon soda |

1 teaspoon vinegar

Mix together 1 cup of the sour cream and a little of the flour. Add the eggs, sugar and salt, and beat thoroughly. Add the rest of the cream and the soda moistened in the vinegar. Add the remaining flour to form a batter which is easily poured. Bake on a hot griddle. Makes about 18 cakes.

## FLANNEL CAKE II

| | |
|---|---|
| 1 teaspoon soda | 2 eggs, separated |
| 1½ cups sour cream or | 1½ cups sweet milk |
| buttermilk | 1 tablespoon butter |

3 cups sifted flour

Dissolve the soda in the sour milk and add to the beaten egg yolks. Stir in the sweet milk, butter, and flour. Fold in the egg whites, beaten stiff. Bake on a hot griddle. Makes about 30 cakes.

## FLANNEL CAKE III

| | |
|---|---|
| 1½ cups sifted flour | 1 egg |
| 1¼ teaspoon baking powder | 1 tablespoon melted butter |
| 1 tablespoon sugar | 2 cups milk |
| ½ teaspoon salt | |

Combine flour, baking powder, and sugar. Add egg, butter, milk and salt, and beat thoroughly. Bake on a hot griddle. Makes about 18 cakes.

## RICE GRIDDLECAKES

| | |
|---|---|
| 1 cup rice | 1 teaspoon baking powder |
| 3 eggs, well beaten | 1 cup flour |
| 2 cups milk | |

Boil the rice until tender. Add the eggs. Sift baking powder with flour and add to rice alternately with the milk. Mix well. Bake on a hot griddle. Makes about 18 cakes.

## OHRFEIGE

### (A Box on the Ear)

| | |
|---|---|
| 4 eggs, separated | Salt |
| ½ cup warm milk | Butter |
| 1 tablespoon flour | Confectioner's sugar |
| Pinch of mace or grated | Strawberry or currant jam, |
| lemon rind | or jelly |
| Cinnamon | |

Beat egg yolks with small amount of milk. Combine flour and remaining milk and beat until smooth. Add mace or lemon rind, and season to taste with salt. Fold in egg whites, beaten stiff, just before baking. Heat butter in pan over low flame, pour batter into pan. Heat the lid and place it on pan. Bake on top of stove for about 10 minutes, or until the top is dry and the bottom a golden yellow. Spread with jam or jelly, fold over and turn onto a small platter. Sprinkle with sugar and cinnamon. Makes 2 large pancakes.

*Henriette Davidis: Praktisches Kochbuch*

## BUTTERMILK WAFFLES

| | |
|---|---|
| 1 tablespoon melted butter | 1 teaspoon salt |
| 5 cups sifted flour | 3 eggs, separated |
| 4 cups buttermilk | 1½ teaspoons soda |
| 1 tablespoon molasses | Hot water |

Combine the butter, flour, buttermilk, molasses, and salt and beat until smooth. Add the egg yolks, well beaten, and the soda which has been dissolved in a small amount of hot water. Fold in egg whites, beaten stiff.

Bake on a hot waffle iron and serve witn maple syrup or honey.  Makes 12 waffles.

## CORN WAFFLES

¾ cup grated fresh corn, or          1 tablespoon melted butter
   ¼ cup dried corn                  1½ cups flour
2 eggs, separated                    2 teaspoons baking powder
1 cup milk                           1 teaspoon sugar
                    ½ teaspoon salt

If dried corn is used, soak the corn in lukewarm water overnight, drain, and force through a food chopper.  Beat the egg yolks, add the milk, butter and corn, and stir until well mixed.  Sift together the flour, baking powder, sugar, and salt and add to corn mixture.  Fold in egg whites, beaten stiff. Bake on a hot waffle iron.  Makes about 6 waffles.

## RICE WAFFLES

1 tablespoon butter                  1 teaspoon salt
1 tablespoon lard                    2 teaspoons baking powder
2 eggs, separated                    1 teaspoon sugar
1 cup boiled rice                    1 teaspoon molasses
2 cups flour                         1 cup milk (about)

Combine butter, lard, and well-beaten egg yolks with the rice, and mix well.  Sift together the flour, salt, baking powder, and sugar and add to rice mixture with molasses and milk.  Batter should be thin enough to pour easily. Fold in egg whites, beaten stiff.  Bake on a hot waffle iron, and serve with maple syrup, or sugar and cinnamon mixed together.  Makes about 6 waffles.

## YEAST WAFFLES

2 cups scalded milk                  ¼ pound butter, melted
4 cups sifted flour                  1 yeast cake
                    Warm water

Combine the milk and flour, and add the butter.  Dissolve yeast in small amount of warm water and add to mixture.  Let rise 3 to 4 hours before baking.  Bake on a hot waffle iron.  Makes about 12 waffles.

# FRITTERS

## FRITTER BATTER
### (With Yeast)

1 yeast cake                         Pinch of salt
¾ cup scalded milk, lukewarm         1½ tablespoons melted butter
2 eggs, separated                    ¾ cup sifted flour

Dissolve yeast cake in warm milk, add egg yolks, well beaten, salt and butter. Beat in flour. Fold in egg whites, beaten stiff. Set aside to rise. Use as cover batter for fruit and meat dishes. Makes about 1 cup batter.

### FRITTER BATTER FOR FRUIT

| | |
|---|---|
| ¾ cup warm milk | 1 tablespoon rum |
| ¾ cup sifted flour | Pinch of salt |
| 4 egg yolks, beaten | 1 tablespoon sugar |
| 1 tablespoon melted butter | 2 egg whites, beaten stiff |

Combine milk and flour, beating until smooth. Add beaten egg yolks, butter, rum, salt, and sugar. Mix well. Fold in egg whites. Use as a cover batter for fruits. Makes about 1¼ cups batter.

### APPLE FRITTERS

| | |
|---|---|
| 2 large tart apples | ½ teaspoon salt |
| 1 egg | 1 cup flour (about) |
| 1 tablespoon sugar | 1 teaspoon baking powder |
| | 1 cup milk |

Pare, core, and cut each apple (preferably Summer Rambo apples) into 8 slices. Beat the egg, add sugar, and salt, and mix well. Sift together the flour and baking powder and add alternately with milk to egg mixture. Dip apple slices in the batter. Drop into hot fat and fry until a golden brown and apples are soft. Serves 4 to 6.

Variation: Cube ½ pound smoked bacon and fry until brown. Remove bacon from fat. Dice the apples. Prepare fritter batter, using buckwheat instead of white flour. Mix apples, bacon, and batter together and drop from spoon into deep hot fat. Fry until well browned, and apples are soft.

*Mrs. Carrie Haas Troutman*

### ELDERBERRY BLOSSOM FRITTERS
#### (Hollerbliet Kichelcher)

| | |
|---|---|
| 2 eggs, well beaten | 2 cups flour |
| 1 cup milk | Elderberry blossom |
| ½ teaspoon salt | Powdered sugar |

Combine eggs and milk and beat until foamy. Add the salt. Stir into the flour and beat until a smooth batter results. Wash the large pannicles of the elder blossoms and break them into small parts. Dip into the batter. Fry in deep hot fat, 360° F., for about 3 minutes, or until a golden brown. Toss the fritters in a brown paper bag containing some powdered sugar. "The blossoms should be eaten while still hot and nice and crisp. You can really eat and eat!"

*Gertrude Meyers Hillenhand*

### BLACK LOCUST BLOSSOM FRITTERS

Prepare batter and proceed as for the above Elderflower Fritters, using the racemes of our native Black Locust tree, when in full blossom and heavy in honey and fragrance. Omit cinnamon. Taste and fragrance not of this earth! Poetry reduced to food!

### GRAPELEAF FRITTERS

Grape leaves
Strawberry, raspberry, or
    currant jam

1 recipe Fritter Batter for
Fruit (see Index)
Sugar

A springtime rhapsody! Select desired number of young grape leaves. Wash and dry them. Spread thinly with jam or fruit preserve. Roll tightly as for a jelly roll. Dip in batter and fry in deep fat until a golden brown. Sprinkle with sugar and serve while hot.

*Das Neue Gothaische Kochbuch, Gotha, 1804*

### PEACH FRITTERS

½ cup sugar
⅓ cup butter
2 eggs, well beaten
2 cups sifted flour
½ teaspoon salt

3 teaspoons baking powder
1 cup milk
½ teaspoon vanilla
½ teaspoon lemon juice
1½ cups chopped peaches

Powdered sugar

Cream together the sugar and butter, add the eggs and mix thoroughly. Sift together the flour, salt, baking powder, and add alternately with the milk to butter mixture. Stir in the vanilla, lemon juice. Add peaches. Drop from a teaspoon into deep hot fat. Fry to a golden brown. Sprinkle with powdered sugar and serve while hot. Serves 6.

### NUNSPUFFS

4 cups milk
4 cups sifted flour

7 eggs, well beaten
1 teaspoon salt

Scald the milk and mix with the flour. Add the eggs and salt, and beat mixture until very light. Drop from large tablespoon into deep, hot fat, 360° F., and fry until brown. Drain on absorbent paper and serve while hot. Sprinkle with powdered sugar, or eat with syrup or honey.

*Mrs. Conrad Hermsted*

### SNOWBALLS

4 cups milk
4 cups sifted flour

12 eggs
½ cup sugar

Heat the milk, and add the flour, stirring vigorously until mixture forms a smooth ball which leaves sides of pan clean. Allow to cool somewhat and then add the eggs, 1 at a time, beating thoroughly after each addition. Add the sugar. Drop from a tablespoon into deep hot fat, 360°F., and fry until brown. The Snowballs will swell as they brown. Serve with syrup or honey, if desired.

## WASHINGTON FRITTERS

| | |
|---|---|
| 4 large potatoes, (white or sweet potatoes) | 2 tablespoons powdered sugar |
| | Juice of 1 lemon |
| 2 tablespoons cream | ½ nutmeg, grated |
| 2 tablespoons sweet white wine | 8 egg yolks |
| | 6 egg whites |

Boil potatoes and peel them. When cool, grate potatoes as fine as possible. Mix together the cream, wine, sugar, lemon juice, and nutmeg. Beat the egg yolks and whites, and add gradually to the creamed mixture. Add grated potatoes. Beat mixture for 15 minutes. Drop from a tablespoon into hot fat and fry until golden brown. Serve immediately with the following sauce:
Sauce:

| | |
|---|---|
| 2 wineglasses white wine | 1 wine glass rose water |
| Juice of 2 lemons | Powdered sugar |
| Nutmeg | |

Mix together the wine, lemon juice and rose water. Sweeten to taste with sugar and sprinkle lightly with nutmeg.

## ONION FRITTERS

| | |
|---|---|
| 4 large onions | Flour |
| 2 teaspoons sugar | 1 cup milk |
| ½ teaspoon salt | 1 egg, well beaten |
| 1 teaspoon baking powder | Cinnamon |

Peel onions and cut into ¼-inch slices. Separate slices into individual rings. Sift the sugar, salt, and baking powder into enough flour to make a light batter. Combine milk and egg, and add alternately to dry ingredients. Dip onion rings into the batter. Fry in deep fat until a golden brown. Sprinkle lightly with cinnamon and serve at once. Serves 6.

## CORN FRITTERS

| | |
|---|---|
| 2 eggs, separated | ¼ teaspoon pepper |
| 2 tablespoons flour | 1 teaspoon salt |
| 1 tablespoon sugar | |
| 2 cups grated corn (fresh or canned) | |

Combine the beaten egg yolks, flour and seasoning. Add to the corn. Fold in egg whites, beaten stiff. Drop from tablespoon into hot frying pan or griddle, and brown on both sides in butter. Serves 6.

## RICE FRITTERS

| | |
|---|---|
| 3 tablespoons rice | 1 teaspoon grated lemon rind |
| 4 eggs, well beaten | Sugar |
| ½ cup currants | Nutmeg |

Sifted flour

Cook the rice in boiling salted water until done. Drain thoroughly. Add the eggs, currants, lemon rind, and sugar and nutmeg to taste. Stir in enough flour to thicken. Drop into hot fat and fry until golden brown. Serves 4.

## RYE MEAL FRITTERS

| | |
|---|---|
| 3 cups rye meal | 1½ cups sour milk |
| 1 teaspoon salt | 2 eggs, well beaten |
| 1 teaspoon soda | ⅓ cup molasses (New Orleans) |

Sift together the rye meal, salt, and soda. Gradually add the milk and mix well. Then add the eggs and molasses. Drop from spoon into deep hot fat and fry until brown, about 4 minutes. Drain on absorbent paper.

## STRAUBEN

| | |
|---|---|
| 1 cup cream | 2 tablespoons sugar |
| 4 eggs, beaten | Flour (about two cups) |

Mix cream, eggs and sugar and add only enough flour to allow dough to be easily rolled. Cut out with small figure cutters and fry in deep fat until golden brown. Powder with sugar and serve hot.

*A Palatine recipe*

The word *Strauben* implies a shagginess or ruffling up (compare the Ger. verb *sträuben*) referring no doubt to the shape taken when the soft dough drops into the hot fat. The word came into the Palatinate via Bavaria and Switzerland. It is interesting to note here that the Palatine dialect form *Streible* has in Lancaster County, presumably under Swiss influence, become *Streivlin*. See recipe below.

## DRECHDER KUCHE I

### (Funnel Cakes)

Known among the plain people in Lancaster County as *Streivlin*. Compare Ger. *Sträublein*, diminutive of *Strauben* (see recipe above).

| | |
|---|---|
| 2 cups milk | 2 cups flour (more or less) |
| 2 eggs, beaten | 1 teaspoon baking powder |

½ teaspoon salt

Mix milk and eggs. Sift one cup of flour with salt and baking powder. Pour milk and egg mixture into the flour and add only as much more flour as is needed to make a batter not too thick to flow. Pour batter into a good-sized funnel and let it drip through the funnel into deep hot fat. Spiral and other forms can be made by dexterous turns of the funnel and control of out-let with finger. Sprinkle with powdered sugar and serve hot. You may how-ever wish to serve it with fried sausage as Tilly Shindledecker did in Elsie Singmaster's delightful story "The End of the World" (in BRED IN THE BONE, Houghton Mifflin Co., 1925).*

### DRECHDER KUCHE II
#### (Funnel Cakes)

| | |
|---|---|
| 1 teaspoon baking soda | 2 eggs, well beaten |
| 1 cup sour cream | Pinch of salt |
| 1 cup sour milk | 2 cups sifted flour |
| 1 cup sugar | Lard |

Dissolve the soda in the milk. Mix the remaining ingredients together, except the lard, and combine with the milk to form a light batter. Place enough lard in a frying pan to cover the bottom of the pan. When lard is hot pour the batter through a funnel into the hot lard, beginning at the center of the pan and working the stream of batter around in a gradually enlarging circle. Be careful not to touch sides of pan or circle of dough. Serve while hot with tart jelly or with molasses.

*(The following few recipes, for want of a better place seek shelter here).*

### FRIED BREAD

| | |
|---|---|
| 6 slices bread | ½ cup milk |
| 2 eggs, well beaten | Salt and pepper |

Use bread which is 1-to 2-days old. Mix together the eggs and milk, and season to taste with salt and pepper. Dip bread slices into the mixture. Fry on both sides in hot fat until golden brown. Serve with molasses or a tart jelly, or sprinkle with sugar. Serves 6.

*Eleazer Herr, self-appointed prophet, had come to his neighbors, the elderly spinsters, Betsey and Tilly Shindledecker, with the dire message: "On Wednes-day at midnight the world will be destroyed. 'For the great day of his wrath is come; and who shall be able to stand?' I'm going to Shankweiler's Hill — the question is, will you be there with me?" Now Tilly was as pious as her sister, but she had both feet on the ground. "Eleazer must eat," said the more earthly Tilly. "A man can't live altogether on religion. He must have strength to climb his hill." She goes to Eleazer's lonely bachelor home, in his absence, carries the wherewithal thither and prepares a substantial supper of *Drechder Kuche* and fried sausage and silently departs. Eleazer returns, sees the tempting food and eats heartily. He straightway falls asleep and misses his terrible midnight vigil on Shankweiler's Hill "when the heavens will be rolled up as a scroll and every-body will appear in judgment." Tilly had unwittingly saved the day and once more expresses her conviction: "These things are too strong for our minds. I would rather read in the front of the Bible where the world is made than in the back where it bursts apart. It's safer."

## EGG BREAD

½ cup butter                           ½ cup milk
½ loaf bread (1-day old)               2 eggs, well beaten
                    Salt and pepper

Melt the butter in a frying pan. Cut bread into cubes and brown in the butter. Mix together the eggs, milk and season to taste with salt and pepper. Pour mixture over bread. Fry until brown. Serve at once. Serves 6.

## CORN-MEAL MUSH

Fried Corn-meal Mush and *Pot Pudding* (see Index) are a favorite breakfast combination of General Dwight D. Eisenhower's. The famous commander of the Allied forces in Europe during World War II is descended on his father's side from a Pennsylvania German ancestor who arrived in this country in 1741 and settled in Elizabethville, near Lancaster. The family removed to Kansas in 1878.

1 cup corn meal                    2 quarts boiling water
                    1 teaspoon salt

Mix the corn meal with enough cold water to form a smooth paste. Stir into the boiling water, add salt, and beat until thoroughly mixed. Cook over a low flame, stirring constantly, for about 10 minutes. Then cook over hot water for about 1 hour. Serve while hot with cream or milk and sugar, or pour hot mush into a well-greased loaf pan and cool.

## FRIED CORN-MEAL MUSH

Cut cold firm mush into desired number of ½-inch slices. Dip in flour, and fry on both sides on a hot griddle until golden brown. Serve with molasses.

# Sweets and Sours

*Er hot gemeent er kennt sie esse;*
*Nau winscht er doch er hett sie gfresse!*

"You're sweet enough to eat!" is what he always said;
He wishes he'd devoured her, now that they are wed!

Bounteous though our tables be we have never met with the "seven sweets and seven sours" served up so generously in books published about the Pennsylvania Germans in recent years. It is a notion to be classed with similar inaccurate pleasantries such as "the blue gate" of the Amish and the *Hexefiess* on our barns.

## AMBROSIA
### (a conserve)

4 cups crushed pineapple        8 cups mashed strawberries
12 cups sugar

Combine all ingredients and simmer until thick. Pour into 6-ounce jelly glasses and seal with paraffin. Makes about 12 glasses.

## APPLE JELLY
### (From Baer's German Almanac, Lancaster, 1877)

Wash, core (but do not pare) as many apples as desired. Cut each apple into 8 pieces and place in a preserving kettle. Add water to cover, and simmer about 15 minutes, or until soft. Do not let them boil to a mush. Strain apples through a muslin bag and measure juice. Add 14 ounces of sugar for each pint of juice. Boil for 20 minutes. Pour into sterilized 6-ounce jelly glasses and seal.

If desired, the juice and rind of 1 lemon may be added before boiling for each 6 pounds of apples. —

[Grandmother would throw in a few leaves of the wasp geranium as the syrup began to jell. They lent a very delicate and unusual flavor.]

**113**

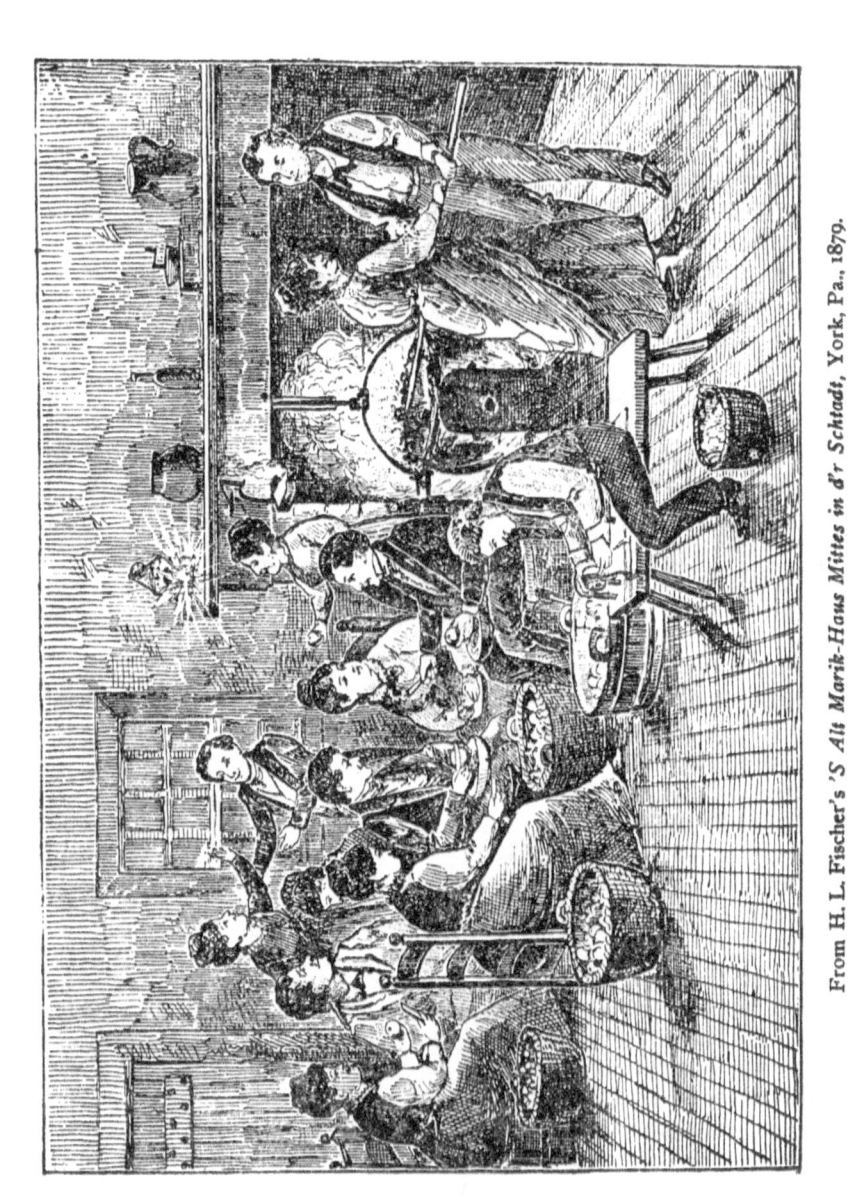

From H. L. Fischer's 'S Alt Marik-Haus Mittes in d'r Schtadt, York, Pa., 1879.

## APPLEBUTTER BOILING

And now the butter-boiling came —
  That set the rural hearts ablaze —
That came as sure as autumn came;
Would that it yet came all the same
  As in those dreamy autumn days —
With fiddle, frolic, dance and play,
With rustic song and rural lay.

Across a rugged bench astride,
  A busy, artless, rustic sits
And pares the apples for the rest,
Who, 'mid the music, song and jest,
  Now cut the apples into snits;
While, two by two, well paired, by turns,
Stir, lest the boiling butter burns.

Good butter must be slowly boiled —
  According to the old-time way;
And so they boiled and stirred it slow,
Until the cocks began to crow,
  And then began the sport and play,
And dance went on and seldom ceased
'Til rosy morn adorned the East.

Before they took the kettle off
  They stirred the fragrant spices in;
And then, with ladle, tin, or gourd,
The boiling mass was dipped and poured;
  Amid the noisy clang and din,
From copper-kettle, burning hot,
Into the well-cooled, earthen pot.

*From a longer poem "Cider-Making and Butter-Boiling"
in H. L. Fisher's OLDEN TIMES: or, Pennsylvania
Rural Life, some fifty years ago, and other poems.
York, Pa. 1888.*

## LATTWAERRICK
### (Applebutter)
#### A recipe arranged for the modern housewife

| | |
|---|---|
| 10 pounds apples | 3 tablespoons cinnamon |
| 6 quarts cider | 2 tablespoons allspice |
| 8 cups sugar | 2 tablespoons ground cloves |

Wash, pare and quarter the apples. Boil the cider for 20 minutes. Add the apples and cook until tender. Press through colander. Add the sugar and spices and cook to the consistency of soft paste, stirring frequently to prevent scorching. Pour into sterilized heated jars and seal.

### More About Applebutter

The German word *Latwerg* (from the Latin *electuarium,* originally a medical term for a paste of some medicinal powder stirred into honey or a sugar solution) came early to be applied in the Rhenish Palatinate of our forefathers to a thick "spread" made from fruits. According to Professor Albert Becker, eminent scholar of Palatine life and lore, the people of the Palatinate made their *Latwerge* of prunes or pears, presumably because the hardy German apples could be kept during the winter months, whereas prunes and pears could not be stored. Therefore the prunes and pears, which were grown in great quantities, were boiled in juices of the same, spiced with cloves and stirred for 48 hours! These long and tedious processes gave the occasion for jolly folk festivities. Our forefathers carried the traditions of *Latwerg* boiling with them to the new world, where a greater abundance of apples and apple cider brought the word to signify applebutter. Originally feminine, *die Latwerge,* the word has in the Pennsylvania German dialect become the masculine *der Latwerg* or *der Lattwaerrick.*

The following verses convey to us of today something of the festive spirit that accompanied the annual event of applebutter boiling. So also this bit of prose, which appeared in The Farmers' Cabinet for Oct. 15, 1838: "Being at the house of a good old German friend in Pennsylvania, in September last, we noticed upon the table what was called apple butter; and finding it an agreeable article, we inquired into the *modus operandi* in making it.

"To make this article according to German law, the host should in the autumn invite his neighbors, particularly the young men and maidens, to make up an apple butter party. Being assembled, let three bushels of fair sweet apples be pared, quartered and the core removed. Meanwhile let two barrels of new cider be boiled down to one-half. When this is done, commit the prepared apples to the cider, and henceforth let the boiling go on briskly and systematically. But to accomplish the main design, the party must take turns at stirring the contents without cessation, that they do not become attached to the side of the kettle and be burned. Let this stirring go on till the liquid becomes concrete — in other words, till the amalgamated cider and apple become as thick as hasty pudding — then throw in seasoning of pulverized allspice, when it may be considered as finished, and committed to pots for future use. This is apple butter — and it will keep sweet for very many years." (By Courtesy of Raymond E. Hollenbach)

Applebutter has been a part of Pennsylvania German cookery since the earliest days. Every fall it was cooked in great quantities. In rural areas it graced the table three times a day. Spread on big slices of homemade bread it accompanied the children to school. Today it is spread nation-wide. Sweet apples such as the Sweet Bough or the Golden Sweet and cider of the same are preferred, but other apples and cider can be used with the aid of sugar. A bit of the root of the wayside sassafras put into the boiling applebutter lends it an exotic and distinctive flavor. But no one knows the full worth of applebutter who has not eaten a slice of homemade rye bread, spread with a substantial layer of *Schmierkaes* (cottage cheese) and over it an equally substantial layer of applebutter.

*Lattwaerrick un Schmierkaes* (see Index) are a favorite combination of General Lewis B. Hershey's, a Pennsylvania German by descent. General Hershey, head of the U. S. Selective Service System during World War II, traces his lineage from Christian Hershey, who settled in the Lancaster area during the first decade of the 18th century. Christian Hershey, like many of the early settlers of Pennsylvania whose descendants are included in the ranks of Pennsylvania Germans, was a native of Switzerland.

## CARROT MARMALADE

| | |
|---|---|
| 1 pound of carrots, boiled and mashed | Grated rind of 1 lemon |
| 2 pounds of sugar | 3 almonds, blanched and grated |
| Juice of 1 lemon | 1 teaspoon almond extract |

Boil carrot pulp and sugar 10 minutes. Add other ingredients. Bring to a boil, pour into containers and seal with paraffin.

*From Mrs. Mary Baumgartner Shepler's book of recipes collected in the Dauphin-Cumberland area a century ago.*

## CHERRY JAM

Wash and weigh desired amount of sour cherries. For each pound of cherries, add ½ cup water. Simmer until tender and force cherries through a colander, discarding stones. Measure pulp and add 2 cups sugar for each quart of pulp. Stir until sugar is dissolved. Place over heat and simmer until mixture is thick and clear, stirring to prevent scorching. Pour into hot sterilized 6-ounce glasses and seal.

## PRESERVED YUDDEKAERSCHE
### (Jerusalem or Ground Cherries)

| | |
|---|---|
| 1 pound Jerusalem or | 1½ cups sugar |
| Ground Cherries | Water |

Remove the lacy, vein-like covering from the cherries. Add the sugar and only enough water to moisten slightly. Boil about 20 minutes, or until the syrup is thick and clear. Pour into 6-ounce jelly glasses and seal.

If desired, 1 lemon may be added, cut in narrow strips, and then more sugar will be required.

## UNCOOKED CURRANT JELLY
### (Baer's German Almanac, Lancaster, 1880)

Crush desired amount of currants and strain through a muslin bag. To each pint of juice add 1 pound of fine white sugar. Stir thoroughly to dissolve sugar. Pour into clean sterilized jars and seal. Stand the jars in hot sun for 2 to 3 days.

## ELDERBERRY JELLY

Elderberries were extensively used in earlier times among the Pennsylvania Germans; elderberry pie is a classic, elderberry jelly a delicious achievement and elderberry wine a nostalgic recollection among the older generation.

Since elderberries are without pectin it is necessary to add some other fruit such as unripe grapes. In earlier days of strict economy apple parings and cores were boiled, the liquid strained and then poured over the berries.

After the fruit is thoroughly boiled, strain through muslin bag and proceed as with other fruit jellies, combining equal portions of sugar and fruit juice. Always make jelly in fairly small quantities, using no more than 6 to 8 cups of juice. Today Certo or some other pectin preparation may be used in making this delicious though difficult jelly.

## GRAPE MARMALADE

Wash desired amount of grapes and remove skins. Place pulp in one pan, the skins in another pan. Bring pulp to a boil and force through a sieve. Grind the skins and add to the pulp. Measure mixture and add equal amount of sugar. Boil for 20 minutes. Pour into sterilized 6-ounce jelly glasses or pint jars, and seal.

## LEMON BUTTER

| | |
|---|---|
| 2 cups sugar | ¼ pound butter |
| 3 eggs, well beaten | Juice of 3 lemons |
| Grated rind of 1 lemon | |

Combine all ingredients and place in top of double boiler, over boiling water. Cook for about 20 minutes. Pour into hot sterilized 6-ounce glasses and seal. Makes about 3 glasses.

## PEACH AND PLUM JAM

16 cups peaches, mashed          12 cups greengage plums, pitted
12 cups sugar

Combine ingredients and simmer slowly until mixture is thick and clear, stirring to prevent scorching. Pour into hot sterilized 6-ounce glasses or pint jars and seal. Makes about 20 glasses.

## BRANDIED PEACHES

8 quarts peaches                 4 cups brandy
Sugar

Select firm, unblemished peaches, peel and weigh them. Use ½ their weight in sugar. In a large crock place a layer of peaches and a layer of sugar, pouring some of the brandy over each layer. Continue process until the ingredients are used. Cover the crock with a cloth and place a lid on top. Set aside in a cool place and let stand for 2 to 3 months before using.

## SPICED PEACHES

3 pounds peaches                 3 cups sugar
½ cup vinegar                    6 sticks cinnamon
12 whole cloves

Remove skins from peaches. Boil vinegar and sugar and drop peaches into liquid, a few at a time. Cook until tender. Transfer peaches to hot clean jars. Add cinnamon and cloves to hot syrup and boil for a few minutes. Pour syrup over the peaches and seal jars.

## PEAR BUTTER

10 pounds Kieffer pears          10 cups sugar
2 cups vinegar

Wash and cook the pears until soft. Force through a colander, discarding skins and seeds. Put pulp in an agate pan and add the sugar and vinegar. Mix thoroughly. Place in a slow oven, 300° F., and bake for 4 hours. During the last hour stir mixture occasionally with a wooden spoon. Test by placing a small quantity on a dish. When juice no longer separates from pulp the pear butter is done. Pour into hot sterilized pint jars and seal. Makes about 10 pints.

*Miss Emma Gable*

## GINGER PEARS

| | |
|---|---|
| 4 pounds pears | Juice and thinly sliced rind |
| 8 cups sugar | of 2 lemons |
| 1 cup water | ¼ pound ginger root |

Select hard, solid pears. Pare, core and cut pears into thin slices. Add the other ingredients and simmer for 1 hour, or until the pears are transparent. If the syrup is not thick, remove pears and cook syrup longer. Then add the pears again. Seal in hot sterilized pint jars and seal. Makes 4 pints.

## QUINCE HONEY

| | |
|---|---|
| 3 large quinces, grated | 1 pound sugar |
| 2 cups water | |

Grate the unpared quinces. Combine sugar and water and bring to a boil. When sugar is dissolved, add quinces and boil for 20 minutes. Pour into hot sterilized 6-ounce glasses and seal with paraffin.

## QUINCE JELLY

| | |
|---|---|
| 12 large quinces | 2 cups water |
| Loaf sugar | |

Boil the quinces in the water until soft and broken. Strain through a muslin bag. Measure juice and to each pint of juice add 1 pound of loaf sugar. Stir mixture until sugar is dissolved. Boil about 30 minutes, or until thick and clear. Pour into hot sterilized 6-ounce jelly glasses and seal. Makes about 5 glasses.

## QUINCE JELLY

Take as many quinces as desired. Wash, core, but do not peel. Cut in small pieces and add sufficient water to float them. Cook until tender. Strain through a muslin bag. Use two-thirds as much sugar as juice. Proceed for jelly making. Add sugar to juice and cook rapidly, thus giving a bright clear jelly, whereas long slow cooking gives a dull dark jelly of inferior quality.

*Carrie V. Bitting*

## QUINCE AND APPLE HONEY

| | |
|---|---|
| 6 large quinces | sugar |
| 4 large apples | 3 pints boiling water |
| Juice of 2 lemons | |

Pare the quinces and apples and grate them. Measure the pulp and use three-fourth as much sugar as pulp. Pour the boiling water over the sugar and stir until almost dissolved. Now add the fruit pulp and lemon juice and cook the mixture until clear  Pour into sterilized hot glasses and when cool cover with paraffin.

*Carrie V. Bitting*

## SPICED QUINCES

7 pounds quinces                    2 cups vinegar
6 cups sugar                        ½ ounce cinnamon
                1¼ ounces whole cloves

Wash and peel the quinces. Combine other ingredients and boil until thickened. Add the quinces and cook until the fruit is tender. Pour into sterilized jars and seal.

*Mrs. David S. Hammond*

## RHUBARB JAM

1½ pounds rhubarb                   ½ cup water
2 cups sugar                        Juice and grated rind of
                                    2 oranges

Wash and skin the rhubarb and cut into small pieces. Add the sugar, water, and orange juice and rind. Simmer for 30 minutes, stirring occasionally. Pour into sterilized 6-ounce jelly glasses and seal. Makes about 3 glasses.

## RHUBARB MARMALADE

2 pounds rhubarb                    1½ pounds loaf sugar
                Grated rind of 1 lemon

Wash and skin the rhubarb and cut into small pieces. Add the sugar and lemon rind. Let stand 24 hours. Strain, and boil the juice for 40 minutes. Add the rhubarb and boil 10 minutes longer. Pour into hot sterilized 6-ounce jelly glasses and seal. Makes about 4 glasses.

## STRAWBERRY JAM

2 quarts strawberries               1 teaspoon powdered alum
8 cups sugar                        1 tablespoon cold water

Wash and hull the strawberries. Mix well with the sugar, being careful not to crush the strawberries. Boil for 10 minutes. Mix the alum and water and add to the berries. Bring to a boil again and boil for 5 minutes. Pour into hot sterilized 6-ounce jelly glasses and seal. Makes 8 glasses.

*Miss Lottie Gable*

## TOMATO JELLY

Select solid, ripe tomatoes and quarter them. Weigh tomatoes and for each pound add the thinly sliced rind of 1 lemon. Boil slowly until soft, then strain tomatoes through a muslin bag. Measure juice and to each pint of juice add 2 cups of sugar and the juice of 1 lemon. Boil for 30 minutes, or until mixture thickens. Pour into hot sterilized 6-ounce jelly glasses and seal. This jelly resembles a West Indian sweetmeat.

### TOMATO PRESERVE

| | |
|---|---|
| 5 pints tomatoes | 6½ cups sugar |

Juice and rind of 3 lemons

Select small ripe tomatoes. Scald and remove the skins. Add sugar and let stand overnight. In the morning drain off the juice that has formed. Add lemon juice and boil rapidly until syrup forms a thread when tested. Add thinly sliced lemon rind and the tomatoes. Boil until mixture is clear and thickened. Pour into hot sterilized jars and seal. Makes about 3½ pints.

*Mrs. David S. Hammond*

### GINGER TOMATOES

| | |
|---|---|
| 6 pounds green tomatoes | 1 teaspoon whole cloves |
| 2 pounds red tomatoes | 3 pieces ginger root |
| 5 pounds sugar | 3 lemons, sliced |

Scald, peel, and quarter the tomatoes. Add the sugar, spices and sliced lemons. Bring mixture to a boil, then reduce heat and simmer until the mixture thickens. Pour into hot sterilized 6-ounce glasses and seal. Makes about 18 glasses.

### PRESERVED WALNUTS

Pare your green walnuts till white appears. Soften in salt water and let lie until sugar is ready. Take 3 pounds of sugar, put in it as much water as will wet sugar and set over charcoal fire. When syrup spins thread, put in walnuts until tender. Lay in dish to cool and tie over with brandied paper.

This old-time recipe must be adjusted to modern usage.

## SOURS

### SOUR BEANS

Wash and string the desired amount of wax beans. Cook in boiling salted water until tender. Drain and pack in jars or crocks. Cover with mild cider vinegar. Add ½ cup sugar to each quart of vinegar, salt, pepper and whole mustard seed, as desired. No sealing is required.

### PICKLED RED CABBAGE

Shred the desired amount of red cabbage. Sprinkle generously with salt and stand in a cool place for 24 hours. Drain thoroughly and place cabbage in the sun for 2 to 3 hours. Estimate the amount of vinegar needed to cover the cabbage. Allow 1 cup of sugar for every two quarts of vinegar, and season with pepper, celery seed, cinnamon, mace and allspice, as desired. Boil liquid for 5 minutes. Pack cabbage in earthen jars and pour liquid over it. Cover and store in a cool place.

### PICKLED CANTALOUPE

Pare the desired number of cantaloupes. Remove seeds and cut cantaloupes into rather large slices. Pack in quart jars. Make a syrup of the following ingredients:

| | |
|---|---|
| 1½ cups sugar | ¼ cup vinegar |
| 1 cup water | |

Bring to a boil and pour mixture over fruit, to within ½ inch of top. Seal the jars, place them in boiling water and process for about 1 hour.

*Mrs. Samuel Smucker*

### SPICED CANTALOUPE

| | |
|---|---|
| 3 pounds cantaloupe | 2 teaspoons mustard seed |
| ½ ounce alum | ½ teaspoon whole mace |
| 8 cups water | 1 stick cinnamon |
| 2 cups vinegar | 4 whole cloves |
| 3 cups sugar | 1 teaspoon allspice |

Pare, remove seeds, and cut cantaloupes into squares. Add the alum to the water and bring to a boil. Add the cantaloupe and boil for 15 minutes. Drain thoroughly. Mix together the remaining ingredients, add the cantaloupe and cook slowly for about 2 hours, or until fruit is clear. Place in hot sterilized jars and seal. Makes about 4 pints.

### PICKLED CHERRIES

Wash and remove stones from desired amount of sour cherries. Cover with vinegar and let stand 24 hours. Drain thoroughly, weigh cherries, and add an equal amount of granulated sugar. Mix well and let stand. Stir cherries about 6 times a day, until the sugar has completely dissolved and formed a thin syrup. (This may take 2 to 3 days.) Place cherries in jars and cover; sealing is not necessary, as the cherries will keep indefinitely. The syrup may be used as a rather sweet cherry vinegar.

*Mrs. F. F. Couch*

### CHOW-CHOW I

| | |
|---|---|
| 1 head cabbage | 2 cups soup beans |
| 1 head cauliflower | 2 cups kidney beans |
| 3 large green peppers | 1 bunch carrots |
| 3 large sweet red peppers | 1 stalk celery |
| 50 small cucumbers | 1 cup sugar |
| 2 quarts Lima beans | 1 cup vinegar |
| 2 quarts string beans | 6 whole cloves |
| 2 quarts wax beans | 1 tablespoon cinnamon |

Prepare the vegetables and cut into medium-sized pieces. Cook in boiling salted water until tender. Drain and return to the kettle. Add the sugar, vinegar, and spices. Mix well and bring to a boil. Pour into hot sterilized jars and seal.

*Miss Katie Spangler*

## CHOW-CHOW II

| | |
|---|---|
| 8 large sour pickles (not dill) | 2 cups salt |
| 1 quart small onions | 4 quarts water |
| 1 stalk celery | 1 cup flour |
| 2 heads cauliflower | 6 tablespoons dry mustard |
| 1 quart green tomatoes | 1 cup sugar |
| 4 green peppers | 1 tablespoon turmeric |

2 quarts vinegar

Dice the pickles. Prepare vegetables and cut into small pieces. Add salt to cold water and add pickles and vegetables. Let stand in brine for 24 hours. Then bring to a boil and cook for a few minutes. Drain thoroughly. Pack vegetables in clean jars. Mix the flour, mustard, sugar and turmeric to a paste with a small amount of cold water. Boil the vinegar and add mixture. Mix well, pour over the vegetables while hot and cover jars. No sealing is necessary.

*Mrs. Paul de Schweinitz*

## CHOW-CHOW III

| | |
|---|---|
| 1 head cabbage | 1 stick horseradish, grated |
| 8 green peppers | ⅓ cup mustard seed |
| Salt | Vinegar |

Sugar

Chop the cabbage and peppers. Place alternate layers of peppers and slightly salted cabbage in quart jars. Sprinkle with the horseradish and mustard seed. Fill jars with vinegar and add a little sugar to taste.

*Mrs. J. Max. Hark*

## CORN RELISH

| | |
|---|---|
| 12 ears corn | ¼ cup salt |
| 2 stalks celery | ¼ teaspoon pepper |
| 1 head cabbage | 1 teaspoon celery seed |
| 12 onions | Sugar |

Vinegar

Cut corn from cobs and chop the other vegetables. Add the salt and let vegetables stand overnight. In the morning, drain, add the pepper, celery seed, and sugar and vinegar to taste. Pack in sterilized jars and seal. Makes 3 quarts.

*Miss Mollie Gable*

### SPICED CRABAPPLES

| | |
|---|---|
| 1 quart crabapples | 1 cup vinegar |
| 2 cups sugar | 1 teaspoon allspice |
| 3 cups water | 1 stick cinnamon |

Select crabapples of uniform size. Wash thoroughly and cut away the dark blossom ends, but do not remove the stems. Pierce each apple 5 or 6 times with a darning needle to prevent skins from bursting when they are cooked. Boil the other ingredients for 5 minutes. Add the apples, keeping them covered with syrup while boiling. When tender, remove the apples and pack them upright in sterilized jars. Fill jars within ¼ inch of top with boiling syrup and seal. Makes 4 pints.

### CUCUMBER RELISH

| | |
|---|---|
| 12 cucumbers | Salt |
| 4 green peppers | Vinegar |
| 6 onions | 1 cup sugar |
| 9 stalks celery | 1 teaspoon turmeric |

Prepare vegetables and force through a food chopper, using a coarse blade. Add salt to taste and let stand overnight. In the morning, drain, cover with vinegar, add the sugar, turmeric and a little salt. Place over heat and boil until fairly thick. Pour into hot sterilized jars and seal.

### CUCUMBER RINGS I

| | |
|---|---|
| 6 large sour pickles | 1 stick cinnamon |
| 2 cups sugar | ½ teaspoon whole cloves |

Cut the pickles into slices, ¼ inch thick. Cover with the sugar and spices and let stand in an earthen jar for 24 hours, stirring frequently. Pack in sterilized jars and seal. Store in a cool place.

### CUCUMBER RINGS II

| | |
|---|---|
| 25 medium-sized cucumbers | 1 stick cinnamon |
| 1½ pints cider vinegar | 1 tablespoon mustard seed |
| 3 pounds light brown sugar | ½ tablespoon allspice |
| ½ tablespoon cloves | |

Place the cucumbers in a strong brine for 3 days. Remove from brine and soak them in fresh water for 3 days, changing the water each day. Remove and slice cucumbers into ½ inch pieces. Cover with vinegar, diluted with water, and heat. (Do not heat for too long, as this tends to make cucumbers soft.) Let them soak in vinegar mixture for 3 days, remove, and drain.

Combine the cider vinegar, brown sugar and spices. If vinegar is very strong dilute with a little water. Bring mixture to a boil and pour over the cucumbers. Let stand for 3 days. Reheat to the boiling point. Pack in hot sterilized jars and seal. Makes about 4 pints.

## SPICED CUCUMBERS

| | |
|---|---|
| 2 green peppers | ¼ cup salt |
| 2 red peppers | 1 teaspoon turmeric |
| 3 onions | 2 cups vinegar |
| 12 cucumbers | ⅔ cup sugar |

2 teaspoons cloves

Cut the peppers and onions into thin slices. Peel the cucumbers and cut into pieces about 1 inch long. Mix all together, sprinkle with salt and let stand for 4 hours. Drain thoroughly. Dissolve the turmeric in a little of the vinegar. Add the sugar, cloves, and the remaining vinegar. Bring to a boil. Add the cucumber mixture and boil about 5 minutes more. Pour into sterilized jars and seal.

## EGGS IN BEET JUICE

| | |
|---|---|
| 10 small beets | ½ cup brown sugar |
| 1 cup vinegar | 6 whole cloves |
| 1 cup water | 1 stick cinnamon |

6 hard-cooked eggs

Boil the beets until tender, and remove skins. Mix together the vinegar, water, sugar, cloves and cinnamon. Boil for 10 minutes. Pour mixture over the beets and let stand for several days. Remove the beets. Remove shells from hard-cooked eggs and place in vinegar mixture. Let stand for 2 days before serving.

[What Pennsylvania German picnic is complete without hard-boiled eggs colored in beet juice?]

## CURRANT CATSUP

| | |
|---|---|
| 3 pints red currant juice | 2 cups sugar |
| 2 cups vinegar | 2 tablespoons cinnamon |

2 tablespoons cloves

Boil the juice for 20 minutes and add the vinegar and sugar. Place the spices in a muslin bag and add them to juice. Boil until thick and clear. Remove spices and pour juice into hot sterilized jars. Seal. Makes about 6 pints.

## PICKLED PEARS

| | |
|---|---|
| 7 pounds pears | 6 cups sugar |
| 2 cups cider vinegar | ½ teaspoon whole cloves |

1 stick cinnamon, broken

Wash, peel, and cut pears in half, removing core. In a saucepan mix together the vinegar and sugar. Add spices tied in a muslin bag, and bring to a boil. Add the pears and cook until fruit is clear and tender. Remove from syrup and pack in hot sterilized jars. Boil the syrup until thick and pour over the pears to within ¼ inch of top. Seal.

### PEPPER CABBAGE

1 stalk celery, chopped             1 head cabbage, chopped
2 small green peppers, chopped      1 tablespoon vinegar
                 Salt and pepper

Combine the celery, peppers, and cabbage. Add the vinegar and season to taste with salt and pepper. Cook until tender. Pour into hot sterilized jars and seal.

### PEPPER RELISH

10 small onions                1½ cups sugar
16 sweet green peppers         2½ teaspoons salt
16 sweet red peppers           4 cups vinegar

Chop the onions and peppers, cover with boiling water, and let stand 5 minutes. Drain, cover again with boiling water and let stand 10 minutes. Then drain overnight in a muslin bag. In the morning, mix the sugar, salt, and vinegar and bring to a boil. Add the onions and peppers and cook for 20 minutes. Pour into hot sterilized jars and seal.

### CABBAGE-FILLED PEPPERS

½ head cabbage             ½ teaspoon mustard seed
6 sweet red peppers        1 teaspoon celery seed
½ tablespoon salt          2 cups vinegar
                ½ cup sugar

Cut off tops of peppers and remove seeds without breaking the peppers. Shred cabbage as for coleslaw, add the salt, sugar, mustard seed and celery seed. Mix thoroughly and stuff cabbage into peppers. Replace the tops on peppers and fasten with tooth picks. Place the stuffed peppers upright in a jar and add vinegar. Cover jar and let stand in a cool place until ready to use. The peppers will keep for several months.

### BREAD AND BUTTER PICKLES

4 quarts sliced pickles        ½ teaspoon turmeric
2 green peppers, chopped       ½ teaspoon cloves
8 small onions                 2 teaspoons mustard seed
½ cup salt                     1 teaspoon celery seed
3 cups sugar                   5 cups vinegar

Place the pickles, peppers and onions in a crock, sprinkle with the salt, cover with a cloth, and lay a heavy weight on top of crock for 3 hours. Mix together the other ingredients and bring to a boil. Add the pickles, peppers, and onions and bring to boiling point again. Pour into hot sterilized jars and seal.

*Mrs. Jonas Martin*

## MUSTARD PICKLES

| | |
|---|---|
| 1 head cauliflower | ¾ cup sugar |
| 1 quart small white onions | ½ pound dry mustard |
| 3 green peppers, chopped fine | ½ ounce celery seed |
| 1 quart green tomatoes, sliced | ¼ ounce turmeric |
| ½ cup salt | 6 cups vinegar |
| ¾ cup flour | 1 quart small sweet pickles |

Separate the flowerets of cauliflower, peel the onions and combine with the tomatoes and peppers. Cover with the salt and let stand overnight. In the morning, drain well, cover with boiling water and cook until soft. Drain. Combine flour, sugar, mustard, celery seed and turmeric. Heat vinegar and pour it over the mixed spices. Stir until thoroughly blended. Add the pickles to the drained vegetables and pour vinegar mixture over all. Cook for 10 minutes, or until mixture thickens. Pour into hot sterilized jars and seal.

## SWEET PICKLES

| | |
|---|---|
| 30 large pickles | 1 tablespoon mustard seed |
| 6 cups cider vinegar | 1 tablespoon celery seed |
| 4 cups sugar | 12 drops oil of spices |

Cut the pickles into 1-inch slices. Combine other ingredients and boil until thickened. Add the pickles and bring to boiling point. Pour into hot sterilized jars and seal.

## PICCALILLI

| | |
|---|---|
| 1 bushel green tomatoes | 2 tablespoons allspice |
| ¾ cup salt | 2 tablespoons cinnamon |
| 2 cups brown sugar | 2 tablespoons dry mustard |
| 1 cup grated horseradish | 4 tablespoons pepper |
| 2 tablespoons cloves | Vinegar |

Chop the tomatoes, sprinkle with salt, and let stand overnight. In the morning, drain, and add the sugar, horseradish, spices, and enough vinegar to cover. Boil mixture for 20 minutes. Pour into hot sterilized jars and seal. Makes about 24 quarts.

## TOMATO KETCHUP I

| | |
|---|---|
| ½ bushel tomatoes | 1 tablespoon celery seed |
| 3 sweet red peppers | 2 teaspoons mustard seed |
| 1 hot red pepper | 1 tablespoon whole allspice |
| 4 teaspoons salt | 2 sticks cinnamon |
| 2 cups sugar | 3 cups vinegar |

Wash and chop the tomatoes and peppers. Combine and boil until soft. Press through a fine sieve. Add the salt and the spices, tied in a muslin bag. Boil mixture rapidly until thick, stirring occasionally to prevent scorching.

Add the vinegar about 5 minutes before removing from heat.  Pour into hot sterilized jars and seal.

## CATSUP II
### (A very old recipe)

| | |
|---|---|
| ½ bushel tomatoes | 1 tablespoon pepper |
| 2 cups vinegar | 1 tablespoon cinnamon |
| ½ cup salt | 1 tablespoon cloves |
| 2 cups sugar | 1 tablespoon celery seed |

Cut the tomatoes into quarters, add the other ingredients and boil until the tomatoes are soft.  Strain.  Return to heat and boil until mixture thickens, stirring to prevent scorching.  Pour into clean hot jars and seal.

## COLD CATSUP III

| | |
|---|---|
| 4 quarts ripe tomatoes | 1 quart cider vinegar |
| 3 green peppers, chopped fine | ½ cup salt |
| 2 stalks celery, chopped fine | ½ cup white mustard seed |
| 1 cup chopped onions | 1 tablespoon black pepper |
| 1 cup ground horseradish | 1 tablespoon celery seed |
| 1 tablespoon cinnamon | |

Wash and peel tomatoes.  Force through a colander.  Combine with other ingredients and mix thoroughly.  Fill clean sterilized jars and seal.  Makes about 6 quarts.

## CHILI SAUCE

| | |
|---|---|
| 3 large onions | 1 cup sugar |
| 3 small green peppers | 3 tablespoons salt |
| 3 sweet red peppers | 1 teaspoon dry mustard |
| 5 pounds tomatoes | ½ teaspoon cayenne pepper |
| 1 teaspoon cinnamon | 1 teaspoon cloves |
| 3 cups vinegar | |

Peel the onions, remove the seeds from the peppers and chop all together. Peel and core the tomatoes and add them together with all other ingredients except the vinegar.  Boil gently for 2 hours, stirring occasionally.  Add the vinegar and cook slowly until mixture thickens.  Pour into clean hot jars and seal.  Makes about 3 quarts.

## DILLED TOMATOES

Fill 5 1-quart jars with small green tomatoes.  To each jar add 1 small stalk of celery, cut into 1-inch pieces, and 3 green peppers cut into large pieces. Combine the following ingredients:

| | |
|---|---|
| 4 cups water | 1 cup salt |
| 4 cups vinegar | ¼ cup dill |

Boil mixture for 5 minutes. Pour the hot liquid over the mixture in the jars and seal. Let stand for 5 weeks before using.

*Mrs. Paul Ellinger*

## GREEN TOMATO PICKLE

| | |
|---|---|
| 1 peck green tomatoes | 1 ounce mustard seed |
| 12 large peppers | ½ ounce cloves |
| 12 large onions | ½ ounce whole ginger |
| Salt | ½ ounce allspice |
| Vinegar | 6 cups brown sugar |
| ½ ounce celery seed | ¼ pound dry mustard |
| ½ ounce turmeric | Flour |

Slice the tomatoes, peppers, and onions, sprinkle with salt, and let stand overnight. In the morning, drain well and cover with vinegar. Add all the remaining ingredients except the mustard and flour. Cook about 2 hours, or until mixture is clear. Then add the mustard. Thicken mixture with a little flour, mixed to a paste with cold water. Pour into hot sterilized jars and seal. Makes about 8 quarts.

## RIPE TOMATO PICKLE

| | |
|---|---|
| 12 ripe tomatoes | 4 tablespoons salt |
| 3 sweet green peppers | 1 stick cinnamon, broken |
| 3 hot red peppers | ½ teaspoon whole cloves |
| 6 onions | 2 tablespoons mustard seed |
| 1 cup sugar | 1 tablespoon celery seed |

3 cups vinegar

Slice the tomatoes, red and green peppers, and onions. Add all other ingredients and boil mixture for 1 hour. Pour into hot sterilized jars and seal. Makes about 2 quarts.

## PICKLED BLACK WALNUTS

Gather the walnuts before the inner shell begins to harden and when it can still be readily pricked with a darning needle.

Scald 100 walnuts and rub off the outer skin. Prepare a heavy brine of four pounds of salt to every gallon of water. After piercing each nut several times with the prongs of a fork, place them in a crock and pour the brine over them. Leave them in the brine for six days, changing the brine every other day, and keeping the crock well covered.

Take of black pepper and of ginger root each an ounce, and of cloves, mace and nutmeg each half an ounce, and two tablespoon of mustard seeds.

Having removed the walnuts from the brine, arrange them in layers in pickling jars, strewing between each layer the above mixed spices.

Boil for five minutes a gallon of good cider vinegar and pour hot over the walnuts. Seal the jars. The walnuts will be ready in a month.

*NOTE — The above recipe can also be applied to white walnuts, known in Pennsylvania as butter-nuts.*

## SPICED BLACK WALNUTS

| | |
|---|---|
| 2 cups sugar | 1 teaspoon cornstarch |
| 1 cup boiled beet juice | 1 cup raisins |
| 1 teaspoon allspice | (seeded or seedless) |
| 1 teaspoon cinnamon | 2 cups black walnut meat |
| 1 teaspoon nutmeg | |

Mix the above ingredients and bring to a boil

*Mrs. Olive Huettinger*

### "STRAWBERRY" CHINA

This colorful china was made at Leeds and Staffordshire for special markets in Pennsylvania. Little of this china is found today in England. Its gaudy designs attracted the Pennsylvania Dutch. Courtesy of Mr. Arthur J. Sussel.

Hand-carved buttermold with heart and tree-of-life motifs
*Courtesy*, Landis Valley Museum, Landis Valley, Pa.

# DUNKES
## Coffeecakes, Crullers
## Doughnuts, Shoofly Pies

*Mer sott net bleed sei am Disch*

Bashfulness is sometimes good —
But not when one sits down to food!

Do you dunk too? We Pennsylvania Germans have long been adepts in the gentle art of dunking. *Dunk* is such a friendly word, a little word to be sure, but it possesses hidden sources of strength, for it has succeeded in entrenching itself firmly in the English language. Lexicographers have been obliged to recognize it and enter it in our dictionaries. Indeed it is the Pennsylvania Germans' great gift to the language of Shakespeare and Milton. The Winston Simplified Dictionary defines *dunk* as a transitive verb meaning "to immerse"; especially to dip (dry food into a liquid, as soup or coffee, before eating it). In Webster's New International Dictionary we find: *dunk*, verb transitive and intransitive — to dip (bread, cake or the like) into coffee, tea, milk, etc., while eating. — But the dictionaries fail to point out that this little word which has found its way into the hearts of millions of Americans scattered over this broad land of ours, from the Atlantic to the Pacific, started forth upon its journey from the Pennsylvania Germans in eastern Pennsylvania. Our dialect verb *"dunke,"* to dip, is related to the High German *tunken*, to dip. The same root occurs in *Dunkers,* or *Dunkards,* the sect which settled in Pennsylvania in 1719 and which like the Baptists, practices immersion in the baptismal rite. — Perhaps you remember the time when you were nearly ostracized socially for having inadvertently dipped your cake or doughnut into your coffee. You may now let yourself go with complete abandonment in the assurance that you belong to an ever-growing body of fellow citizens. The National Dunking Association, established some years ago, now numbers over three millions, among whose charter members are such conspicuous names as Bing Crosby, Carveth Wells, Gracie Allen, Bob Hope, Dwight Fiske and Congressman Jennings Randolph.

Why were our forefathers so given to dunking? While breaking bread into soup and milk was common among the peasants of Europe from early times, we can only think that dipping became a general practice with the introduction of coffee. The use of coffee and the serving of a second breakfast, the Pennsylvania German *nein Uhr Schtick,* no doubt, were factors in the evolution of that large body of delightful Pennsylvania German creations whose very nature invites to dipping and which have here been gathered under the general heading of DUNKES, or, baked things that lend themselves to dunking.

## BUTTERSEMMELN
### (Butter Rolls)

| | |
|---|---|
| ½ cup mashed potatoes | 2 eggs, well beaten |
| ½ yeast cake | ½ cup butter and lard |
| ¼ cup warm water | ¼ teaspoon salt |
| 1 cup sugar | 6 cups flour, sifted twice |
| 2 cups scalded milk, lukewarm | Melted butter |

At about 6 p.m. mix the mashed potatoes, the yeast which has been dissolved in the warm water and half the sugar. Cover and let rise for 4 hours. Then add the milk, eggs, shortening, salt and remaining sugar. Sift in the flour. Toss onto a floured board and knead until the dough blisters and drops clean from the palm of the hand. Cover and let rise overnight in a warm place. In the morning, turn onto floured board and pat out ¼ inch thick, brush with melted butter and cut into 2-inch squares. Lap the four corners to center of each square and place the resulting squares on a greased baking sheet, about 2 inches apart. Let rise until very light. Bake in a hot oven, 400° F., for 15 to 20 minutes. Remove from the oven, brush the tops with melted butter and sprinkle with granulated sugar and cinnamon. Makes about 5 dozen rolls.

## KAFFEE KRANZ
### (Coffee Wreath)

| | |
|---|---|
| 1 cup sugar | 1 yeast cake |
| 4 eggs, well beaten | ½ cup lukewarm water |
| ¾ cup butter and lard | 7 cups sifted flour |
| 2 cups scalded milk, lukewarm | Milk |

Sugar

Combine the sugar, eggs and shortening and mix well. Add the milk. Dissolve yeast cake in lukewarm water and add to mixture. Stir in 4 cups of the flour and beat well. Cover and set in a warm place for about 1½ hours. When light, add the remaining flour to form a dough just stiff enough to stir with a spoon. To make the *Kranz,* or wreath, place about 2 cups of dough on a well-floured board. Divide dough into 3 equal parts and braid like a wreath. Form wreaths out of the remaining dough, place on greased baking sheets, and let rise for 1½ hours. Brush the tops with milk and sprinkle with sugar. Bake in a moderately hot oven, 375° F. to 400° F., for about 20 to 25 minutes. Makes 3 to 4 wreaths.

## BAKING POWDER COFFEECAKE

| | |
|---|---|
| ½ cup sugar | ½ cup milk |
| 1 egg, well beaten | ½ cup water |
| ¼ teaspoon salt | Brown sugar |
| 2½ teaspoons baking powder | Cinnamon |
| 3 cups flour | Butter |

Combine the sugar, egg and salt. Sift together the baking powder and flour and add alternately with the milk and water. Pour batter into greased baking pans. Dot the top with butter about 2 inches apart and sprinkle with brown sugar and cinnamon, mixed. Bake in a moderate oven, 350° F., for about 30 minutes.

## EEPIES CAKE

### (Not to be confused with the Eepies, or A. P. Cookies)

| | |
|---|---|
| 4 cups pastry flour | Pinch of salt |
| 1 cup granulated sugar | 1 cup shortening |
| 1 cup light brown sugar | 1 egg, well beaten |
| 1 teaspoon baking soda | 1 cup sour milk, or buttermilk |
| ¼ teaspoon cream of tartar | Cinnamon and sugar, mixed |

Sift together the dry ingredients and cut in the shortening. Combine the egg and sour milk and add to the first mixture. Pour batter into 5 medium-sized greased pie tins. Sprinkle with cinnamon and sugar. Bake in a moderate oven, 350° F., for about 30 minutes.

## FASSNACHT KUCHE I
### (Doughnuts)

Shrove Tuesday, the day before Ash Wednesday, ushering in the Lenten season, is the German *Fastnacht,* known among the South Germans, hence also among the Pennsylvania Germans, as *Fassnacht.* Since the Pennsylvania Germans are chiefly of the Protestant faith, old-world traditions that prevail in the Catholic areas of Germany such as carnivals and mummeries are absent, except for the baking of doughnuts. The baking of *Fassnacht* or *Faasenacht Kuche,* known also as *Fassnacht Kichelcher* or *Fettkuche,* is a custom that was brought from across the sea by our Palatine forefathers and continues in Pennsylvania and in the Palatinate to this day. Dr. Edwin M. Fogel, in his book, Pennsylvania German Superstitions, points out that the cakes baked and eaten at this time are closely related to the cakes baked in pre-Christian times in celebrating the advent of Spring. In the Palatinate the housewife fries her cakes in deep fat in the afternoon of Shrove Tuesday and the festivities of the day continue until midnight. In Pennsylvania the housewife sets her dough the day before and the cakes are fried on Tuesday morning. Both there and here the cakes are made of a yeast dough and tradition requires that they be baked in squares or rectangles with slits cut in them. The Pennsylvania housewife drops the last bit of formless dough into the fat and fries it for that member of the family who is the last to get up on Shrovetide morning. He is called *Die Fassnacht*. In the Palatinate these cakes are eaten on Shrove Tuesday evening and those left over are eaten with coffee at breakfast next morning. Here large quantities are baked to be eaten in the following days. Although some prefer them fresh they are good at any time, as the old proverb indicates: *Kalt un waarm sin sie yo am beschte!* (They are best both cold and warm!)

| | |
|---|---|
| 2 cups sugar | 1 cup scalded milk, lukewarm |
| ½ cup shortening, melted | 2 cups Potato Yeast (see Index) |
| 2 eggs, well beaten | 4 cups sifted flour (about) |

Combine sugar, shortening, and eggs, and mix well. Add milk and yeast. Beat in enough flour to form a stiff dough. Set aside to rise. Turn onto floured board and roll out ½ inch thick. Cut into rectangular shapes with slit in the middle and let rise again. Fry in hot, deep fat, 360° F., for 2 to 3 minutes, turning several times. Drain on absorbent paper. Makes about 2 dozen. — To be eaten with the good table molasses one still finds in our country stores.

*Mrs. Norman H. Hoffman*

### FASSNACHT KUCHE II
### (Doughnuts)

| | |
|---|---|
| 3 medium-sized potatoes | 2 cups scalded milk, lukewarm |
| 4 cups sifted flour | 4 eggs, well beaten |
| 1 yeast cake | ½ cup melted butter |
| ¼ cup warm water | 1 cup sugar |

Wash and pare the potatoes. Cover with water and boil until tender. Remove potatoes from water, reserving the water. Mash the potatoes. Add 2 cups of the flour to the potato water, scald, and combine with the potatoes. Cool. Dissolve yeast in warm water and add. Set aside to rise for about 5 hours. Combine remaining flour with the milk, forming a batter which drops readily from a spoon. Add to yeast mixture and let rise overnight. In the morning, add the egg, butter, and sugar. Knead dough until stiff enough to roll and let rise until double in bulk. Turn out onto floured board and roll ½ inch thick. Cut with floured cutter and let rise again. Fry in hot, deep fat, 360° F., for 2 to 3 minutes, turning several times. Drain on absorbent paper. Makes about 3 dozen.

### FASSNACHT KUCHE III
### (Doughnuts)

| | |
|---|---|
| 2 cups sugar | ¾ cup melted butter |
| 1 cup hot mashed potatoes | 1 cup potato water |
| 1 cup Potato Yeast (see Index) | 2 eggs, separated |
| 3 cups sifted flour (about) | |

Combine 1 cup of the sugar and the hot mashed potatoes, reserving the
water in which the potatoes were boiled.  Add the yeast and set aside for 4
hours to rise.  Add the melted butter, remaining cup of sugar, and 1 cup of
the potato water.  Add the egg yolks, which have been well beaten, and fold
in the stiffly beaten egg whites.  Add enough flour to form a fairly stiff dough.
Turn out onto a lightly floured board and knead.  Form into a loaf, brush
the top with butter and let stand in a warm place overnight.  In the morning,
turn onto a lightly floured board and roll out ¼ inch thick.  Cut with a floured
cutter and let stand until light.  Fry in hot, deep fat, 360° F., for 2 to 3
minutes, turning several times.  Drain on absorbent paper.  Makes about 2
dozen.

*Mrs. George D. Sell*

### FASSNACHT KUCHE IV
#### (Doughnuts)

| | |
|---|---|
| 1 cup mashed potatoes | 1 yeast cake |
| 1 cup potato water | ½ cup warm water |
| 2½ cups sugar | 9 cups sifted flour (about) |
| 1 teaspoon salt | 4 eggs |
| 1 quart milk | ¼ cup melted butter |

¾ teaspoon ginger

Combine the mashed potatoes, potato water, 1 cup of the sugar, and salt.
Add the milk.  Dissolve the yeast cake in the warm water and add.  Add
enough of the flour to form a thin batter.  Let rise 2½ to 3 hours.  Add the
eggs, slightly beaten, the remaining 1½ cups sugar, and the butter.  Stir in the
remaining flour, just enough to form a dough which is fairly stiff.  Add the
ginger with the last of the flour.  Divide the dough into 2 or 3 portions and
let rise overnight.  Turn out onto a lightly floured board and roll out ¼ inch
thick.  Cut with floured cutter and let rise until double in bulk.  Fry in deep,
hot fat, 360° F., for 2 to 3 minutes, turning several times.  A few whole cloves
may be added to the fat for a delicious flavor, if desired.  Drain on absorbent
paper.  Makes about 7½ dozen.

"I have used the above recipe possibly twenty-five years.  I remember that
both my grandmothers just took some of their bread dough, adding a bit of
sugar and a bit of shortening, then letting it rise.  They cut the rolled out
dough into squares with two slits in them and fried them in lard."

*Mrs. Emory M. Moyer*

*Eat a doughnut on Shrove Tuesday and live a year longer.*

### FASSNACHT KUCHE V
#### (Doughnuts)

| | |
|---|---|
| 2 cups milk | 1 cup sugar |
| 1 yeast cake | 3 eggs, well beaten |
| ½ cup warm water | ¼ cup melted butter |
| 6 to 7 cups sifted flour (about) | 1 teaspoon salt |

Scald the milk and set aside to cool. Dissolve the yeast cake in warm water and add ½ cup flour. Mix well. Add the batter to the milk and stir in 1 teaspoon of the sugar. Add about 3 cups of the flour and set aside in a warm place to rise overnight. In the morning, add the eggs, butter, remaining sugar, and salt. Mix thoroughly. Stir in enough of the remaining flour to form a fairly stiff batter. Set aside to rise until light. Turn out onto a well-floured board and roll out ¼ inch thick. Cut in desired shapes. Let rise again until double in bulk. Fry in deep, hot fat, 360° F., for 2 to 3 minntes, turning several times. Drain on absorbent paper. Makes about 5 dozen.

*Hannah C. Evans*

## CRULLERS

It is sad but true that most doughnuts are only crullers. They may both be round with a neat hole in the middle, but for the Pennsylvania German they are not doughnuts unless they are made of yeast-risen dough. Less wholesome than the doughnut, the cruller has triumphed commercially over the doughnut. No cruller recipe, however else it may differ, calls for yeast. It lends itself to the busy housewife. It can be made rapidly with the aid of baking powder or soda. It has even taken the place of the Shrovetide yeast doughnuts in some households. Both doughnut and cruller figure prominently in the art of dunking.

## CRULLERS I

### A recipe used in Lehigh County for Shrovetide Doughnuts.

| | |
|---|---|
| ¾ cup sour cream | 1 egg, well beaten |
| ¾ cup thick sour milk | 1½ teaspoons baking soda |
| ¼ cup sugar | 4 cups sifted flour (about) |

Combine sour cream and milk, and add the sugar and egg. Beat until well mixed. Combine baking soda with the flour and add gradually to first mixture to form a fairly stiff dough. Turn out on a floured board and roll out ¼ inch thick. Cut into 2-inch squares and prick each square of dough with a fork. Fry in hot, deep fat, 360° F., for 2 to 3 minutes, turning several times. Drain on absorbent paper. Makes about 2 dozen.

*Mrs. Cora I. Hollenbach*

Mrs. Hollenbach used this recipe religiously only once a year, namely for the "Faasenacht" or Shrovetide baking. The *approved* manner of serving them is to split each doughnut in half and spread it with a generous portion of *Gwidde Hunnich* (quince honey). If this is not available, good apple jelly will do. If eaten without jelly or jam the amount of sugar in the recipe should be increased.

## CRULLERS II

3 tablespoons melted butter  
1 cup sugar  
1 egg, well beaten  
½ teaspoon salt  

1 teaspoon baking soda  
¼ cup vinegar  
3½ cups sifted flour  
1 cup thick sour milk  

Combine butter, sugar, egg and salt. Dissolve the soda in the vinegar and add. Then add flour and milk alternately, stirring until ingredients are combined. Turn out on a floured board and roll ½ inch thick. Cut into 1-inch strips or cut in rounds with floured cutter. Fry in hot, deep fat, 360° F., for 2 to 3 minutes, turning several times. Drain on absorbent paper. When cold roll crullers in powdered sugar. Makes about 2 dozen.

*Mrs. F. F. Bartholomew*

## CRULLERS III

½ cup butter  
1 cup sugar  
2 eggs, well beaten  
3½ teaspoons baking powder  

¼ teaspoon nutmeg  
½ teaspoon salt  
3½ cups sifted flour (about)  
1 cup milk  

Cream together the butter and sugar. Add the eggs and mix well. Sift the baking powder, nutmeg, and salt with 1 cup of the flour and add alternately with the milk to the first mixture. Add enough of the remaining flour to form a fairly stiff dough. Turn out on a floured board and roll ½ inch thick. Cut as desired with floured cutter. Fry in hot, deep fat, 360° F., for 2 to 3 minutes, turning several times. Drain on absorbent paper. When cold sprinkle with sugar, if desired. Makes 2 dozen.

*Mrs. F. F. Bartholomew*

## FUNNY CAKE or COCOA CAKE

½ cup sugar  
⅓ cup cocoa  

¼ cup milk  
⅓ teaspoon vanilla  

1 unbaked pastry shell

Blend the sugar and cocoa, and stir in the milk. Add the vanilla. Pour mixture into unbaked pastry shell and top with the following batter. Bake in a moderate oven, 350° F., for about 30 minutes.

**Batter**

¾ cup sugar  
¼ cup butter  
1 egg, well beaten  

⅓ cup flour  
⅔ teaspoon baking powder  
⅓ cup milk  

⅓ teaspoon vanilla

Cream together the sugar and butter, and add the egg. Mix well. Stir together the flour and baking powder and add alternately with the milk to the creamed mixture. Add the vanilla.

## KUGELHOPF
### (Turkish Cap)

Known in Switzerland as *Gugelhopf*, but whether *Kugel*-(sphere) or *Gugel*-(monk's hood), the word no doubt refers to the spherical and piled-up form the dough takes in the process of baking.

| | |
|---|---|
| 2 cups milk | 4 cups sifted flour |
| ½ pound butter | 1 yeast cake, crumbled |
| 8 eggs, well beaten | 1 tablespoon sugar |

Pinch of salt

Combine milk, butter and eggs in a saucepan. Place over a low heat. When thoroughly warm add the flour, yeast, sugar and salt. Turn out onto a floured board and knead. Place in a well-greased round baking mold and let rise until double in bulk. Bake in a slow oven, 300° F., for about 1 hour. Turn it out at once and sprinkle thickly with confectioner's sugar.

Raisins, currants, citron and almonds may be added, if desired. — Bake in an old earthenware Turk's Head, if you are so fortunate as to have one.

## MOLASSES CAKE

| | |
|---|---|
| 1 cup molasses | 2 tablespoons warm water |
| ¾ cup sugar | 2 cups flour |
| 2 tablespoons shortening | 1 teaspoon ginger |
| 1 egg, well beaten | ¼ teaspoon salt |
| 1 teaspoon baking soda (scant) | 1 cup sour milk |

Combine the molasses, sugar, and shortening, and add the egg. Dissolve the soda in the warm water and add. Sift together the flour, ginger, and salt and add alternately with the sour milk. Pour batter into 2 greased pie tins. Bake in a moderate oven, 350° F., for about 25 minutes.

## MORAVIAN SUGARCAKE

A favorite delicacy of the late J. Fred Wolle, organizer and leader of the famous Bach Choir of Bethlehem, and a Pennsylvania German by descent. Dr. Wolle's great-great-grandfather, Matthias Weiss, a native of Switzerland, settled in Bethlehem in 1743, just two years after the founding of that Moravian town.

Named for the Moravians, or Unitas Fratum, a group of German Pietists, who, under Count Zinzendorf, founded Bethlehem in 1741, and soon thereafter further settlements at Lititz, Nazareth and Emmaus.

| | |
|---|---|
| 2 yeast cakes | 1½ cups melted butter |
| 1 cup lukewarm water | 1 cup hot mashed potatoes |
| 1 cup granulated sugar | 7 cups sifted flour (about) |
| 1 teaspoon salt | 2 cups brown sugar |
| 2 eggs, well beaten | 5 teaspoons cinnamon |

Dissolve the yeast cakes in the lukewarm water. Mix together the granulated sugar, salt, eggs, and 1 cup of the butter. Add the hot mashed potatoes. Add alternately the dissolved yeast and enough flour to form a light dough. Beat well and set aside to rise overnight. In the morning, place the dough in deep greased pie tins, spreading dough about ¾ inch thick. Let it rise again for about 1½ hours, or until quite light. Make indentations in top of dough, about 2 inches apart, and fill holes with brown sugar and cinnamon, mixed, and the remaining butter. Bake in a moderate oven, 350° F., for about 20 to 25 minutes.

## MORAVIAN SUGAR CAKE

| | |
|---|---|
| 1 cup hot mashed potatoes | ¼ cup lard (melted) |
| 1 cup sugar | 2 eggs, slightly beaten |
| 1 yeast cake | 4 cups flour |
| ½ cup butter | 1 teaspoon salt |

Measure flour before sifting. Dissolve yeast cake in a cup of lukewarm water drained from the boiled potatoes.

Now mix above ingredients in order given and place dough in warm place, letting it rise to double size. Spread it out in ¾ inch deep pans. Let rise again until puffy. Make holes and fill with pats of buttter. Spread top generously with brown sugar and sprinkle with cinnamon.

Bake in oven at 350° F. until brown.

*Mrs. F. F. Couch*

*The above two old recipes are said to have been brought to Bethlehem by the early Moravian settlers and handed down from mother to daughter through successive generations.*

## MORAVIAN CAKE

| | |
|---|---|
| 1½ cups scalded milk, lukewarm | 1 teaspoon nutmeg |
| | ⅔ cup shortening |
| 2 yeast cakes | ¾ tablespoon salt |
| 1 cup warm mashed potatoes | 7½ cups sifted flour (about) |
| 1 cup sugar | Butter |
| 2 eggs, well beaten | |

### Cinnamon and brown sugar, mixed

Dissolve the yeast cakes in the lukewarm milk. Add the mashed potatoes and sugar, and mix well. Add the eggs, nutmeg, shortening, salt, and flour. Set aside in a warm place to rise. Turn out onto a floured board and knead for a few minutes. Return to bowl and let dough rise again until double in bulk. Then pat out dough and place in 5 greased shallow pans (8 x 10) and let it rise again. When light, make small indentations in top, close together, and place bits of butter in each hole. Sprinkle generously with cinnamon and brown sugar. Bake in a moderate oven, 350° F., for about 30 minutes.

*Mrs. Preston A. Barba*

## RIWWELKUCHE
### (Crumb Cake)

| | |
|---|---|
| 1¼ cups sugar | 2 eggs, separated |
| ¾ cup butter and lard | 1 cup sour milk |
| 2 cups sifted flour | 1 teaspoon melted butter |
| 2 teaspoons baking powder | Cinnamon |

Mix with the hands the sugar, butter, flour and baking powder to form a crumbly mixture. Reserve ¾ cup of the mixture and to the remainder add the well-beaten egg yolks and the milk. Beat the egg whites until stiff and fold into the batter. Pour into 2 well-greased cake pans and scatter the crumb mixture over the top. Bake in a moderately hot oven, 375° F. to 400° F., for about 45 minutes. Remove from oven and dust lightly with cinnamon.

## SCHNECKE
### (Snails)

| | |
|---|---|
| ¼ cup sugar | 1 egg white |
| 1 teaspoon salt | 2 egg yolks |
| 1 yeast cake, crumbled | ¼ cup melted butter |
| 1 cup scalded milk, lukewarm | Sugar and cinnamon, mixed |
| 1½ cups sifted flour | ½ cup seedless raisins |
| ¼ cup melted butter | ½ cup shredded almonds |

Brown sugar (optional)

Combine the sugar, salt, and yeast with the lukewarm milk and let stand for 5 minutes. Add the flour and beat well. Cover, and let rise until light. Then add the first ¼ cup butter, egg yolks and egg white, and enough additional flour to form a soft dough. Let rise. Turn out dough onto a lightly floured board and roll out ½ inch thick. Brush with some melted butter, sprinkle with sugar and cinnamon, mixed, and the raisins and almonds. Roll up like a jelly roll and cut into 1-inch slices. Place the slices, cut side down, on a baking sheet. Brush top with some of the melted butter and sprinkle with additional sugar and cinnamon, mixed. Bake in a moderately hot oven, 375° F. to 400 ° F., for about 15 to 20 minutes.

To make the *Schnecke* sticky, place brown sugar on the bottom of the baking pan, dot with butter, and then lay the pieces of dough on top.

## SCHWENKFELDER CAKE

Named for the Schwenkfelders, a sect founded by Luther's contemporary, Caspar Schwenkfeld. They emigrated from Silesia to Pennsylvania in 1733-34 and settled for the most part in the valley of the Perkiomen.

General Henry Harley Arnold, commanding general of the U. S. Army Air Forces during World War II, remembers Schwenkfelder Cake as one of his favorite childhood treats. General Arnold was born and reared in Montgomery County, and claims Pennsylvania German antecedents on both sides of his family tree.

| | |
|---|---|
| 2 cups sugar | ½ cup butter |
| 1 cup hot mashed potatoes | ½ cup lard |
| 1 yeast cake | 3 eggs, well beaten |
| ¼ cup warm water | 1 teaspoon salt |
| 1 cup sifted flour | Melted butter |

**Brown sugar**

Combine 1 cup of the sugar with the mashed potatoes and set aside to cool. Dissolve the yeast cake in warm water and add with the flour to the potato mixture. Beat well and set aside to rise for 3 hours. Combine the butter, lard, eggs, salt, and remaining sugar, and beat into the potato mixture. Beat vigorously until mixture is stiff. Set aside to rise overnight. In the morning, place the dough in greased cake pans. Brush top with melted butter and sprinkle with brown sugar. Bake in a moderate oven, 350° F., for about 25 minutes.

## SHOOFLY PIE

This, one of the triumphs of the Pennsylvania German kitchen and unknown elsewhere, is in reality not a pie, but a cake baked in a pastry shell. The connotation of the word "shoofly" is not clear. It has been suggested that it is a corruption of the French *choufleur,* cauliflower, since the texture of its crumb-besprinkled surface resembles a head of cauliflower. Since the Palatinate borders on France and other French words have crept into our dialect, this explanation were plausible enough if the shoofly pie were known there. Perhaps the philologist will detect in it a distorted form of the dialect word *Schubel,* diminutive *Schubli* or *Schufli,* signifying a small part of a larger whole, here the surface crumbs commonly used on other German coffee cakes (see *Streiselkuchen*). It is called by various names in different parts of Pennsylvania, such as shoofly cake, molasses crumb pie, molasses crumb cake, molasses shoofly pie and molasses pie, to name a few.

More important than the name is the baking. There are several schools of thought when it comes to baking shoofly pie. Some *Hausfraas* insist that the finished product should come from the oven with a distinctly damp zone at the bottom, which appeals particularly to the male members of the family; others claim that it should be dry and cakelike throughout. Some cooks put the liquid portion in the pie shell first, with the crumbs sprinkled evenly on top; others fill in the crumbs and pour the liquid over them; still others fill the pie shell with alternate layers of liquid and crumbs. There are numbers of recipes, each differing slightly. The 4 recipes given here will illustrate the various methods of procedure.

### SHOOFLY PIE I

| | |
|---|---|
| ¾ cup flour | ½ cup boiling water |
| ½ cup sugar | ¼ cup molasses |
| ¼ tablespoon butter | ½ teaspoon baking soda |

**1 unbaked pastry shell**

Mix together with the hands the flour, sugar, and butter. Mix well until a crumbly mixture is formed. Combine the water, molasses, and baking soda. Beat until foamy. Pour into unbaked pastry shell and add crumbly mixture, stirring well. Bake in a moderate oven, 350° F., for about 30 to 35 minutes.

### SHOOFLY PIE II

| | |
|---|---|
| 2 eggs, well beaten | ½ recipe Basic Pastry |
| 1 cup molasses | (see Index) |
| 1 teaspoon baking soda | 1½ cups flour |
| 1½ cups hot coffee | 2 tablespoons butter |
| 2 cups brown sugar | Pinch of salt |

Combine the eggs and molasses and add the soda which has been dissolved in the coffee. Add 1 cup of the brown sugar. Line a 9-inch pie tin with pastry and pour in the mixture. Sprinkle with crumbs made by rubbing together with the hands the flour, butter, salt, and remaining brown sugar. Bake in a moderate oven, 350° F., for about 45 minutes.

### SHOOFLY PIE III

| | |
|---|---|
| ½ cup butter | ½ teaspoon nutmeg |
| 1 cup sugar (scant) | ½ recipe Basic Pastry |
| 1 cup sifted flour | (see Index) |

2 tablespoons molasses

Form crumbs of the butter, sugar, flour, and nutmeg, by rubbing mixture through the hands. Line a 9-inch pie tin with pastry and place crumbs in the bottom of the pan. Pour the molasses over the crumbs. Bake in a moderately hot oven, 375° F., for about 35 minutes.

### SHOOFLY PIE IV

This was the favorite Shoofly Pie recipe of Milton S. Hershey, "the chocolate king," who was a Pennsylvania German born and bred.

| | |
|---|---|
| 5 cups sifted flour | 1 cup molasses |
| 2 cups brown sugar | 1 teaspoon baking soda |
| 2 tablespoons butter | Pinch of salt |
| 1½ cups boiling water | 3 recipes Basic Pastry |
| | (see Index) |

Combine the flour and brown sugar into a crumbly mixture. Mix together the butter, water, molasses, soda, and salt, until thoroughly blended. Line 6 9-inch tins with pastry. Place a layer of liquid mixture in each pastry shell, then a layer of crumbs, until pastry shells are filled. Bake in a moderate oven, 350° F., for about 45 minutes. Makes 6 pies.

*Mrs. Norman H. Hoffman*

## STREISELKUCHE

*Streisel* refers to the sweet crumbs strewn over the top of these coffeecakes. It originates from the German *streuen,* meaning, to strew or sprinkle.

| | |
|---|---|
| ½ cup shortening | 5 cups sifted flour |
| ½ cup mashed potatoes | 1 yeast cake |
| ½ cup potato water | ½ cup lukewarm water |
| 1 cup sugar | 2 eggs, well beaten |

**Melted butter**

Combine the shortening, mashed potatoes, potato water (water in which potatoes were cooked) and ½ cup of the sugar. Add 3⅓ cups of the flour. Dissolve the yeast cake in the lukewarm water and add. Mix well and set aside in a warm place to rise over night. In the morning, add the eggs and the remaining sugar and flour. Set aside to rise until light. Turn out onto a floured board and roll out 1 inch thick. Cut into pieces, 6 by 8 inches, and place on greased baking sheets. Brush the tops with melted butter and sprinkle with crumbs, made as follows:

| | |
|---|---|
| 1 cup sifted flour | ½ cup sugar |

**1 egg, well beaten**

Combine ingredients and rub through a coarse sieve to form crumbs. Sprinkle over top of cakes. Bake in a hot oven, 400° F., for about 20 minutes.

## STRICKLE SHEETS

| | |
|---|---|
| 2 cups scalded milk | ½ cup lukewarm water |
| 4 eggs, well beaten | 1 teaspoon salt |
| 4 tablespoons butter | 2 cups sugar |
| 1 yeast cake | 7 cups sifted flour (about) |

Combine the milk, eggs, and butter and set aside to cool. Dissolve the yeast in the lukewarm water and add with the salt, sugar, and enough of the flour to make a thin batter. Beat vigorously for about 7 minutes. Cover and set in a warm place to rise for 7 to 8 hours. Then add enough additional flour to form a soft dough. Knead lightly and set aside to rise again. When light, turn out onto a lightly floured board and roll out 1 inch thick. Cut with a floured biscuit cutter and place on greased baking pans to rise. Spread with the following topping. Bake in a moderate oven, 350° F., for about 20 minutes.

**Topping**

| | |
|---|---|
| 2 cups sugar | ½ cup butter |
| 4 tablespoons flour | 4 tablespoons boiling water |

Combine the sugar, flour and butter. Add the boiling water and beat until smooth and creamy. Spread over the cakes before baking.

## STRUMPFBAENDER
### (Literally: Garters)

½ pound butter
2 cups powdered sugar

6 eggs, well beaten
½ teaspoon cinnamon

4 to 5 cups sifted flour

Cream together the butter and sugar. Add the eggs and gradually sift in the cinnamon and enough flour to make a stiff dough. Turn out onto a lightly floured board and roll out very thin. Cut with a jagging iron into 1- by 5-inch strips. Tie each strip into a loose knot, leaving a small hole in the center of each knot. Fry in very hot, deep fat, 360° F., for 1 to 2 minutes. (They should rise almost immediately to the surface.) Drain on absorbent paper. When cool, sprinkle with powdered sugar. *Strumpbänder* are better on the second day than on the first.

*Mrs. Paul de Schweinitz*

# Loaf and Layer Cakes

*Batsche, batsche Kuche/ Der Becker hot gerufe/*
*Wer will gude Kuche backe/ Der muss hawwe siwwe Sache/*
*Zucker un Sals/ Oier un Schmals/*
*Millich un Mehl/ Saffran macht die Kuche gehl/\**

## APPLESAUCE CAKE

| | |
|---|---|
| 2 cups flour | ½ teaspoon nutmeg |
| 1 teaspoon baking soda | 1 cup light brown sugar |
| ¼ teaspoon salt | ½ cup butter (scant) |
| 1 teaspoon cinnamon | 1 cup unsweetened applesauce |
| ½ teaspoon cloves | 1 cup chopped raisins |

Sift together the flour, baking soda, salt, and spices. Cream together the brown sugar and butter until soft and smooth. Gradually add the sifted dry ingredients alternately with the applesauce, beating well after each addition. Add the raisins last. Pour batter into a greased loaf pan. Bake in a moderate oven, 350° F., for 35 to 40 minutes.

## EBBELSCHNITZ KUCHE

### (Dried-Apple Cake)

| | |
|---|---|
| 3 cups dried apples | 2 teaspoons baking soda |
| 3 cups sugar | 2 teaspoons cinnamon |
| 1 cup water | 1½ teaspoons cloves |
| 1 cup butter | 2 teaspoons allspice |
| 2 eggs, well beaten | 1 teaspoon nutmeg |
| 4 cups flour | 1 cup sour milk |

Cut the apples into small pieces, add 1½ cups of the sugar and the water. Cook until apples are tender. Cream together the remaining sugar and the

*\*This children's rime, remembered in various forms by our older generation, is freely rendered: Patty cake, patty cake, the baker cried: Whoever would bake good cakes must have these seven ingredients: Sugar and salt, eggs and lard, milk and flour — and saffron to give the cake a golden color. — Saffron can still be purchased in some of our apothecary shops.*

butter until smooth. Add the eggs and stir until well mixed. Sift together the dry ingredients and add alternately with the sour milk to the creamed mixture. Stir in the cooked apples. Pour into greased loaf pans. Bake in a slow oven, 325° F., for about 1 hour. Makes 2 loaves.

*Mrs. Emma Bach*

### ARMER MANN'S KUCHE

#### (Poor Man's Cake)

| | |
|---|---|
| 2 cups sugar | 2 cups chopped raisins |
| 1 cup lard | 2 tablespoons cinnamon |
| 3 teaspoons baking soda | 1 nutmeg, grated |
| 1 cup hot water | 4 cups sifted flour |

Cream together the sugar and lard. Dissolve the baking soda in the hot water and add together with the raisins and spices. Let batter stand until cold. Then gradually stir in the flour. Pour into a greased loaf pan. Bake in a slow oven, 325° F., for about 45 minutes.

*Mrs. Albert T. von Trott*

### BLACK WALNUT CAKE

| | |
|---|---|
| 1 cup sugar | 1 cup ground walnuts |
| ½ cup butter and lard | 2 cups flour |
| 2 eggs, well beaten | 2 teaspoons baking powder |
| ½ cup milk | |

Cream together the sugar and shortening. Add the eggs and ground nuts. Mix well. Sift together the flour and baking powder and add alternately with the milk to the creamed mixture. Pour batter into a greased loaf pan. Bake in a moderate oven, 350° F., for about 1¼ hours.

*Mrs. Paul Ellinger*

### CARAMEL CAKE

| | |
|---|---|
| 1 cup butter | ½ cup cornstarch |
| 1½ cups powdered sugar | 2 teaspoons baking powder |
| 2 cups flour | 1 cup milk |
| 4 egg whites, beaten stiff | |

Cream together the butter and sugar. Sift together the flour, cornstarch, and baking powder. Add alternately with the milk to the creamed mixture. Fold in the egg whites. Pour batter into a greased loaf pan. Bake in a moderate oven, 350° F., about 50 minutes. Cool and frost with the following icing:

Icing

| | |
|---|---|
| 1 cup light brown sugar | ¼ cup milk |
| ½ tablespoon butter | ¼ teaspoon vanilla |

Combine the ingredients and boil until a small amount dropped in cold water forms a soft ball. Remove from the heat and beat until creamy.

## CIDER CAKE

| | |
|---|---|
| 2 cups sugar | ½ teaspoon cinnamon |
| ½ cup butter | ½ teaspoon allspice |
| 1½ teaspoons baking soda | ½ teaspoon cinnamon |
| 4 cups flour | 1 cup cider |
| 3½ cups chopped raisins | |

Cream together the sugar and butter. Sift together the baking soda, flour, and spices. Add to cream mixture alternately with the cider, beating well after each addition. Add the raisins. Pour batter into a greased loaf pan. Bake in a moderate oven, 350° F., for about 1 hour.

## CHOCOLATE LOAF

| | |
|---|---|
| 2 cups brown sugar | 1 teaspoon baking soda |
| ¾ cup butter and lard | 1 cup warm water |
| 2 eggs, well beaten | 3 cups sifted flour |
| Pinch of salt | ½ cup sour milk |
| ½ cup melted chocolate | 1 teaspoon vanilla |

Cream together the brown sugar and shortening. Add the eggs, salt, and melted chocolate. Dissolve the soda in the warm water and add to creamed mixture. Add the flour alternately with the sour milk to the creamed mixture. Add the vanilla. Pour batter into a loaf pan lined with waxed paper. Bake in a moderate oven, 350° F., for about 40 minutes.

## FEATHER CAKE

| | |
|---|---|
| 2 cups sugar | 2 eggs, well beaten |
| 4 tablespoons butter | 3 cups flour |
| 1 cup sour milk | 1 teaspoon cream of tartar |
| ½ teaspoon baking soda | |

Combine the sugar and butter and add the sour milk and eggs. Sift together the flour, cream of tartar, and baking soda and add gradually to first mixture, beating well after each addition. Pour batter into a greased loaf pan. Bake in a moderate oven, 350° F., for about 35 minutes.

*Mrs. David S. Hammond*

## WALNUT GINGERBREAD

| | |
|---|---|
| 1 cup light brown sugar | 2 teaspoons baking soda |
| ½ cup shortening | ½ teaspoon cloves |
| ½ cup molasses | ½ teaspoon cinnamon |
| 1 cup boiling water | ½ teaspoon ginger |
| 3½ cups flour | 2 eggs |
| ¾ cup chopped black walnuts | |

Cream together the sugar and shortening. Add the molasses and water and beat until well mixed. Sift together the flour, baking soda, and spices and add to first mixture, beating well after each addition. Beat in the eggs, one at a time. Add chopped walnuts. Pour batter into a greased loaf pan. Bake in a moderate oven, 350° F., for about 35 to 40 minutes.

## WEICHE LEBKUCHEN

### (Soft Gingerbread)

| | |
|---|---|
| 1 cup sour milk or buttermilk | 2 eggs, well beaten |
| 1 cup molasses | 1 teaspoon nutmeg |
| 1 cup butter, melted | 1 teaspoon cinnamon |
| 1 teaspoon baking soda | 1 tablespoon ginger |
| 1 tablespoon hot water | 2 cups flour (about) |

Combine milk, molasses, and butter. Dissolve soda in the hot water and add with eggs to first mixture. Sift together the dry ingredients and add gradually to form a smooth batter. Pour into a greased 9-inch square pan. Bake in a moderate oven, 350° F., for about 35 to 40 minutes.

*Die Geschickte Hausfrau, Harrisburg, Pa. (1852)*

## HICKORY NUT CAKE

| | |
|---|---|
| 1 cup butter | 2 cups finely chopped |
| 2 cups sugar | hickory nuts |
| 8 eggs | 2 tablespoons flour |
| 2 cups sifted flour | 1 wineglass brandy |

Cream together the butter and eggs. Slowly add the eggs, one at a time. Stir in 1 tablespoon flour after each egg is added and mix well for about 5 minutes. Then add remaining flour. Dust the nuts with the 2 tablespoons of flour and stir them into the batter. Add the brandy last. Pour batter into a well-greased loaf pan. Bake in a moderate oven, 350° F., for 1½ hours, or until a cake tester inserted in center of cake comes out dry and clean.

## LEMON CAKE

| | |
|---|---|
| ½ cup butter and lard | ½ teaspoon baking soda |
| 1½ cups sugar | 1 teaspoon cream of tartar |
| 3 eggs, separated | Juice and grated rind of |
| 2 cups flour | ½ lemon |

½ cup milk

Cream together the sugar and shortening, and add the well-beaten egg yolks. Sift together the flour, baking soda, and cream of tartar. Add dry ingredients alternately with the milk to the first mixture. Add the lemon juice and grated rind. Fold in the stiffly beaten egg whites. Pour batter into greased loaf pan. Bake in a moderate oven, 350° F., for 45 to 50 minutes.

## LOAF CAKE

| | |
|---|---|
| 1 cup sugar | 2 cups flour |
| ½ cup lard | 2½ teaspoons baking powder |
| | 1 cup milk |

Cream together the sugar and lard. Sift together the flour and baking powder and add alternately with the milk to creamed mixture. Pour batter into greased loaf pan. Bake in a moderate oven, 350° F., for 45 to 50 minutes. When cake is cool, frost with following icing:

**Icing**

| | |
|---|---|
| 1½ cups confectioner's sugar | ½ teaspoon vanilla |
| 2 tablespoons butter | Water |

Cream together the sugar and butter. Add the vanilla and enough water to make proper spreading consistency.

## MARBLE CAKE

| | |
|---|---|
| 1 cup sugar | 2 teaspoons baking powder |
| ⅓ cup butter | ½ cup milk |
| 2 eggs, well beaten | 1 tablespoon butter |
| 1½ cups flour | 1 square chocolate |
| | 1 teaspoon vanilla |

Cream together the sugar and butter. Add the eggs and mix well. Sift together the flour and baking powder and add alternately with the milk to the first mixture. Mix well after each addition. Melt 1 tablespoon of butter with the chocolate and add ⅓ of the batter. Add the vanilla to the remaining batter. Place spoonfuls of batter in a greased loaf pan, alternating light and dark mixtures. Bake in a moderate oven, 350° F., for about 45 minutes.

## SPANISH BUN

| | |
|---|---|
| 1 cup butter | 1 tablespoon cream |
| 3 cups sugar | 1 teaspoon baking soda |
| 4 eggs, well beaten | 1 cup brandy |
| 4 cups sifted flour | ½ cup chopped raisins |
| 1 cup milk | ½ cup chopped currants |
| | ½ cup chopped citron |

Cream together the butter and sugar, and add the eggs. Stir in the flour alternately with the milk and cream, mixing well after each addition. Dissolve baking soda in the brandy and add together with the fruit. Pour batter into a large well-greased loaf pan. Bake in a slow oven, 300° F., for about 1 to 1½ hours.

*Mrs. J. Max. Hark*

## KING'S CAKE

(From an old Pennsylvania German almanac)

| | |
|---|---|
| 2 cups heavy cream, whipped | 2 cups raisins |
| 16 egg yolks, well beaten | 2 cups currants |
| 2 cups sugar | ½ cup finely chopped citron |
| 4 cups sifted cake flour | 9 egg whites, beaten stiff |

Combine the whipped cream, egg yolks, and sugar. Stir for 1 hour. Gradually add the flour and stir for ½ hour. Wash and thoroughly dry the raisins and currants, and add together with citron. Fold in egg whites. Pour batter into 2 well-greased pans. Bake in a moderate oven, 350° F., for about 1 hour.

## QUEEN'S CAKE

(From an old Pennsylvania German almanac)

| | |
|---|---|
| 2 cups sugar | Cinnamon |
| 1 pound butter | 1 nutmeg, ground |
| 8 eggs, separated | 4 cups flour |
| | 1 cup currants |

Cream together the sugar and butter. Beat the egg yolks for 30 minutes and add to creamed mixture. Measure an equal amount of cinnamon and nutmeg, sift together with the flour and stir into first mixture. Add the currants. Beat the egg whites for 20 minutes and fold in last. Pour batter into a well-greased pan. Bake in a moderate oven, 350° F., for about 1 hour.

## POUND CAKE

| | |
|---|---|
| 1 cup butter | 1 teaspoon lemon juice |
| 1 cup sugar | 5 eggs, separated |
| 1 teaspoon vanilla | 2 cups flour |
| | 1 teaspoon baking powder |

Cream the butter until soft and smooth. Add sugar gradually, creaming until very fluffy. Add vanilla and lemon juice. Add well-beaten egg yolks, beating very thoroughly. Fold in stiffly beaten egg whites, then add the flour and baking powder, sifted together 3 times. Turn into greased loaf pan. Bake in a moderately slow oven, 325° F., for 1 to 1¼ hours.

*Mrs. David S. Hammond*

## SPICECAKE I

| | |
|---|---|
| 2 cups brown sugar | 2 teaspoons cloves |
| 4 eggs, well beaten | 2 cups flour |
| 1 teaspoon baking soda | ½ cup butter, melted |
| 1 teaspoon cream of tartar | 1 cup sour milk |

Combine the brown sugar and eggs and mix until soft and smooth. Sift together the dry ingredients and add alternately with the sour milk to first mixture. Add melted butter last. Pour batter into a greased loaf pan. Bake in a moderate oven, 350° F., for 30 to 40 minutes.

*Mrs. Walter Sechrist*

## SPICECAKE II

| | |
|---|---|
| 2 cups brown sugar | 2 teaspoons cinnamon |
| ½ cup butter and lard | 1 teaspoon allspice |
| 2 eggs, well beaten | 1 teaspoon nutmeg |
| 2½ cups flour | 1 cup sour milk |
| 1 teaspoon baking soda | ¾ cup raisins and currants |

Cream together the sugar and shortening and add the eggs. Mix well until smooth and creamy. Sift together the dry ingredients and add alternately with the sour milk to first mixture. Fold in raisins and currants. Pour batter into a greased loaf pan. Bake in a moderate oven, 350° F., for 30 to 40 minutes.

*Mrs. M. M. Kutz*

## CITRON CAKE

| | |
|---|---|
| 1 cup sugar | 1¼ teaspoons baking powder |
| ½ cup butter | 2 tablespoons water |
| 4 eggs, well beaten | ¼ pound citron, sliced thin |
| 1½ cups flour | Almond flavoring |

Cream together the sugar and butter, and add the eggs. Mix well until smooth and creamy. Sift together the flour and baking powder and add to first mixture. Moisten with the water. Fold in the citron and almond flavoring to taste. Pour batter into a greased loaf pan, lined with waxed paper. Bake in a moderate oven, 350° F., for about 45 minutes.

## ANGEL CAKE

| | |
|---|---|
| 1¼ cups powdered sugar | 1 cup egg whites |
| ½ cup flour | 1 teaspoon cream of tartar |
| ½ cup cornstarch | (scant) |
| | Vanilla or almond flavoring |

Sift the sugar several times. Sift together the flour and cornstarch several times. Combine with the sugar and sift twice. Beat the egg whites to a froth, sprinkle cream of tartar over top and continue beating until whites are just stiff enough to form peaks, but not dry. Add flavoring to taste. Fold egg whites into dry mixture. Turn into ungreased tube pan. Place in cold oven, set heat control to 325° F. and bake for 1¼ hours. Invert pan on rack until cake is cold, about 1 hour.

## SPONGECAKE

| | |
|---|---|
| ¾ cup flour | Grated rind of 1 lemon |
| 6 eggs, separated | 1½ cups sugar |

Sift the flour 3 or 4 times. Beat egg yolks until thick and lemon-colored. Add lemon rind and continue beating until thick. Stir in the flour gradually and mix well. Fold in egg whites which have been beaten stiff with the sugar. Pour batter into an ungreased tube pan. Bake in a moderately slow oven, 325° F., for about 1 hour. Invert pan on a rack until cake is cold, about 1 hour.

*Mrs. Albert T. von Trott*

## CUSTARD SPONGECAKE

| | |
|---|---|
| 2 cups sugar | 4 eggs, well beaten |
| ½ teaspoon salt | 1 teaspoon baking soda |
| 2 teaspoons cream of tartar | 1 cup cold water |
| 3 cups sifted flour | Juice of 1 lemon |

Sift together the sugar, salt, cream of tartar, and ½ of the flour. Stir mixture into the eggs. Dissolve the soda in the water, add the lemon juice and remaining flour. Stir into the first mixture. Pour batter 2 inches deep into 2 ungreased pans. Bake in a moderate oven, 350° F., for about 25 minutes. When cake is cool, split each layer and spread custard filling between the halves.

### Custard Filling

| | |
|---|---|
| 2 cups milk | 1 cup sugar |
| 2 tablespoons cornstarch | 1 egg, well beaten |
| Water | Vanilla |

Place the milk in top of double boiler over hot water and heat. Mix the cornstarch in a little water to form a paste. Add the sugar and egg, and flavor to taste with vanilla. Stir into the hot milk. Continue cooking for about 15 minutes, stirring constantly. Cool and spread on the layers of Custard Spongecake.

## POTATO SPONGECAKE

| | |
|---|---|
| ½ pound potatoes | 1 teaspoon grated lemon rind |
| 8 eggs, separated | Bread crumbs |
| 1 cup sugar | Confectioner's sugar |

Boil the potatoes until cooked. Peel, and when cold, grate them. Beat egg yolks until thick and lemon-colored. Add the sugar and beat until thoroughly mixed. Add grated potatoes and lemon rind. Beat egg whites until stiff but not dry. Fold into potato mixture. Butter a deep cake dish, sprinkle bottom and sides with fine bread crumbs, and pour batter into dish. Bake in a moderately slow oven, 325° F., for about 1¼ hours. Invert pan on rack and let stand about 1 hour to cool. Sprinkle confectioner's sugar over cake before serving.

*Vollmer's Vollständiges deutsches Vereinigten Staaten Kochbuch,*
*Philadelphia, 1865.*

# LAYER CAKES

## APPLE CREAM CAKE

| | |
|---|---|
| 2 cups sugar | 3 cups flour |
| 2 tablespoons butter | 2 teaspoons baking powder |
| 3 eggs, separated | 1 cup milk |

### Vanilla or lemon juice

Cream together the sugar and butter, and add the egg yolks. Beat until well mixed. Sift together the flour and baking powder, and add alternately with the milk to creamed mixture. Add vanilla or lemon juice to taste. Pour batter into 2 greased layer cake pans. Bake in a moderate oven, 350° F., for about 25 minutes. Frost with the following icing:

### Icing

| | |
|---|---|
| 1 egg white | 1 apple, grated |
| 1 cup sugar | Juice of 1/4 lemon |

Beat the egg white until stiff, add the sugar and beat thoroughly. Add the grated apple and lemon juice and beat until mixture is light and foamy. Chopped nuts may be added, if desired.

## CHOCOLATE LAYER CAKE

| | |
|---|---|
| 1 cup brown sugar | 1/2 cup butter |
| 1/2 cup unsweetened chocolate, grated | 2 eggs, well beaten |
| | 2 cups flour |
| 1 1/4 cups milk | 2 teaspoons baking powder |

### 1 teaspoon vanilla

Combine 1/2 cup of the brown sugar with the chocolate and 3/4 cup of the milk. Cook over hot water until slightly thickened. Cream together the remaining sugar with the butter, and add the eggs, milk, and vanilla. Mix well. Combine with the chocolate mixture. Sift together the flour and baking powder. Add to chocolate mixture and mix well. Pour batter into 2 greased layer cake pans. Bake in a moderate oven, 350° F., for about 30 minutes. Spread filling between the layers.

### Filling

| | |
|---|---|
| 1 1/2 cups powdered sugar | 1 tablespoon melted butter |
| 2 1/2 tablespoons cocoa | Cold coffee |

### Vanilla

Combine the sugar, cocoa, and butter. Add enough coffee to form a smooth paste. Flavor to taste with vanilla.

## SCHWARZ KUCHE

### (Literally: Black Cake)

| | |
|---|---|
| ½ cup grated chocolate | 3 eggs, separated |
| 2 cups milk | 1 teaspoon baking soda |
| ½ cup butter | 3 cups flour |
| 1½ cups sugar | 1½ teaspoons baking powder |

1 teaspoon vanilla

Combine the chocolate with 1 cup of the milk. Cook over hot water until slightly thickened. Cool. Cream together the butter and sugar, and add the well-beaten egg yolks. Dissolve the soda in the remaining cup of milk. Sift together the flour and baking powder. Add dry ingredients alternately with the milk to chocolate mixture. Fold in stiffly beaten egg whites. Pour batter into 3 greased layer cake pans. Bake in a moderate oven, 350° F., for about 30 minutes. Spread filling between the layers.

**Filling**

| | |
|---|---|
| ½ cup sugar | ⅔ teaspoon cornstarch |
| ½ cup milk | 1 egg yolk |

2 squares unsweetened chocolate

Combine all the ingredients and cook until thick enough to spread between layers of cake.

## COCONUT LAYER CAKE

| | |
|---|---|
| ½ cup butter and lard | 1 teaspoon baking soda |
| 2 cups sugar | 2 teaspoons cream of tartar |
| 3 egg yolks, well beaten | 2 cups flour |

1 cup milk

Cream together the shortening and sugar, and add the egg yolks. Beat until smooth and creamy. Sift together the soda, cream of tartar, and flour, and add alternately with the milk to the creamed mixture. Pour batter into 3 greased layer cake pans. Bake in a moderate oven, 350° F.. for about 30 minutes. Frost with the following icing:

**Icing**

| | |
|---|---|
| 3 egg whites | 1¼ cups powdered sugar |

1 cup shredded coconut

Beat egg whites until stiff, add the sugar and beat thoroughly. Spread on cake and sprinkle coconut over the top.

## ICE-CREAM CAKE
### (From Baer's German Almanac, Lancaster, 1883)

| | |
|---|---|
| 1 cup butter | 3 cups flour |
| 2 cups sugar | 3 teaspoons baking powder |
| | 1 cup milk |

Cream together the butter and sugar. Sift together the flour and baking powder and add alternately with the milk to the creamed mixture. Mix well after each addition. Pour batter into 3 greased layer cake pans, forming thin layers. Bake in a moderate oven, 350° F., for about 25 to 30 minutes. Frost with the following icing:

**Icing**

| | |
|---|---|
| 3 cups sugar | 5 egg whites |
| | 1 teaspoon vanilla extract |

Dissolve the sugar in a little water and boil until mixture spins a thread. Cool and pour in a thin stream over unbeaten egg whites, beating constantly until proper consistency is formed.

## LADY BALTIMORE CAKE

| | |
|---|---|
| ½ cup butter | 3 teaspoons baking powder |
| 2 cups sugar | 1 cup milk |
| 3 cups flour | 6 egg whites, beaten stiff |

Cream the butter and gradually add the sugar, creaming until light and fluffy. Sift together the flour and baking powder and add alternately with the milk, mixing well after each addition. Fold in egg whites. Pour batter into 3 greased layer cake pans. Bake in a moderately hot oven, 375° F., for about 20 minutes. Frost with the following icing:

**Icing**

| | |
|---|---|
| 3 cups sugar | 1 cup chopped raisins |
| 1 cup boiling water | 1 cup chopped almonds |
| 3 egg whites, beaten stiff | 1 cup chopped English walnuts |
| | 1 teaspoon vanilla |

Combine sugar and boiling water and cook until mixture spins a thread. Pour syrup in a thin stream over egg whites, beating constantly until thick and creamy. Fold in raisins, nuts, and vanilla.

*Mrs. J. Max. Hark*

## ORANGE LAYER CAKE

| | |
|---|---|
| ½ cup butter and lard | 3 eggs, separated |
| 1½ cups sugar | 2½ cups flour |
| Grated rind of 1 orange | 2½ teaspoons baking powder |
| | 1 cup milk |

Cream shortening and gradually add sugar, creaming until light and fluffy. Add orange rind and well-beaten egg yolks. Sift together the flour and baking powder and add alternately with the milk, to the creamed mixture, mixing well after each addition. Fold in egg whites, beaten stiff. Pour batter into 2 greased layer cake pans. Bake in a moderately hot oven, 375° F., for about 25 minutes. Frost with the following icing:

**Icing**

| | |
|---|---|
| 1 egg white, beaten stiff | Juice and grated rind of 1 orange |
| 2 cups sugar | |

Combine egg white with juice and grated rind and gradually stir in the sugar. Beat until well mixed and creamy.

## SHELLBARK LAYER CAKE

| | |
|---|---|
| ½ cup butter | 1½ teaspoons baking powder |
| 1½ cups sugar | 2 cups flour |
| 3 eggs | ¾ cup water (about) |
| 1 cup chopped shellbark meats | |

Cream the butter and gradually add the sugar, mixing well until smooth. Beat in the eggs, one at a time, reserving 1 egg white for the icing. Sift together the baking powder and flour and add alternately with the water to the creamed mixture. Add just enough of the water to form a fairly stiff batter. Pour some of the batter into 2 greased layer cake pans. Add nut meats to remaining batter and pour into 3rd layer cake pan. Bake in a moderate oven, 350° F., for about 30 minutes. Frost with following icing, placing layer containing nut meats in the middle.

**Icing**

| | |
|---|---|
| 1 cup sugar | 1 egg white, beaten stiff |
| 4 tablespoons cold water | 1 teaspoon vanilla |

Combine sugar and water and boil until mixture forms a thread. Pour over beaten egg white, beating constantly until thick and creamy. Add vanilla.

## DELICATE CAKE

| | |
|---|---|
| ¾ cup butter | 4 teaspoons baking powder |
| 2 cups sugar | 1 cup milk |
| 4 cups cake flour | 4 egg whites, beaten stiff |
| 1 teaspoon vanilla | |

Cream butter and gradually add sugar, beating well. Sift together the flour and baking powder and add alternately with the milk to the creamed mixture. Fold in beaten egg whites and vanilla. Pour batter into 3 greased layer cake pans. Bake in a moderately hot oven, 375° F., for about 25 minutes.

## ROTATION CAKE

| | |
|---|---|
| ½ cup butter | ½ cup sour milk |
| 1½ cups sugar | 2 cups cake flour |
| 3 eggs | 1 teaspoon baking soda |

1½ teaspoons cream of tartar

Cream butter and gradually add the sugar, mixing well. Beat in eggs, one at a time, reserving 1 egg white for icing. Add sour milk and beat until thoroughly mixed. Sift together the flour, baking soda, and cream of tartar and add gradually, stirring after each addition. Pour batter into 1 greased 8-inch square pan. Bake in a moderate oven, 350° F., for about 35 minutes. Frost with icing (see Shellbark Layer Cake).

## STRAW CAKE

| | |
|---|---|
| ½ cup butter | 3 teaspoons baking powder |
| 2 cups sugar | 3 cups cake flour |
| 3 eggs, well beaten | 1 cup milk |

1 teaspoon vanilla

Cream butter and gradually add the sugar, mixing well. Add egg yolks and beat until well mixed. Sift together baking powder and flour and add alternately with milk to creamed mixture. Add vanilla. Pour batter into 3 greased layer cake pans. Bake in a moderately hot oven, 375° F., for about 25 minutes. Frost with following icing:

**Icing**

| | |
|---|---|
| 1 cup sugar | 1 egg white, beaten stiff |
| ½ cup water | 1 teaspoon vanilla |

Combine sugar and water and boil until mixture spins a thread. Pour syrup in a thin stream over beaten egg white, beating constantly until thick and creamy. Add vanilla.

## SCRIPTURE CAKE

| | |
|---|---|
| 1 cup butter (Judges 5:25) | 1 tablespoon honey |
| 3 cups sugar (Jeremiah 6:20) | (Exodus 16:21) |
| 6 eggs (Isaiah 10:14) | 1 cup water (Genesis 24:17) |
| 3½ cups flour (I Kings 4:22) | 2 cups raisins (I Samuel 30:12) |
| Pinch of salt (Leviticus 2:15) | 2 cups figs (I Samuel 30:12) |
| Spices to taste (I Kings 10:10) | 1 cup almonds (Genesis 43:11) |

Follow Solomon's advice for making good boys and you will have a good cake (Proverbs 23:14).

*Mrs. A. W. Davis*

*If you want your cakes to be light,*
*Stir them only from left to right.*

# Cookies, Drop Cakes and Cupcakes

*Die Fraa kann meh verduh als ihr Mann beischaffe kann*
A careless cook can waste and burn
More than her thrifty man can earn.

Few of the following recipes can be claimed by the Pennsylvania Germans as being peculiarly their own. In the fatherland they probably knew the luxury of cookies and small cakes only on special holidays. With the greater plenty of butter, eggs and milk they soon cultivated in their new homes more elaborate baking. Those recipes that have no leavening agent, but call for a large number of eggs are no doubt among the oldest; so also those that call for soda and sour milk. Baking powder came to be more widely used only after the Civil War. Interesting is the use of pearlash and hartshorn in the Honey Cake Recipe. The recipes for cookies and cakes definitely associated with the Christmas season are found in the next chapter.

## BUTTERSCOTCH COOKIES

| | |
|---|---|
| 3 cups brown sugar | 1 teaspoon salt |
| 2 cups butter and lard | 6½ cups flour |
| 2 teaspoons baking soda | 1 tablespoon vanilla |
| 2 teaspoons cream of tartar | 3 eggs, well beaten |

Cream together the sugar and shortening. Sift together the dry ingredients and stir into the creamed mixture. Add the vanilla and beaten eggs and mix well. Shape the dough into rolls about 2 inches in diameter. Wrap in waxed paper and chill overnight. Cut rolls into ⅛-inch slices and place on ungreased cooky sheet. Press each cooky with a metal potato masher to make a design. Bake in a moderately hot oven, 375° F., for 8 to 10 minutes. Makes approximately 12 dozen cookies.

*Mrs. Samuel Smucker*

## SOUR CREAM COOKIES

| | |
|---|---|
| ¼ pound butter | 2 cups sugar |
| 1 cup sour cream | 4 cups flour |
| 1 teaspoon baking soda | 1 egg, well beaten |

Cream the butter, and beat into it the sour cream. Mix well. Sift together the sugar and flour and add to first mixture. Roll out dough on a lightly floured board and cut into small rounds. Place on ungreased baking sheet and brush top of each cooky with beaten egg. Bake in a moderate oven, 350° F., for about 10 minutes. Makes approximately 8 dozen cookies.

### CHOCOLATE COOKIES

| | |
|---|---|
| 2 cups brown sugar | 2 eggs, well beaten |
| ½ cup butter | 1 teaspoon baking soda |
| 6 squares chocolate, melted | 3 cups sifted flour (about) |

Cream together the sugar and butter, and add the melted chocolate and eggs. Dissolve the soda in a little warm water and stir into creamed mixture. Add gradually enough flour to form a fairly stiff dough, mixing well after each addition. Roll out on a lightly floured board and cut into rounds. Place on an ungreased cooky sheet. Bake in a moderate oven, 350° F., for about 10 minutes. Makes approximately 6 dozen cookies.

### SCHPRITZKUCHE
#### (Squirt Cookies)

| | |
|---|---|
| 1 cup butter | Pinch of salt |
| 1 cup sugar | 3 cups sifted flour (about) |
| 2 eggs, well beaten | 1 tablespoon water |
| 1 teaspoon vanilla | |

Cream together the butter and sugar, and add the eggs and salt. Add the flour alternately with the water and vanilla to the creamed mixture, but only enough flour to make a very soft dough. Put dough into pastry bag and squeeze out on cooky sheet in S-shaped forms. Sprinkle the top of each cooky with red sugar. Bake in a moderate oven, 350° F., for about 10 minutes. Makes approximately 5 dozen cookies.

*Mrs. Walter Erdman*

### PEANUT COOKIES

| | |
|---|---|
| 2 tablespoons butter | ¼ teaspoon salt |
| 1 cup sugar | 1¼ teaspoons baking powder |
| 3 eggs, well beaten | 1¼ cups flour |
| 2 cups ground peanuts | 2 tablespoons milk |

Cream the butter and add the sugar. Mix well. Add the eggs and peanuts. Sift together the dry ingredients and add alternately with the milk to the first mixture. Roll out on a lightly floured board and cut into small rounds. Place on an ungreased cooky sheet. Bake in a moderately hot oven, 375° F., for about 8 to 10 minutes. Makes approximately 4 dozen cookies.

## ENGLISH WALNUT COOKIES

| | |
|---|---|
| 1 tablespoon butter | ¾ cup bread crumbs |
| 1 cup sugar | Pinch of allspice |
| 2 eggs, well beaten | Milk |
| 1 pound chopped English walnuts | |

Cream the butter and gradually add the sugar. Mix well. Add the eggs and beat until creamy. Combine the bread crumbs and allspice, and add enough milk to moisten mixture. Add to creamed mixture. Fold in chopped nuts. Roll out ½-inch thick on lightly floured board. Cut into 3-inch rounds. Place on an ungreased cooky sheet. Bake in a moderate oven, 350° F., for about 10 minutes. Makes approximately 1½ dozen cookies.

## FILLED COOKIES

| | |
|---|---|
| 2 cups brown sugar | Pinch of salt |
| ¾ cup shortening | 1 teaspoon baking soda |
| 3 eggs, well beaten | 4 cups flour |
| 1 teaspoon vanilla | |

Cream together the sugar and shortening, and add the eggs. Sift together the dry ingredients and stir into creamed mixture. Add vanilla. Roll out ¼-inch thick on lightly floured board and cut into small rounds. Place on an ungreased cooky sheet. Bake in a moderately hot oven, 375° F., for about 10 minutes. Place 1 teaspoon of the following filling on a cooky, place another cooky on top and press together. Makes approximately 4 dozen filled cookies.

### Filling:

| | |
|---|---|
| 1½ cups chopped raisins | 1½ cups water |
| 1½ cups brown sugar | ½ cup cornstarch |

Combine ingredients and boil until mixture thickens. Cool before spreading on cookies.

## GINGERSNAPS

| | |
|---|---|
| 1 cup molasses | 4 cups flour |
| ½ cup sugar | 1 teaspoon baking soda |
| 3 tablespoons butter | 1 teaspoon cloves |
| 3 tablespoons lard | 1 teaspoon cinnamon |
| 2 tablespoons milk | 1 teaspoon ginger |
| 1 teaspoon salt | |

Pour molasses into a saucepan and bring to a boil. Add the sugar, shortening and the milk. Sift together dry ingredients and stir into liquid mixture. Chill overnight. Roll out ⅛-inch thick on a lightly floured board. Cut into rounds. Place on an ungreased cooky sheet. Bake in a moderate oven, 350° F., for about 10 minutes. Makes about 10 dozen gingersnaps.

*Mrs. Jonas Martin*

## COCONUT SNAPS

| | |
|---|---|
| 2½ cups sugar | 1 cup molasses |
| ⅓ cup butter | 1 cup grated coconut |
| ½ teaspoon baking soda | 3 cups sifted flour |

Cream together the sugar and butter. Dissolve the baking soda in the molasses and add with the coconut to the creamed mixture. Stir in the flour. Roll out dough on a lightly floured board and cut into small rounds. Place on an ungreased cooky sheet. Bake in a hot oven, 400° F., for about 10 minutes or until golden brown. Let cool thoroughly before removing from the sheet. Makes approximately 10 dozen cookies.

## SUGAR SNAPS

| | |
|---|---|
| 2 cups sugar | 3 eggs, well beaten |
| ½ pound butter | ½ teaspoon soda |
| ½ pound lard | ¼ cup sherry |
| 6 cups sifted flour | |

Cream together the sugar and shortening, and add the eggs. Dissolve the soda in the sherry and add alternately with the flour to the creamed mixture. Mix well. Roll out the dough on a lightly floured board and cut into 3-inch rounds. Place on an ungreased cooky sheet. Bake in a moderate oven, 350° F., for about 10 minutes.

## MRS. HUMMEL'S BUTTER COOKIES

| | |
|---|---|
| ½ lb. butter | 2 egg yolks |
| ½ lb. margarine | grated lemon rind |
| ¾ lb. sugar | 4 cups flour |

Cream butter and sugar, add egg yolks and grated lemon rind. Stir in the flour. Cool dough, roll and cut out, and bake at 350° F.

## HEIFER TONGUES
### (Rinnszung Kuche)

| | |
|---|---|
| 2 cups brown sugar | 1 teaspoon baking soda |
| 1 cup shortening | ½ cup warm water |
| 1 cup molasses | 1 teaspoon cinnamon |
| 5 cups pastry flour | |

Cream together the sugar and shortening and add the molasses. Dissolve the soda in the warm water. Sift the cinnamon with the flour and add alternately with the warm water to the creamed mixture. Mix well. Fashion dough into a long roll about 2½ inches in diameter, flatten it slightly and chill overnight. Cut into ¼-inch slices and place on an ungreased cooky sheet. Sprinkle with granulated sugar. Bake in a moderately hot oven, 375° F., for about 12 minutes. Makes approximately 50 cookies.

*Mrs. Lloyd A. Moll*

## JUMBLES I

| | |
|---|---|
| 1 pound butter | 1 teaspoon baking soda |
| 2 cups sugar | 1 teaspoon cream of tartar |
| 4 eggs, well beaten | 1 nutmeg, grated |
| 4 cups flour | 1 cup sour milk |

Cream together the butter and sugar, and add the eggs. Sift together the flour, baking soda, cream of tartar, and nutmeg, and add alternately with the sour milk to the creamed mixture. Mix well. Roll small portions of the dough between the hands, making sections about 9 inches long and ¾ inch thick. Twist each section into a circle and place on baking sheet. Bake in a moderate oven, 350° F., for about 15 to 20 minutes.

*Mrs. David S. Hammond*

## JUMBLES II

| | |
|---|---|
| 1½ cups sugar | 3¾ cups flour |
| 1½ cups butter | ¼ teaspoon cinnamon |
| 2 eggs, well beaten | 1 tablespoon rose water or wine |

Cream together the butter and sugar, and add the eggs. Sift together the flour and cinnamon and add to the creamed mixture with the rose water or wine. Mix well. Roll out ¼ inch thick on a lightly floured board and cut into 3-inch rounds. Place on a baking sheet. Bake in a slow oven, 300° F., for about 15 minutes. Makes approximately 4 dozen.

*Mrs. J. Max. Hark*

## HONEY CAKES
### (An ancient recipe)

| | |
|---|---|
| 2½ pounds honey | ½ ounce salt of hartshorn |
| 1½ pounds brown sugar | (ammonium carbonate) |
| 1 ounce pearlash | 4 eggs, well beaten |
| (potassium bicarbonate) | 3¾ pounds flour |

Mix honey and sugar and bring to boiling point. Pour gradually into flour. Add pulverized pearlash dissolved in a little water. When cooled somewhat, add eggs. Add the hartshorn dissolved in a little water. Mix thoroughly and chill overnight. Roll out ½ inch thick on floured board and cut into 4-inch rounds. Place on baking sheet and bake in a moderate oven, 350° F., for about 12 to 15 minutes.

*Mrs. John Kunsman*

## SMALL RICE CAKES

| | |
|---|---|
| 2 cups sugar | 3 eggs, well beaten |
| 1 pound butter | 4 cups rice flour |
| Sugar and cinnamon, mixed | |

Cream together the sugar and butter, and add 2 of the beaten eggs. Stir in the rice flour and mix well. Turn out on a board lightly dusted with flour and powdered sugar. Roll very thin and cut into small rounds. Place on a baking sheet, brush each cake with beaten egg and sprinkle with sugar and cinnamon. Bake in a moderate oven, 350° F., for 8 to 10 minutes. Makes approximately 5 dozen cakes.

### SHREWSBURY CAKES

| | |
|---|---|
| 2 cups sugar | ½ teaspoon baking soda |
| ¾ cup butter | ¼ cup sherry |
| 4 eggs, well beaten | 5 cups sifted flour |
| 1 tablespoon caraway seeds | |

Cream together the sugar and butter and add the eggs. Dissolve the baking soda in the sherry and add alternately with the flour to the creamed mixture. Stir in the caraway seeds. Roll out thin on a lightly floured board and cut into small rounds. Place on a baking sheet and sprinkle with sugar. Bake in a moderate oven, 350° F., for about 10 minutes. Makes approximately 10 dozen cakes.

# DROP COOKIES

### CHOCOLATE DROPS

| | |
|---|---|
| 2½ cups sugar | 2½ cups sifted flour |
| 1½ cups grated chocolate | 8 egg whites, beaten stiff |

Combine the sugar and chocolate, and stir in the flour. Fold in beaten egg whites and mix well. Drop from a teaspoon onto ungreased, paper-covered baking sheet. Bake in a slow oven, 300° F., for about 15 to 20 minutes.

### CURRANT DROPS

| | |
|---|---|
| ¾ pound butter | 1 teaspoon baking soda |
| 2½ cups powdered sugar | 1 cup sour cream |
| 5 eggs, well beaten | 4½ cups sifted flour |
| 2 cup currants | |

Cream together the butter and sugar, and add the eggs. Dissolve the soda in the sour cream and stir into creamed mixture. Gradually add the flour, mixing well. Stir in the currants last. Drop from a teaspoon onto a greased baking sheet. Bake in a moderately hot oven, 375° F., for 8 to 12 minutes. Makes approximately 5 dozen drops.

### LOVE DROP CAKES

| | |
|---|---|
| 3 cups sugar | 1 cup grated coconut |
| 1 cup butter and lard | 2½ teaspoons baking powder |
| 1 cup milk | 4 cups flour |
| 6 egg whites, beaten stiff | |

Cream together the sugar and shortening. Add the milk and coconut and mix well. Sift together the baking powder and flour and add to first mixture. Fold in beaten egg whites. Drop from a teaspoon onto a well-greased baking sheet. Bake in a moderate oven, 350° F., for about 8 to 12 minutes. Makes approximately 5 dozen cakes.

*Miss Edna Martin*

### SPUNIGAL DROP CAKES

| | |
|---|---|
| 2 cups brown sugar | 1 tablespoon warm water |
| 4 eggs, well beaten | 3 cups flour |
| 1 teaspoon baking soda | 1 teaspoon cinnamon |
| 1 teaspoon aniseed | |

Combine the sugar and eggs and mix well. Dissolve the baking soda in the warm water and add. Sift together the flour and cinnamon and stir into egg mixture. Stir in aniseed. Drop from a teaspoon onto an ungreased, paper-covered baking sheet. Bake in a slow oven, 300° F., for 15 to 20 minutes.

*Miss Emma Martin*

### RAISIN DROPS

| | |
|---|---|
| ¼ cup shortening | 1½ cups flour |
| ¾ cup sugar | ¼ teaspoon nutmeg |
| 1 egg, well beaten | ¼ teaspoon cinnamon |
| ½ teaspoon baking soda | ¼ teaspoon salt |
| 1 tablespoon hot water | 1 cup chopped raisins |

Cream together the shortening and sugar, and add the egg. Mix well. Dissolve the baking soda in the hot water and add to creamed mixture. Sift together the dry ingredients and stir into creamed mixture. Fold in the chopped raisins. Drop from a teaspoon onto a greased baking sheet. Bake in a moderate oven, 350° F., for about 8 minutes. Makes approximately 4 dozen cakes.

### SPONGE DROPS

| | |
|---|---|
| 4 eggs | 1⅓ cups flour |
| 1¼ cups sugar | 1 teaspoon baking powder |
| Lemon Juice | |

Beat the eggs to a stiff froth and gradually stir in the sugar. Sift together the flour and baking powder and gradually add to the egg mixture. Flavor to taste with lemon juice. Drop from a tablespoon onto a greased baking sheet. Bake in a hot oven, 400° F., for about 8 minutes, watching carefully that they do not burn. Makes approximately 1½ dozens.

### BLACK WALNUT COOKIES

| | |
|---|---|
| 2 cups brown sugar | ½ teaspoon salt |
| 4 eggs, well beaten | ½ teaspoon baking powder |
| ½ cup flour | 1 pound black walnuts, chopped |

Combine the sugar and eggs and beat until smooth. Sift together the flour, salt, and baking powder and gradually stir into the egg mixture. Fold in the chopped nuts. Drop from a spoon onto a greased baking sheet. Bake in a moderate oven, 350° F., for about 12 minutes. Makes approximately 2 dozen cookies.

### MOLASSES CAKES

| | |
|---|---|
| 2 cups molasses | 2 tablespoons hot water |
| 1 cup lard | 6 cups sifted flour |
| 2 tablespoons sugar | 2 tablespoons pearlash* |
| 1 tablespoon baking soda | 1 cup sour milk |
| 1 egg, well beaten | |

Mix together the molasses, lard, and sugar. Dissolve the soda in the hot water and add to first mixture. Stir in the flour and pearlash, mixing well. Add the sour milk. Drop from a tablespoon onto a greased baking sheet. Brush the top of cakes with beaten egg. Bake in a moderate oven, 350° F., about 15 minutes. Makes approximately 100 cakes.

*Mrs. Conrad Hermsted*

### COCONUT MOLASSES CAKES

| | |
|---|---|
| 5 cups brown sugar | 2 cups molasses |
| ¾ cup butter | 4 cups sifted flour |
| 1 coconut, grated | |

Cream the sugar and butter, and mix well until smooth and creamy. Add the molasses and flour alternately. Stir in the grated coconut last. Drop from a teaspoon onto a greased baking sheet. Bake in a moderate oven, 350° F, for about 12 minutes. Makes approximately 8 dozen cakes.

### OATMEAL COOKIES

| | |
|---|---|
| 1 cup sugar | 2 teaspoons baking powder |
| 1 teaspoon butter | ½ teaspoon salt |
| 2 eggs, well beaten | 2½ cups oatmeal |
| 1 cup flour | ½ teaspoon vanilla |

Cream together the sugar and butter, and add the eggs. Mix well. Combine the baking powder, salt, and oatmeal and stir into creamed mixture. Flavor with vanilla. Drop from teaspoon onto greased baking sheet. Bake in a moderately slow oven, 325° F., for about 20 minutes. Makes approximately 2 dozen cookies.

———

*Pearlash, also known as potash and salt of tartar, is an unrefined form of potassium carbonate, formerly obtained from ashes of wood.—See your apothecary.

## ROCKS CAKES

| | |
|---|---|
| 1½ cups sugar | 3 cups sifted flour |
| 1 cup butter | 1 teaspoon cloves |
| 3 eggs, well beaten | 1 teaspoon cinnamon |
| 1 teaspoon baking soda | ¾ pound chopped raisins |
| 1 tablespoon hot water | ½ pound chopped English walnuts |

Cream together the sugar and butter, and add the eggs. Mix well. Dissolve the baking soda in hot water and stir into creamed mixture. Combine flour, cloves, and cinnamon and gradually stir into mixture. Fold in raisins and walnuts. Drop from a teaspoon onto a greased baking sheet. Bake in a moderately hot oven, 375° F., for about 8 minutes. Makes approximately 4 dozen cakes.

## TAYLOR CAKES

| | |
|---|---|
| 2 cups sugar | 3⅓ cups flour (about) |
| 1 cup butter and lard | 1½ teaspoons cinnamon |
| 2 cups molasses | 1½ teaspoons cloves |
| 1 tablespoon baking soda | 2 cups sour milk |
| 3 eggs, well beaten | |

Cream together the sugar and shortening. Heat the molasses and add the baking soda. Stir until soda is dissolved. Sift together the flour, cinnamon, cloves, and add alternately with molasses to the creamed mixture. Stir in the sour milk. Add more flour if necessary for a drop dough. Drop from spoon onto a greased baking sheet and brush top of cakes with beaten egg. Bake in a moderate oven, 350° F., for about 12 minutes. Makes approximately 6 dozen cakes.

## BROWN HERMITS

| | |
|---|---|
| ⅔ cup butter | 2½ cups flour (about) |
| 2 cups brown sugar | 1 teaspoon nutmeg |
| 2 eggs, well beaten | 1 teaspoon cloves |
| 1 teaspoon baking soda | 1 teaspoon cinnamon |
| 1 cup sour cream | 1 cup chopped raisins |

Cream together the butter and sugar, and add the eggs. Mix well. Dissolve the baking soda in the sour cream. Sift together the flour and spices and add alternately with sour cream to the creamed mixture. Fold in the chopped raisins. Drop from a teaspoon onto buttered baking sheet. Bake in a moderate oven, 350° F., for about 8 minutes. Makes approximately 6 dozen cakes.

## DATE AND NUT CAKES

| | |
|---|---|
| 3 eggs | 1 teaspoon baking powder |
| 1 cup sugar | 1 cup chopped dates |
| 1 cup flour | 1 cup chopped nuts |

Powdered sugar

Beat the eggs until light and gradually stir in the sugar. Sift together the flour and baking powder and add to the egg mixture. Stir in the dates and nuts. Spread a thin layer of batter on greased square baking pans. Bake in a moderately slow oven, 325° F., for about 35 minutes. Cut into squares while warm and roll each piece in powdered sugar. Makes approximately 20 squares.

## CHOCOLATE KISSES

| | |
|---|---|
| 3 egg whites | 2½ cups powdered sugar |

½ pound chocolate, grated

Beat the egg whites until stiff and stir in the sugar and chocolate. Drop from teaspoon onto an ungreased, paper-lined baking sheet. Bake in a slow oven, 275° F., for 40 to 50 minutes. Makes approximately 2½ dozen kisses.

## NUT KISSES

| | |
|---|---|
| 6 egg whites | 2 tablespoons flour |
| 2½ cups powdered sugar | 2 cups finely chopped nuts |

Beat the egg whites until stiff and gradually add the sugar, beating until well mixed. Add the flour and nuts and mix well. Drop from a teaspoon onto an ungreased, paper-lined baking sheet. Bake in a slow oven, 275° F., for 40 to 50 minutes. Makes approximately 3½ dozen kisses.

## SHELLBARK KISSES

| | |
|---|---|
| 1 cup shellbark nuts, ground | 1 egg, well beaten |
| 1 cup sugar | ¼ teaspoon salt |

Combine all the ingredients and mix well. Drop from a teaspoon onto an ungreased, paper-lined baking sheet. Bake in a slow oven, 275° F., for about 40 to 50 minutes. Makes approximately 2 dozen kisses.

## VANILLA KISSES

| | |
|---|---|
| 2½ cups confectioner's sugar | 6 egg whites |

Vanilla

Combine the sugar and egg whites and beat for 40 minutes until mixture is stiff. Flavor with vanilla. Drop from a teaspoon onto an ungreased, paper-lined baking sheet. Bake in a slow oven, 275° F., for about 40 to 50 minutes. Nut meats may be added before baking, if desired. Makes approximately 2 dozen kisses.

### ALMOND MACAROONS

½ pound almonds       1¼ cups powdered sugar
4 egg whites, beaten stiff

Blanch and chop almonds. Combine with the sugar and place over heat, stirring constantly until a light brown. Fold in egg whites. Drop from a teaspoon onto greased baking sheet. Bake in a slow oven, 300° F., for about 25 minutes. Makes approximately 2 dozen macaroons.

### HICKORY NUT MACAROONS

3 egg whites       1 cup granulated sugar
1 teaspoon salt       1 cup light brown sugar
2 cups hickory nuts, chopped

Combine egg whites and salt, and beat until a stiff froth. Gradually stir in the sugar and nuts, beating well after each addition. Drop from a teaspoon onto an ungreased, paper-lined baking sheet. Bake in a moderate oven, 350° F., for about 20 minutes. Makes approximately 3½ dozen macaroons.

### SHELLBARK MACAROONS

1 lb. shellbark kernels       7 tablespoons flour
   (hickory nut)       6 egg whites beaten stiff
1 lb. confectioner's sugar

Mix nuts with sugar, add to egg whites and then add flour. Drop on greased cooky sheet. Bake in moderate oven, 300° F.

*Mrs. Kensie N. Yoder*

# CUPCAKES

### LITTLE CRUMB CAKES

½ cup sugar       ¾ teaspoon baking powder
¼ cup butter       ½ teaspoon nutmeg
1 egg yolk       ½ cup milk
1¼ cups fine bread crumbs       ¼ cup black walnuts,
           chopped fine

Cream together the sugar and butter, and add the beaten egg yolk. Mix well. Sift together the bread crumbs, baking powder, and nutmeg and add alternately with the milk to creamed mixture. Stir in chopped nuts. Turn into greased muffin pans. Bake in a moderate oven, 350° F., for about 25 minutes. Makes approximately 8 cupcakes.

## GINGER CAKES

| | |
|---|---|
| 1 cup brown sugar | 1 tablespoon boiling water |
| 1 cup butter and lard | 4 cups flour |
| 2 eggs, well beaten | 1 teaspoon ginger |
| 1 teaspoon baking soda | 1 cup molasses |

Cream together the sugar and shortening, and add the eggs. Mix well. Dissolve the baking soda in boiling water and add. Sift dry ingredients and add alternately with molasses to creamed mixture. Turn into greased muffin pans. Bake in a moderate oven, 350° F., for about 20 to 25 minutes. Makes approximately 20 cupcakes.

## SPOON CAKES

| | |
|---|---|
| 2 cups sugar | 2½ cups flour |
| 1 teaspoon butter | 2 teaspoons baking powder |
| 2 eggs, well beaten | 1 cup milk |

Combine sugar and butter and mix well. Add eggs and stir until smooth. Sift together the flour and baking powder and add alternately with the milk to first mixture. Turn into greased muffin pans. Bake in a moderate oven, 350° F., for about 25 minutes. Makes approximately 20 cupcakes.

## SMALL SPONGECAKES

| | |
|---|---|
| 6 eggs, separated | ½ teaspoon salt |
| 1 cup sugar | ½ teaspoon baking powder |
| ¾ cup flour | Lemon juice |

Beat the egg yolks, add the sugar and continue beating until thick and creamy. Beat the egg whites until stiff. Sift together the flour, salt, and baking powder. Add to egg yolks alternately with egg whites and flavor to taste with lemon juice. Turn into ungreased muffin tins. Bake in a moderately slow oven, 325° F., for about 25 minutes. Makes approximately 2 dozen cupcakes.

## SNOWBALL CAKES

| | |
|---|---|
| 1 cup sugar | 1 teaspoon baking soda |
| ½ cup butter | 1 tablespoon warm water |
| 3 egg whites, beaten stiff | 1 cup sifted flour (about) |

Cream together the sugar and butter, and add the beaten egg whites. Dissolve baking soda in warm water and add. Stir in enough flour to make a soft batter which drops easily from the spoon. Turn into greased muffin pans. Bake in a moderate oven, 350° F., for about 25 minutes. Makes approximately 8 cupcakes.

# Christmas Cakes and Cookies

Christmas holidays are a period of rejoicing throughout the Christian world, but nowhere in America are they attended by so much delightful "cult" as among the Pennsylvania Germans. Bethlehem, Pa., is the Christmas city of the United States. Eastern Pennsylvania is the *non plus ultra* area of Christmas "putzes" and of Christmas baking. In fact, but for scattered instances, there are no other communities in which one finds the "putz" and cookies cut or fashioned into all sorts of figures and designs. During the Advent weeks the Pennsylvania German housewife is busy with her baking. A sense of mystery pervades the house despite the telltale fragrance of spices that are rarely used at other times. From groceries and apothecary shops come currants, sultanas, citron, almond paste, pearlash, hartshorn, anise and cardamom seeds, and other unusual products. Old cutters and molds that delighted the children of earlier generations are once more brought forth from their attic hidings. The housewife little suspects that some of these designs — horses, riders, roosters are faint echoes from out of the remote pre-Christian past when animals, either actual, or in token forms fashioned out of dough, were sacrificed to Wodan, god of life and death, who with his myriad hosts rode through the stormy winter skies, just as little as she suspects that the signs, the so-called *Hexefiess*, which adorn the barn, are also left-overs from out of the ancient sun cult of our pagan ancestors who lived through the long winters of northern Europe 2000 years ago. But with the advent of Christianity in later centuries other familiar figures were added to cake and cooky forms — stars, sheep, shepherds, camels, the Palm Sunday ass, St. Nicholas and others. In the museum at Kaiserslautern in the Palatinate is preserved a small round stone, used as a cake mold some 500 years ago. On it is engraved the scene of the Flight into Egypt.

To the German of the 18th century almonds, raisins, currants, citron and orangepeel, and spices were precious articles, associated particularly with the Christmas season. With their exotic flavors and fragrance they conjured forth distant lands and climes. They had journeyed across the seven seas. From Arabia, Persia and the Indies they had brought sunny phantasies into the long winter months of northern Europe. They were too precious for common use. Here in Pennsylvania, land of plenty, in a day that hardly distinguishes

An old *Springerle* mold carved in wood
Photo by Mr. Guy F. Reinert
Courtesy, Miss M. Alice Schwaninger

any longer between summer and winter, some of these recipes have invaded other seasons of the year. However, most of them are still regarded by the Pennsylvania German housewife as distinctly reserved for the Christmas season. Like the Pennsylvania German pioneers themselves, these recipes come to us from Switzerland, the Palatinate, the Rhenish provinces and even from more distant Saxony. Some few like *Speculatius* and *Leckerle* may only have been brought by later immigrants. They present a varied array. May they long survive to delight the young and restore fond childhood memories to the old with each recurring Christmas season.

## LEBKUCHEN I

One of the oldest of Christmas bakings. The word itself is of ancient origin. The first component *leb* — comes from the Latin *libum*, which originally meant a consecrated cake, a cake offered to the gods. Although often translated as gingerbread, ginger is not its main ingredient (in some recipes not present at all), nor is it a soft cake as the English word implies.

| | |
|---|---|
| 1 pound honey | ½ teaspoon ground cloves |
| 1 pound brown sugar | ½ teaspoon mace |
| ¼ pound butter | ½ teaspoon ground |
| 2½ pounds white flour | cardamom seed |
| ½ teaspoon salt of hartshorn | ¼ pound chopped candied |
| 1 teaspoon cinnamon | citron |

¼ pound chopped almonds

Heat honey and add butter. Sift flour, hartshorn and spices. Add to honey and butter mixture, and stir thoroughly. Add citron and almonds. Knead dough. Cover in a bowl and set aside for a week. Roll out in sheets ¼-inch thick. Place on greased baking sheets and bake in moderate oven until dark brown. Remove from oven, brush lightly with diluted honey, and cut into squares or rectangles while still warm.

In 1556 the Abbess of Rosenthal sent her brother the ruling Count of Nassau a New Year's gift of *Latwerg* and *Lebkuchen*. In what shape this *Lebkuchen* was baked we do not know, but to this day the Rhinelanders prefer their *Lebkuchen* cut in the form of hearts.

## LEBKUCHEN II

| | |
|---|---|
| 2 cups dark brown sugar | 2 teaspoons baking powder |
| 3 eggs, well beaten | 4 cups flour |
| 3 egg yolks, well beaten | 1 cup citron, chopped fine |

1 cup chopped English walnuts

Combine the sugar, beaten eggs and egg yolks, and mix well. Sift together the baking powder and the flour, and add to sugar mixture together with the citron and nuts. Roll out the dough ½ inch thick on a lightly floured board and cut into 4-inch rounds. Place on greased baking sheet. Bake in a moderately slow oven, 325° F., for about 20 minutes. Cool and frost with the following icing:

### Icing

| | |
|---|---|
| 2 cups sugar | ½ cup water |
| 3 egg whites, beaten stiff | |

Combine sugar and water and boil for 7 minutes. Pour syrup in a thin stream over beaten egg whites, beating constantly until smooth and creamy.

*Mrs. George Light*

## WHITE LEBKUCHEN

### (An old recipe, circa 1750)

| | |
|---|---|
| 1 pound sugar | 1 pound flour |
| 8 eggs | 1 teaspoon cinnamon |
| 1 pound almonds, blanched | ½ teaspoon nutmeg |
| and ground fine | ½ teaspoon mace |

Combine sugar and eggs, beating in 1 egg at a time until thoroughly blended. Stir in the almonds. Sift together the flour and spices and gradually add to egg mixture, beating thoroughly after each addition. Spread dough on well-greased baking tins, lined with waxed paper. Bake in a moderately slow oven, 325° F., for about 20 minutes, or until a light brown. Cut into squares when partly cooled.

## LECKERLE

### (A South German word denoting a delicious morsel)

| | |
|---|---|
| 4½ teaspoons baking soda | 4 teaspoons cloves |
| Warm water | 6 teaspoons cinnamon |
| 3 cups light molasses | ½ pound almonds, chopped fine |
| 1½ cups brown sugar | ½ cup citron, chopped fine |
| 2 tablespoons butter | 12 cups sifted flour |
| ½ cup brandy | |

Dissolve the soda in a little warm water and combine with the molasses. Stir in the sugar, butter, spices, nuts, and citron. Add the flour, a small amount at one time, mixing well after each addition. Moisten with the brandy as dough gets stiffer and harder to work. (The last few cups of flour will probably have to be worked in with the hands by one of the men of the household). Cover the dough and set aside for about two weeks to age. Then roll out the dough ½ inch thick on a lightly floured board and cut into rectangles about 4 inches square. Place on greased baking sheets and brush each cake with milk. Bake in a moderate oven, 350°F., for 15 to 20 minutes. These cakes will keep more than 2 months (if you hide them).

## PEFFERNISS

### (Spice Nuts)

These cookies are rich in spices and made only for the Christmas season. The recipe is large and meant to furnish an ample supply both for the household and the casual holiday visitors, when treated to a glass of dandelion, elder, or currant wine. The modern housewife may wish to reduce this recipe by one-half. It is well to make the dough three weeks before Christmas.

| | |
|---|---|
| 1½ pounds honey | ¼ pound candied orange and |
| 2 pounds brown sugar | and lemon peel mixed |
| ½ cup butter | (chopped fine) |
| 1 cup water | ¼ pound citron (chopped fine) |
| 14 cups flour | 3 teaspoons salt |
| 2 teaspoons ground anise seed | 1 ounce pearlash (potassium |
| 2 teaspoons ground cardamom | bicarbonate) |
| seed | ½ ounce salt of hartshorn |
| 3 teaspoons ground cinnamon | (ammonium carbonate) |
| 1 teaspoon ground cloves | 6 egg yolks, well beaten |

Mix honey, sugar and butter and bring to a boil. Sift flour, spices and salt and add chopped fruits. Pour the boiling mixture into the bowl with sifted flour and other ingredients and stir thoroughly. Dissolve pearlash in a little water and add to the above. When the mixture is cooled, add the egg yolks. Lastly dissolve the salt of hartshorn in a little water, add to the above and stir and knead thoroughly. Set aside in room temperature for two weeks to ripen flavor. Roll portions of dough into long thin rolls ¾ inch in diameter. Put in cold place to chill. Then cut the roll in ¼ inch slices and bake at 350°F. for about 12 minutes. Cool and frost with the following icing:

Icing:

| | |
|---|---|
| 1 cup sugar | 1 egg white, beaten stiff |
| 4 tablespoons cold water | 1 teaspoon vanilla |

Combine the sugar and water and boil until mixture spins a thread. Pour in thin stream over beaten egg white, beating constantly until smooth and creamy. Flavor with the vanilla.

## SPRINGERLE

The beauty of these cookies, with their detailed designs in high relief, veritable cameos in dough, charms young and old. The name itself brings with it faint echoes out of the dim pagan past. In pre-Christian times the Germanic tribes of the north celebrated their *Julfest* at the time of the winter solstice, the period of the holy nights, when animals were sacrified to the Germanic gods. The poor made their sacrifices by token, in the form of animals and other figures fashioned out of dough. The word *Springerle* is the

A metal *Springerle* mold
Photo by Mr. Guy F. Reinert
By courtesy of the same

South German diminutive of *Springer*, charger or horse. The horse was sacred to Wodan, god of gods (for whom we have named Wednesday) who rides on the storm-clouds at the head of his wild hosts, "der ewig Jaeger", or the wild huntsman of legendry. In these ancient rites we find the beginnings of the German custom of baking Christmas cookies in the form of animals and other figures. The man on horseback is a familiar figure among our old Christmas cooky cutters. But it is a long way from Wodan riding his horse to the dainty little designs we find on the *Springerle* molds today. Many such molds linger among the descendants of old Pennsylvania German families, beautiful designs delicately engraved into pearwood or some other hard and close-grained wood. Most of them are imported from Germany and are occasionally for sale in our large department stores.

The old recipes for *Springerle* are rather unpractical. Few housewives would wish to beat the eggs and sugar clockwise for an hour! Our recipe is attuned to less leisurely days. The modern housewife need not fear to make these most unusual cookies. The following recipe requires a little practice but no great artistry.

### SPRINGERLE RECIPE

| | |
|---|---|
| 2 eggs | 2 cups flour |
| 1 cup granulated sugar | ½ teaspoon baking powder |
| Grated rind of 1 lemon | ¼ teaspoon salt |
| 2 teaspoons aniseed | |

Beat eggs very light. Add slowly the sugar and beat for 15 minutes. Add grated lemon rind. Stir in gradually the sifted flour, baking powder and salt. Add the aniseed and mix well. If the dough is still rather soft, knead into it a little more flour. Roll out to ¼ inch thickness and as nearly as possible to fit the form of the *Springerle* mold, so that there may be little waste. The dough should be rerolled as little as possible. Flour surface of the dough well, then press the mould down hard upon the dough. Cut into little individual picture squares. Place on greased and floured baking sheets. Set aside overnight to dry out and to set the impressions on the dough. Bake in moderate oven of 325°F., for 15 minutes. They should remain very pale.

### A.P.'S

#### (Eepies)

This pale-faced cooky with the elusive name occupies a favored place on the list of Pennsylvania German Christmas bakings. The name occurs in a variety of forms: *Apees, apeas, apise* and *apiece*. Marcus B. Lambert in his Pennsylvania German Dictionary enters it as *Eepies* and relates it to the French *épice* (*pain d'épice*, gingerbread). It must in fairness be pointed out that the cooky contains no spices and that it is not known among the Palatines. John F. Watson, in his Annals of Philadelphia, states that one Ann Page, a

Philadelphia dame, first made them and impressed upon them her own initials. This seems plausible enough, even though the cooky seems to have fled from Philadelphia and found a permanent home among the Pennsylvania Germans, where it is being made after half a dozen different recipes. There still remains the difficult problem of the pronunciation of the name, for all Pennsylvania Germans accent the first syllable. We cffer here two excellent recipes. The results of either will make you indifferent as to the name.

### Recipe I

| | |
|---|---|
| 2 cups granulated sugar | ½ cup sour cream |
| 1 cup butter | 1 teaspoon baking soda |
| 2 eggs, beaten | 6 cups flour (about) |

Cream together the sugar and butter, and add the eggs. Dissolve the baking soda in a little warm water and add to creamed mixture. Add flour alternately with milk. Chill overnight. Roll out on a lightly floured board and cut with figure cutters. For this dough it was a tradition to use the less complicated figure cutters: hearts, stars, leaves, circles with scalloped edges. Place on an ungreased cooky sheet. Bake in a moderate oven, 350°F., for about 8 to 10 minutes.

### Recipe II

| | |
|---|---|
| 2 pounds confectioner's sugar | 1 teaspoon baking soda |
| 1 pound butter | 1 teaspoon cream of tartar |
| 6 eggs, beaten | 9 cups flour (about) |

Cream together sugar and butter, and add the eggs. Sift flour, soda and cream of tartar. Add flour gradually and stir thoroughly. Chill overnight. Roll out on floured board and cut out as indicated in first recipe. Place on an ungreased cooky sheet. Bake in a moderate oven, 350°F., for about 8 to 10 minutes.

### FRUITCAKE
#### (From an old Lancaster County almanac)

| | |
|---|---|
| 2 cups butter | 1 teaspoon ground nutmeg |
| 2 cups powdered sugar | 1 tablespoon cinnamon |
| 6 eggs, well beaten | 1 tablespoon cloves |
| 2 cups molasses | 2 cups currants |
| 7 cups flour | 2 cups raisins |
| 1 cup preserved citron | |

Cream together the butter and sugar, and add the eggs. Mix well. Stir in the molasses. Sift together the flour and spices and add. Fold in the currants, raisins, and citron. Mix thoroughly. Turn into greased loaf pans, lined with waxed paper, filling about ¾ full. Bake in a very slow oven, 250°F., for about 3 hours. Wrap in waxed paper when cake is cold and place in a covered tin for at least 1 month before using. Makes approximately **6 pounds fruit-cake.**

## DARK FRUITCAKE

| | |
|---|---|
| 2 cups seeded currants | 1 teaspoon nutmeg |
| 2 cups seedless raisins | 1 tablespoon cloves |
| 1 cup figs, chopped | ½ teaspoon salt |
| 1 cup dates, chopped | 2 cups butter |
| 1 cup citron, chopped | 2 cups brown sugar |
| 5 cups flour | 5 eggs, well beaten |
| ½ teaspoon baking soda | 1 cup sour cream |
| 1 tablespoon cinnamon | ½ cup molasses |

½ wineglass brandy

Wash the currants and raisins in hot water to plump them. Drain and dry them. Add the figs, citron, and dates. Sift together the flour, baking soda, spices, and salt. Add to fruit mixture. Cream together the butter and sugar, and add the eggs. Mix well. Add the floured mixture, alternately with the sour cream and molasses to the creamed mixture. Mix well after each addition. Turn into 2 large cake pans, lined with waxed paper, filling about ¾ full. Place the cake pans in larger pans containing 1 inch of hot water. Bake in a slow oven, 250°F., for about 2½ hours. Remove the pan of hot water and continue baking for 30 minutes more. Wrap in waxed paper, when cakes are cold, and cover with a cloth soaked in the brandy. Store in a tightly covered tin.

## WHITE FRUITCAKE

| | |
|---|---|
| ½ pound butter | 1 cup milk |
| 2½ cups powdered sugar | 1 cup citron, chopped fine |
| 4 cups flour | 1 cup raisins |
| 2 teaspoons baking powder | 1 cup currants |

5 egg whites, beaten stiff

Cream together the butter and sugar and beat until smooth. Sift together 2 cups of the flour with the baking powder and add alternately with the milk to creamed mixture. Sift remaining flour over the citron, raisins and currants and mix well. Add to first mixture. Fold in beaten egg whites. Turn into 2 greased loaf pans. Bake in a slow oven, 300°F., for about 1½ hours. Cool in pans and let stand overnight before cutting.

### GRANDMOTHER KLEISER'S FRUITCAKE

| | |
|---|---|
| 1 cup butter | 1 teaspoon baking soda |
| 3 cups sugar | 1 cup sour milk |
| 5 eggs, well beaten | ½ cup molasses |
| 4 cups flour | 1 cup citron, chopped fine |
| 1 teaspoon cloves | 1 lemon, chopped fine |
| 1 teaspoon cinnamon | 2 cups currants |
| 1 nutmeg, grated | 2 cups raisins |

1 teaspoon brandy

Cream together the butter and sugar, and add the eggs. Mix well. Sift together the flour, spices, and baking soda. Add to creamed mixture alternately with sour milk and molasses. Mix thoroughly after each addition. Fold in fruit and add brandy last. Turn into a large greased cake tin, lined with waxed paper, filling ¾ full. Bake in a slow oven, 300°F., for 1½ to 2 hours, or until done. Wrap in waxed paper, when cake is cold, and store in covered tin.

### HUNNICHBROT
#### (Honey Bread)

| | |
|---|---|
| 2 pounds honey | 1 teaspoon ground cardamom |
| 1 cup water | seed |
| 1 cup sugar | 1 teaspoon cinnamon |
| 4 eggs, well beaten | 1 teaspoon baking powder |
| 2 tablespoons olive oil | 1 teaspoon baking soda |
| 8 cups flour (about) | 1 teaspoon cloves |

1 teaspoon vanilla

Combine honey, water, and sugar in a saucepan and bring to boiling point. Remove from heat, cool to room temperature, and add beaten eggs and olive oil. Sift together the dry ingredients and add gradually to the honey mixture, mixing well after each addition. Stir in the vanilla last. Turn into 4 greased bread pans. Bake in a moderately slow oven, 325°F., for about 2 hours, raising temperature to 350° during last 30 minutes of baking. Makes 4 medium-sized loaves.

*Mrs. Leo von den Driesch*

### HUTZELBROT I
#### (Dried-Fruit Bread)

| | |
|---|---|
| 3 cups dried pears | ½ cup butter |
| 1 yeast cake | 1 cup brown sugar |
| 3 cups sifted flour | 2 eggs, well beaten |
| ½ teaspoon salt | 1 pound raisins |
| ⅓ teaspoon baking soda | 1 teaspoon fennel seed |
| ¼ cup lard | 2 teaspoons cinnamon |

Melted butter

Cover the pears with water and simmer for 30 minutes. Remove pears from the juice. Dissolve yeast cake in small amount of warm water and add to pear juice. Combine 2 cups of the flour and the salt. Add to yeast mixture, cover, and let stand overnight. In the morning, dissolve the baking soda in a small amount of warm water and add to yeast mixture. Cream together the shortening and sugar, and add the eggs. Dice the pears, sprinkle with a small amount of flour, and add the raisins, fennel, and cinnamon. Add to creamed mixture and mix well. Then combine creamed mixture and yeast mixture, adding enough of the remaining flour to form a stiff dough. Knead and let rise again. Shape into 4 loaves and place in greased loaf pans. Brush top of each loaf with melted butter. Bake in a moderate oven, 350°F., for 1 to 1½ hours, or until done.

### HUTZELBROT II

| | |
|---|---|
| 1½ cups sugar | ¼ cup warm water |
| ¾ cup butter | 7 cups sifted flour (about) |
| 1 cup mashed potatoes | 1 cup dark raisins |
| ¾ tablespoon salt | 1 cup light raisins |
| 1 teaspoon nutmeg | 2½ cups chopped dried fruits |
| 1½ cups scalded milk, lukewarm | 1½ cups chopped candied lemon, orange, and citron peel, mixed |
| 2 eggs, well beaten | |
| 2 yeast cakes | 1 egg white |

Combine suger, butter, mashed potatoes, salt, and nutmeg and beat until well mixed. Add scalded milk and beaten eggs. Dissolve yeast cakes in warm water and add. Add enough of the flour to form a sponge, cover, and set in a warm place to rise until light. Add dark and light raisins, dried fruits (prunes, peaches, apricots, etc.) and chopped candied peel. Add remaining flour, knead, and set aside to rise again until double in bulk. Shape into 6 loaves and place in greased loaf pans. Let rise again until double in bulk. Brush the top of each loaf with egg white. Bake in a moderate oven, 350°F., for about 1 hour.

*Mrs. Preston A. Barba*

### STRIETZ
#### (A German Christmas Loaf)

Known in Austria, Bavaria and Wuerttemberg as *Strützel*.

| | |
|---|---|
| 2 yeast cakes | 1 cup citron, chopped fine |
| 2 cups scalded milk, lukewarm | ½ pound butter |
| 12 cups sifted flour | ¼ pound lard |
| 4 cups raisins | 1½ cups sugar |
| 2 cups currants | 3 eggs, well beaten |

Dissolve the yeast cakes in a little warm water and combine with the milk and about 4 cups of flour. Cover, and set aside overnight to form a sponge. In the morning combine the remaining flour with the fruit and mix well. Cream together the shortening and sugar, and add the eggs. Combine the sponge, floured fruit, and creamed mixture and let rise again for about 10 hours. Turn into greased bread pans, filling about ½ full, and let rise once more until light. Bake in a moderate oven, 350° F., for about 1 hour. Makes 4 to 5 loaves.

*Mrs. Paul de Schweinitz*

## ANISE COOKIES

| | |
|---|---|
| 6 eggs, separated | 1 cup sifted flour |
| 1 cup powdered sugar | 3 teaspoons aniseed |

Beat the egg yolks until thick and lemon-colored. Beat the egg whites until stiff and combine with egg yolks. Gradually add the sugar, mixing well after each addition. Add the flour and aniseed, mixing well. Drop from a teaspoon onto a greased baking sheet, spacing about 1 inch apart. Let stand in a cold place overnight. Bake in a slow oven, 300°F., for about 12 minutes. Makes approximately 2 dozen cookies.

## SNICKER DOODLES

| | |
|---|---|
| 1 cup shortening | 2¾ cups flour |
| 1½ cups sugar | ½ teaspoon salt |
| 2 eggs | 1 teaspoon soda |

Cream shortening, sugar and eggs. Sift flour, salt, cream of tartar and soda. Mix with the above ingredients  Roll in balls the size of a walnut (or smaller). Roll balls in mixture of 2 tablespoons of granulated sugar and 2 tablespoons of cinnamon.

Place on cooky tin 2 inches apart and bake at 375° F.

*Miriam Metzger*

## BELLYLAPS I
### (An old-time Christmas cooky)

The curious name of this unsophisticated Christmas cooky is veiled in obscurity. The proportions of the recipe bespeak a generous housewife, large families, and many guests.

| | |
|---|---|
| 1 quart dark molasses | 2 tablespoons baking soda |
| ¾ cup butter or lard, melted | (about) |
| 2 eggs, well beaten | 8 cups flour (about) |

Combine molasses, melted shortening, and beaten eggs. Sift together the baking soda and flour and add to molasses mixture. Roll out the dough about ¼ inch thick on a lightly floured board. In the olden days it was customary to make large cookies of this particular dough and they were cut into the shapes of hearts, stars, eagles, horses and their riders. Place cookies on greased baking sheets. Bake in a moderate oven, 350°F., for about 12 minutes.

*Mrs. Robert A. Wertman, Sr.*

## BELLYLAPS II

The recipe for Bellylaps which I found in my mother's old cookbook reads as follows: "Add 1 pint of New Orleans molasses to 2 well-beaten eggs, beat well. Then add 1 cup yellow sugar; stir in some of the flour. Next dissolve 1½ tablespoons of baking soda in 6 tablespoons of vinegar, and add to the above. Now add flour enough to stiffen the dough. Roll out about ⅛ inch thick and cut out with round cooky cutter, about 3 inches in diameter."

*Carrie V. Bitting*

## BELSNICKELKUCHE
### (Belsnickel Cakes)

So-called because the *Belsnickel,* and masked and gaily costumed revelers, who went from house to house among the Pennsylvania Germans during Christmas week, were always treated to these and similar cookies and other holiday refreshments.

| | |
|---|---|
| 2 cups sugar | 3 cups flour |
| 1 cup melted butter | 1 teaspoon baking soda |
| 4 eggs | Pinch of salt |

Cream together the sugar and butter, and add the eggs 1 at a time, beating well after each addition. Sift together the flour, baking soda, and salt, and stir into creamed mixture. Chill the dough for about 1 hour. Roll out thin on a lightly floured board and cut into small rounds. Place on greased baking sheets and sprinkle generously with granulated sugar. Bake in a hot oven, 400°F., for about 10 minutes. Makes approximately 200 small cookies.

## ZIMMTSTERNE
### (Cinnamon Stars)

| | |
|---|---|
| 6 egg whites | 1 cup chopped almonds, |
| 2½ cups powdered sugar | unblanched |
| 2 teaspoons cinnamon | |

Beat the egg whites to a froth. Gradually beat in sugar and cinnamon, about ¼ cup at a time. Beat mixture for about 30 minutes. Divide mixture in half and add almonds to one part, forming a stiff dough. Roll out lightly on a board dusted with powdered sugar, and cut into small stars. Brush the top of each star with some of the remaining mixture. Place on baking sheet. Bake in a moderate oven, 350°F., for about 20 minutes, or until lightly browned. Makes approximately 1½ dozen cookies.

## MORAVIAN BROWN CHRISTMAS CAKES

| | |
|---|---|
| 2 cups sugar | ¼ cup cream |
| 1 pound butter | 16 cups flour |
| 1⅓ cups molasses | 2 tablespoons ginger |
| 2¾ cups dark syrup | 2 tablespoons cinnamon |
| 1 teaspoon cloves | |

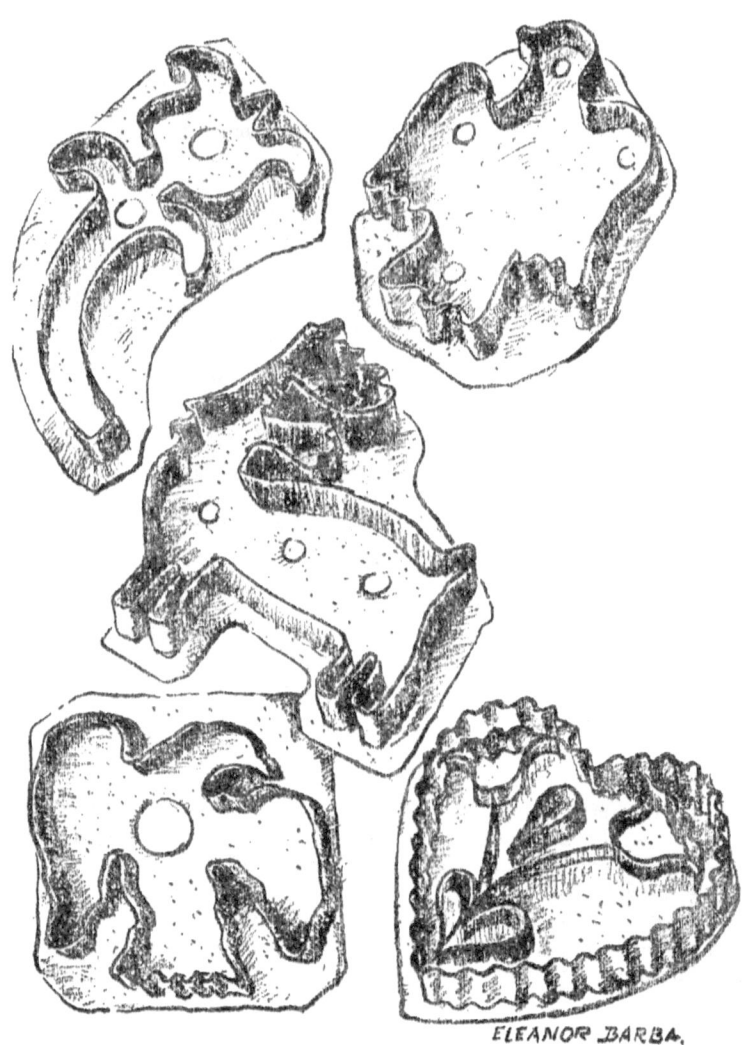

ELEANOR BARBA.

Old tin cookie cutters
Courtesy, Mr. Titus C. Geesey

Cream together the sugar and butter, until smooth and creamy.  Add the molasses, syrup, and cream and mix until well blended.  Sift together the flour and spices and stir into creamed mixture.  Roll out very thin on a lightly floured board and cut in various shapes.  Place on greased baking sheets.  Bake in a moderate oven, 350°F., for about 12 minutes.

## MORAVIAN WHITE CHRISTMAS CAKES

| | |
|---|---|
| 2½ cups sugar | 2 tablespoons sherry |
| ½ pound butter | 4 cups flour |
| 4 eggs, well beaten | ½ teaspoon cinnamon |
| ¼ nutmeg, grated | |

Cream together the sugar and butter, and add the eggs; mix well.  Add the sherry.  Sift together the flour and spices and stir into creamed mixture.  Roll out very thin on a lightly floured board and cut in the shape of stars, hearts, and diamonds.  Place on a greased baking sheet.  Bake in a moderate oven, 350°F., for about 12 minutes.

## FRUIT COOKIES

| | |
|---|---|
| 1 cup butter | 3½ cups flour (about) |
| 2 cups sugar | 2 tablespoons cinnamon |
| 2 eggs, well beaten | 1 tablespoon allspice |
| 2 cups raisins, chopped fine | 1 tablespoon baking soda |

Cream together the butter and sugar, and add the eggs.  Mix well.  Stir in the raisins.  Sift together the dry ingredients and add to creamed mixture to form a fairly stiff dough.  Roll out ½ inch thick on a lightly floured board and cut in desired shapes.  Place on a greased baking sheet.  Bake in a moderate oven, 350°F., for about 10 minutes.  Makes approximately 5 dozen cookies.

## GINGER NUTS
### (Of close kin to Pefferniss)

| | |
|---|---|
| ¾ pound butter | 8 cups flour (about) |
| 1½ cups sugar | 4 teaspoons ground ginger |
| 1 teaspoon baking soda | 1 teaspoon nutmeg |
| 2 cups molasses | 2 teaspoons cinnamon |

Cream together the butter and sugar until smooth.  Dissolve the baking soda in the molasses.  Sift together the dry ingredients and add alternately with the molasses to the creamed mixture.  Add enough of the flour to form a stiff dough.  Roll out ½ inch thick on a lightly floured board and cut into small rounds, about ½ inch in diameter.  Place on a greased cooky sheet.  Bake in a slow oven, 300°F., for about 15 minutes.

## MRS. HUMMEL'S HAZELNUT COOKIES

| | |
|---|---|
| 2 egg whites | 1 teaspoon cinnamon |
| ½ lb. confectioner's sugar | ½ lb. ground hazelnuts |

To the stiffly beaten egg whites add the sugar and beat until firm. Chill the dough and form into small balls. Roll in sugar and bake at 300° F. on waxed paper until light brown.

## MANDELSPITZEN
### (Almond Points)

| | |
|---|---|
| ½ pound butter | 3 egg yolks, well beaten |
| ¾ cup powdered sugar | 3 tablespoons cream |
| 4 cups sifted flour | |

Cream together the butter and sugar, and add the egg yolks. Mix well and add the cream. Stir in the sifted flour and mix well. Turn out onto a board, lightly sprinkled with flour and powdered sugar, and roll out ¼ inch thick. Cut crisscross into diamond shapes. Place on a baking sheet. Bake in a moderate oven, 350°F., for about 12 minutes. Cool and frost with the following icing:

Icing:

| | |
|---|---|
| 2 egg yolks | 1 pound almonds, blanched |
| 2 tablespoons water | and chopped |
| Powdered sugar | |

Beat the egg yolks and water until well mixed. Add enough powdered sugar to thicken. Spread on top of cakes and sprinkle with chopped almonds. Return to the oven for a few mniutes to dry the icing.

## SAND TARTS

| | |
|---|---|
| 4 cups sugar | 1 teaspoon baking soda |
| 1½ pounds butter | 1 egg yolk, well beaten |
| 3 eggs, well beaten | Cinnamon and sugar, mixed |
| 4 cups flour | Chopped nuts |

Cream together the sugar and butter, and add the eggs. Mix well. Sift together the flour and baking soda and stir into creamed mixture. Moisten dough with hot water. Roll out thin on a lightly floured board and cut into 3-inch rounds. Place on baking sheet and brush tops with beaten egg yolk. Sprinkle with cinnamon and sugar, and chopped nuts. Bake in a moderately hot oven, 375°F., for about 8 to 10 minutes.

## SLAP JACKS

| | |
|---|---|
| 1 cup baking molasses | ¼ teaspoon salt |
| 1 cup sugar | ½ teaspoon baking soda |
| 1 cup butter | 1 teaspoon baking powder |
| 2 cups flour | ½ cup finely chopped |
| | black walnuts |

Combine molasses, sugar and butter. Bring to a boil and boil 1 minute. Add the sifted flour, salt, soda and baking powder, and the walnuts. Stir thoroughly. Keep batter warm by setting it in a vessel of hot water. Drop scant teaspoons of this batter 3 inches apart on well-greased cookie tins and bake 10 minutes at 350° F. Remove with spatula while still warm.

## SPECULATIUS
### (A native of the Rhineland)

| | |
|---|---|
| ½ pound butter | Grated rind of 1 lemon |
| 1 pound sugar | 1 pound flour |
| 3 eggs | 1 teaspoon cinnamon |

1 teaspoon baking powder

Cream together the butter and sugar, and beat until smooth. Add 1 egg at a time and beat well after each addition. Add lemon rind. Sift together the dry ingredients and stir into creamed mixture. Chill overnight in refrigerator. Roll out ⅛ inch thick on lightly floured board and cut into desired shapes. Place on baking sheet and brush with beaten egg white and sprinkle with sugar. Bake in a moderate oven, 350° F., for about 12 minutes.

*Mrs. Leo von den Driesch*

## BROWN SPICE COOKIES

| | |
|---|---|
| 1 cup butter | 8 cups flour (about) |
| 1½ cups brown sugar | 1 teaspoon cloves |
| 3 teaspoons baking soda | 1 teaspoon cinnamon |
| 2 cups dark molasses | 1 teaspoon allspice |

1 wineglass whisky

Cream together the butter and sugar until smooth and creamy. Dissolve the baking soda in the molasses. Sift together the dry ingredients and add alternately with molasses to the creamed mixture. Stir in the whisky. Let dough stand overnight. Roll out very thin on a lightly floured board and cut into desired shapes. Place on a baking sheet. Bake in a moderate oven, 350°F., for about 12 minutes.

This is a large recipe which calls for a big stone crock, well beyond the reach of little hands. The longer you keep them the better they get.

*Mrs. Robert A. Wertman, Sr.*

## SOFT CHRISTMAS CAKES

| | |
|---|---|
| 1½ cups molasses | ½ cup warm water |
| ½ cup lard, melted | 5 cups flour |
| ½ cup sour milk | 1 teaspoon allspice |
| ½ teaspoon baking soda | 1 teaspoon cinnamon |

½ teaspoon cloves

Combine the molasses, lard, and sour milk. Dissolve the baking soda in the water. Sift together the flour and spices and add alternately with the water to first mixture. Drop from a tablespoon onto a greased baking sheet. Bake in a slow oven, 300°F., for about 15 minutes. Makes approximately 10 dozen cakes.

## CHRISTMAS DOUGHNUTS

| | |
|---|---|
| 1 cup sugar | 4 teaspoons baking powder |
| 5 tablespoons shortening, | 1 teaspoon salt |
| melted | 1 teaspoon nutmeg |
| 3 eggs, separated | 3 cups flour |

1 cup milk

Combine the sugar, melted shortening, and beaten egg yolks and mix well. Sift together the dry ingredients and add alternately with the milk to the first mixture. Fold in stiffly beaten egg whites. Drop from a teaspoon into deep hot fat, 360° F., and fry for 2 to 4 minutes, turning occasionally. Remove from fat and drain on absorbent paper. Roll in confectioner's sugar.

*Mrs. Harry Hess Reichard*

## LITTLE FRUITCAKES

| | |
|---|---|
| ⅔ cup butter | 1 teaspoon cloves (scant) |
| 1 cup sugar | 1 teaspoon cinnamon (scant) |
| 2 eggs, well beaten | 2 cups chopped raisins |
| 1 teaspoon baking soda | 2 cups chopped English |
| 1 tablespoon hot water | walnuts |
| 2 cups sifted flour | |

Cream together the butter and sugar, and add the eggs. Mix well. Stir in the flour and spices. Then add the raisins and nuts and mix thoroughly. Drop from a teaspoon onto buttered baking sheet, spacing far apart as batter spreads somewhat in baking. Bake in a moderate oven, 350°F., for about 25 to 30 minutes. Makes approximately 3 dozen cakes.

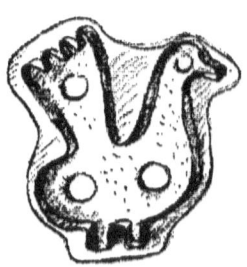 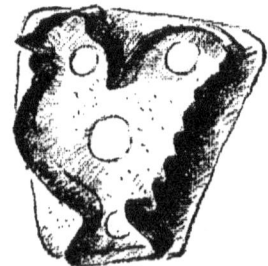

# Pies and Tarts

*Yuscht sei gedroscht un net vergesse,*
*Der Abbedit kummt mit em Esse.*

When appetite may wanting be,
Good, hearty food provides the key.

The eastern counties of Pennsylvania constitute the piebelt of America. In this area more and better pies are eaten in greater variety than anywhere else on this terrestrial globe. We Pennsylvania Germans eat pie at breakfast, at dinner, at supper, and the midnight snack is not without it. And yet pie is an anomalous item in the Pennsylvania German cuisine. It was unknown to our forefathers before they arrived in Pennsylvania. "The pie," writes Harriet Beecher Stowe (OLDTOWN FOLKS, 1869), "is an English institution, which planted on American soil, forthwith ran rampant and burst forth into an untold variety of genera and species." The word crept into Middle English literature as early as the 14th century as *pye*, meaning perhaps a mixture (compare the adjectives *piebald* and *pied*), and was probably first applied to a pastry dish of meat or fish or fowl. In English usage today pastry with fruit is called "tart" from the Latin past participle *tortus*, twisted, some twisted form of dough.

The nearest approach to pie in the German fatherland were the *Obstkuchen,* large wagon-wheel flats made of yeast dough, on the top of which were baked the fruits in season, cherries, apples, plums, which continue to this day to add a festive note to the afternoon coffee table. Although our pioneer *Hausfraas* no doubt baked these yeast-dough fruit *Kuchen* of their native land during the early period in Pennsylvania, English pie seems to have made rapid inroads into our rural areas and became a very popular dish. The Reverend Israel Acrelius, Provost of the Swedish congregations on the Delaware (1749-56) finds the early settlers in Pennsylvania baking pies of apples, cherries and peaches.

Since our dialect had no word for pie, an English adaptation in the form of *Boi* came into usage. This poses a fascinating problem for the philologist. Since the English dialect form *poi* is found in Yorkshire, Leicestershire and in the Midlands, it is to be assumed that this form was also prevalent in the American colonies in the 18th century and that our Pennsylvania German settlers heard this word from their Anglo-Saxon neighbors. Be that as it may, the fact is that English pie in its new environs took its own course of development.

It is in the baking of pie, not indigenous to her kitchen, that the Pennsylvania German housewife has outdone herself. Here her genius has asserted itself as nowhere else. Here she creates with the fancy and imagination of the artist. The home economist's attempt at scientific standardization has not yet inhibited the style of the *Hausfraa* of the older generation. Her touch is sensitive to the degree of grittiness of her flour, whether of winter or of summer wheat, and to the richness of the shortening she cuts into it. Nothing is measured, but all is mixed with the subtlety of long experience. The prepared filling at her side is of the greatest variety. She nimbly fits the pastry into her scalloped pattypans, and with the aid of her brass or bone *Boiraedel* (pie-wheel) she crimps and curls and twists and performs surface arabesques and initials worthy of the Fraktur-artist of an earlier day.

Who will name the endless varieties of pies and tarts that went forth from under the hands of our grandmothers? But for lemons and raisins the fruits came from the nearby gardens, fields and orchards. There were pies for all seasons of the year. With the breath of spring came rhubarb and the now extinct sorrel pie, followed in time by strawberry and cherry pies, both of the red sour and of the native black and red sweet cherries, currant and gooseberry, used both green and ripe, with their sweet dough strips or floating "dollars," raspberry, blackberry, elderberry, and early apple; and always there were plain custard and cheese pies; late fall and early winter brought the pumpkin and the mince meat, diluted with good Yankee rum. But the provident housewife during the long winter months drew upon her large store of fruits and berries she had during the summer months carefully dried in the oven after her weekly bakings or, in later days, canned and stored on cellar shelves.

It is a congenital weakness of the human male to remind his mate of the pie mother used to bake. There are those who remember with nostalgia the pies that used to be baked in the great outdoor ovens in gently-sloping earthen pie dishes and with the fragrance of applewood ashes clinging to them. Those days are no more. The modern housewife prefers to bake in smaller quantities and abhors a pie that has "slept over night." Her pie may lack in variety but not in quality.

The English-speaking housewife who chats with her Pennsylvania German neighbor hears in wonderment a most confusing pie terminology. In English "pie" is a general word applied both to meat and fruit pies, and if to the latter then a pie with a top crust is implied. If it is an open fruit pie, then the word "tart" is in order. But the Pennsylvania German *Hausfraa* speaks of apple cakes and pumpkin and cheese cakes, for the simple reason that she has been accustomed to speak of them in the dialect as *Ebbelkuche, Kaerbse kuche* and *Kaeskuche,* which is quite understandable when we recall that the yeast-risen dough flats on which fresh fruits were baked were known as *Obstkuchen.* So also when a cake batter is baked in a pastry shell it is for her *Shoofly Cake* and not *Shoofly Pie.*

We trust that the limited recipes offered in the following pages will give our readers a glimpse of the gay and motley pie pageantry in a Pennsylvania German kitchen.

### BASIC PASTRY

| | |
|---|---|
| 2 cups flour | ½ cup shortening |
| ½ teaspoon salt | ¼ cup cold water (about) |

Sift together the flour and salt, and rub in the shortening. Add water in small amounts to dry material, using only enough water to make dough hold together. Roll dough ⅛ inch thick on lightly floured board and use for pies and tart shells. Makes 1 two-crust 8-inch pie or about 12 4-inch tart shells.

### BASIC PASTRY FOR MEAT DISHES

| | |
|---|---|
| 2 cups flour | 1½ tablespoons butter |
| ¼ teaspoon baking powder | 1 egg, well beaten |
| ½ teaspoon salt | ⅛ cup milk or water |

Sift together the dry ingredients. Cut in the butter until well mixed and crumbly. Add beaten egg and just enough liquid to hold the dough together. Roll out thin on a lightly floured board and let stand for ½ hour before cutting into desired shape. Makes enough pastry to cover two 8-inch casseroles.

### SWEET DOUGH I

| | |
|---|---|
| 1 cup flour (about) | ½ teaspoon baking soda |
| Pinch of salt | ½ cup sour milk or buttermilk |
| 1½ cups brown sugar | ½ cup shortening |

Sift together the flour and salt, and combine with the sugar. Dissolve the baking soda in the sour milk. Cut the shortening into the dry ingredients until well blended and crumbly. Gradually add the sour milk, adding just enough to hold dough together. The dough should not be too stiff. Roll out on a lightly floured board and cut in strips for top of fruit pies, such as elderberry, currant and lemon pies.

### SWEET DOUGH II

| | |
|---|---|
| 2 cups flour | ½ cup shortening |
| 1½ teaspoons baking powder | 1 egg, well beaten |
| 1 cup sugar | ½ cup milk |

Sift together the flour and baking powder, and combine with the sugar. Cut in the shortening and mix until well blended. Combine the egg and milk, and gradually add to first mixture. Roll out on a lightly floured board and cut in strips, or cut with a round floured cutter. "Dollars, we used to call them." For top of fruit pies: elderberry, lemon, raisin, rhubarb.

*Mrs. Robert A. Wertman, Sr.*

### SWEET CRUMBS

| | |
|---|---|
| ¾ cup flour | ¼ teaspoon salt |
| ⅔ cup sugar | ⅓ cup butter |
| ½ teaspoon cinnamon | |

Combine all ingredients and mix with a fork until mixture is crumbly and well blended. These crumbs are used on fruit tarts. Nutmeg may be substituted for the cinnamon, or spice may be omitted entirely.

*Mrs. Harry Hess Reichard*

### APPLE CRUMB PIE

| | |
|---|---|
| 2½ cups flour | ⅓ cup ice water (about) |
| 1 teaspoon salt | 8 medium-sized apples |
| ¾ cup shortening | ½ cup brown sugar |
| ¼ teaspoon cinnamon | |

Sift together the flour and salt, and cut in the shortening. Mix well until blended. Reserve ½ cup of the mixture. To the remaining, gradually add just enough ice water to make a dough which holds together. Roll out on a lightly floured board and line a pie tin with the pastry. Pare, core, and slice the apples and place them in pastry shell. If the apples are sour, sprinkle with sugar to taste. Combine the brown sugar, cinnamon and ½ cup of reserved mixture. Sprinkle mixture over the apples. Bake in a hot oven, 450° F., for 10 minutes, then reduce heat to 350° F. and bake about 30 minutes longer. Fresh peaches may be substituted for apples, if desired.

*Mrs. Walter Sechrist*

### APPLE PIE

#### (Ebbelboi)

Our Pennsylvania German housewives did not want for native apples of fine cooking and baking quality. Great favorites were the Summer Rambo and the Smokehouse, the Baer or Hiester of Berks County, the Lehigh Greening, the Krauser, also of Berks, Smith's Cider Apple of Bucks, and the Handwerk and Herter, both of Lehigh County. Some of these are forgotten apples and deserve to be restored by our modern orchardists.

| | |
|---|---|
| 5 or 6 apples | 1 recipe Basic Pastry |
| 2 tablespoons flour | (see Index) |
| ¾ cup sugar | ½ teaspoon cinnamon |
| Butter | |

Peel, core and slice 5 or 6 apples, depending on size.  Line pie plate with pastry.  Mix 1 tablespoon of flour and ¼ cup sugar and sprinkle into the pastry shell.  Fill the apples into the shell.  Mix remaining flour, sugar and the cinnamon and sprinkle over the apples.  Dot generously with butter.  Wet edge of lower crust, cover with upper crust, press edges together and crimp. Puncture upper crust.  Bake 15 minutes at 450° F., then reduce to 350° F., and bake 30 more minutes.

> *Es gebt nix Schenners zu meim Aag,*
> *Wie'n Ebbelboi, gewiss ich saag.*
> *Der zackich Ranft, schee brauni Gruscht,*
> *Ken Wunner gebt's eem grossi Luscht;*
> *Aus Gawwellecher owwe druff*
> *Kocht Budder, Zucker unne ruff;*
> *Un ei, du Welt! der gut Geruch!*
> *Was wessert's Maul fer en Versuch!**
> —RALPH S. FUNK

## APPLE TART
### (Ebbelkuche)

| | |
|---|---|
| 5 large apples | 1 unbaked pastry shell |
| 2 tablespoons flour | 2 teaspoons butter |
| ¾ cup sugar | ¼ teaspoon nutmeg |

Peel and quarter the apples.  Many of our housewives insist on using halves!  Sprinkle the flour and ¼ cup of the sugar in an unbaked pastry shell. Place the apples in the pastry shell, cover with remaining sugar.  Dot with butter and sprinkle top with nutmeg.  Bake in a moderate oven, 350° F., for about 35 minutes, or until apples are soft.

## APPLE PIES BAKED ON CABBAGE LEAVES

This is an ancient and almost forgotten procedure.  Form circles of pastry, about 9 inches in diameter.  Fill one half with sliced apples, adding the desired amount of sugar.  Sprinkle with flour, some butter, and cinnamon. Moisten edges and fold over to form a semi-circle, crimping edges tightly with the end of the *Boiraedel* (little pie-wheel).  Place each of these pies on a green outer cabbage leaf, and place flat on the bottom of the oven.  A rare flavor is thus added to the pies.  And, incidentally, there are no pie pans to wash!

*Mrs. Milton E. Staudt*

*There's nothing that will please the eye
Quite like old-fashioned apple pie.
The good brown crust, edge crimped a bit,
No wonder that we long for it;
Through fork holes in the lid there toils
The butter, sugar, as it boils;
When baked, the smell is sheer delight —
My mouth just waters for a bite!
—Tr. by Martin Birmelin*

## APFELSTRUDEL

### (Apple Whorl)

| | |
|---|---|
| 2½ cups flour | 2 tablespoons butter |
| ½ teaspoon salt | ½ cup dry grated bread |
| 3 tablespoons shortening | 1 cup brown sugar |
| 1 egg | 1 cup raisins |
| ½ cup lukewarm water | ½ cup grated almond |
| 6 diced apples | 1 teaspoon cinnamon |

Sift flour and salt into bowl. Add beaten egg, mix well, adding water gradually. Remove to pastry board and knead and beat dough until it forms blisters. Let it rest on board and cover with an inverted heated dish. Set aside in warm place for 15 minutes. Prepare the filling: fry the grated bread in butter, add apples, sugar, raisins, almonds and cinnamon. Return to dough and divide into two parts. Roll out each part on a floured napkin or teatowel as thin as noodle dough. Spread evenly with the apple mixture and roll up, wetting sides and pressing together to prevent oozing out. Place the two rolls on greased baking tins, brush tops with butter and sprinkle with sugar. Bake in hot oven, 450° F., for 15 minutes, reduce to 350° F. and bake 25 minutes longer.

This popular dish is an importation on the part of later German immigrants into Pennsylvania.

## SCHNITZ BOI

### (Dried Apple Pie)

For many a Pennsylvania German household *Schnitz* (cuts, cf. Ger. *schneiden*, to cut) formed the mainstay for winter pastry. In summer and fall vast quantities of the various sorts of sour apples were pared, sliced in quarters or eighths, dried and suspended in bags under the attic rafters for winter use.

| | |
|---|---|
| 1 pound of Schnitz | 2 cups sugar |
| Water | 3 teaspoons cinnamon |
| Rind of lemon or orange | 1 recipe Basic Pastry |
| | (see Index) |
| Butter | |

Cover *Schnitz* with water to soak over night. Add rind of lemon or orange and more water, if necessary, and boil until soft. Put through collander, add sugar and cinnamon. Line pie tin with pastry and pour cooled mixture into tin. Dot with butter. Cover with top crust, or with strips of pastry. The *Schnitz* filling should be only about ½ inch deep. Bake in a hot oven, 450 F., for 10 minutes, then reduce heat to 350° F. and bake 30 minutes longer. There will be left-over filling for the next recipe!

## SCHNITZ CRUMB PIE

Line a pie tin with pastry. Fill with the dried apple filling of the above recipe as denoted. Now prepare 1 recipe Basic Sweet Crumbs (see Index) and sprinkle the crumbs over the top of the Schnitz filling. Bake in a hot oven, 450° F., for 10 minutes, then reduce to 350° F. and bake 20 minutes longer.

Variation: Proceed as above, but instead of the crumbs, take ½ recipe for Basic Sweet Dough (see Index), roll out and cut in strips. Twist and criss-cross over top of pie. Bake in a hot oven, 450° F., for 10 minutes, then reduce to 350° F. and bake 20 minutes more.

## APPLEBUTTER PIE

3 cups applebutter              ½ teaspoon cinnamon
1 cup water                     ¼ cup sugar
2½ tablespoons flour            2 unbaked pastry shells
            1 recipe Sweet Pastry (see Index)

Combine the applebutter and water. Sift together the dry ingredients and add to applebutter mixture. Pour into two unbaked pastry shells and top with narrow twisted strips of the Sweet Pastry. Bake in a moderate oven, 350° F., for about 35 minutes.

*Miss Lottie Gable*

## SOUR CHERRY PIE

*Good appetite perfects the rudest meal,*
*Nor can the cook the appetite supply;*
*A feast for kings in old-time harvest field*
*Was cold sweet milk and fresh-baked cherry pie.*
            From "Harvesting" in H. L. Fisher's OLDEN
            TIMES, York, Pa., 1888.

1½ cups sugar                   1 recipe Basic Pastry
½ cup flour                          (see Index)
                                4 cups sour cherries, pitted

Combine sugar and flour and mix well. Line a pie tin with pastry and sprinkle ⅓ of the mixture on the pastry. Fill with cherries and sprinkle remaining mixture over the top of the fruit. Cover with top crust and slit crust in several places to allow steam to escape. Bake in a hot oven, 450° F., for 10 minutes, then reduce heat to 350° F. and continue baking for about 35 minutes longer.

## YUDDEKARSCHE PIE

### (Jerusalem (or Ground) Cherry)

A favorite dish of Cornelius Weygandt, well-known writer, whose great-great-great-grandfather came to this country in 1736 from Osthofen-on-the-Rhine, Bavaria, and settled in Germantown.

| | |
|---|---|
| 2 cups Yuddekarsche | ½ cup light brown sugar |
| (Jerusalem cherries) | 1 tablespoon flour |
| ¼ cup sugar | 1 unbaked pastry shell |

Remove the veil-like covering from the cherries and combine them with the dry ingredients. Pour mixture into the unbaked pastry shell, and if desired, place narrow strips of pastry on top. Bake in a hot oven, 400° F., for about 45 minutes, or until filling is thickened.

*Gertrude Meyers Hillenhand*

## GREEN CURRANT PIE

| | |
|---|---|
| 2 tablespoons flour | 2 cups green currants |
| ⅔ cup sugar | 2 tablespoons currant jelly |
| 1 recipe Basic Pastry | 2 tablespoons water |
| (see Index) | |

Mix together the flour and ½ of the sugar. Line a pie tin with pastry and sprinkle mixture over the pastry. Fill with currants. Add the jelly, remaining flour mixture, and the water. Cover with top crust. Bake in a moderate oven, 350° F., for about 35 minutes.

Variation: Proceed as above, but use ripe currants, 1 cup sugar and no jelly. Cover with strips made from ½ recipe of Sweet Dough I or II (see Index).

## ELDERBERRY PIE

| | |
|---|---|
| 2 cups ripe elderberries | Juice of ½ lemon |
| ¾ cup brown sugar | ¼ teaspoon salt |
| ¼ cup flour | 1 unbaked pastry shell |
| ¼ teaspoon cinnamon | Butter |
| ½ recipe Sweet Dough (see Index) | |

Combine elderberries with sugar, flour, cinnamon, lemon juice, and salt. Pour mixture into unbaked pastry shell and dot with butter. Cut the Sweet Dough into strips and arrange them over top of fruit. Bake in a hot oven, 450° F., for 10 minutes, then reduce heat to 350° F. and bake about 30 minutes longer.

## GOOSEBERRY PIE

| | |
|---|---|
| 1 recipe Basic Pastry (see Index) | 2½ cups green or ripe goose-berries |
| 2 tablespoons flour | ½ teaspoon cinnamon |
| ¾ cups sugar | Butter |

Line pie tin with pastry and sprinkle 1 tablespoon flour over bottom. Mix sugar, remaining flour and fruit, and pour into pastry. Dot with butter, sprinkle with cinnamon and cover with top crust. Bake in hot oven, 450° F., for 20 minutes, reduce to 350° F., and bake 25 minutes longer.

Variation: Ripe gooseberries in an unbaked pastry shell. Proceed as above. Instead of top crust cover with strips made of ½ Sweet Dough recipe (see Index).

## GRAPE PIE

| | |
|---|---|
| 4 cups grapes | 1 tablespoon butter |
| 1 cup sugar | 2 tablespoons flour |
| 1 recipe Basic Pastry (see Index) | |

Wash grapes and remove skins. Cook the pulp for about 10 minutes, or until tender, and force through a sieve. Combine with the grape skins, sugar, and butter. Line a pie tin with pastry and sprinkle with ½ of the flour. Pour in the grape mixture and sprinkle remaining flour over top. Cover with top crust and slit in several places to allow steam to escape. Bake in a hot oven, 450° F., for 10 minutes, then reduce heat to 350° F. and continue baking for 30 minutes longer.

## HUCKLEBERRY PIE

| | |
|---|---|
| 3 cups huckleberries | ½ cup sugar |
| 1 recipe Basic Pastry (see Index) | 1 teaspoon flour |
| | ½ teaspoon salt |
| Nutmeg | |

Wash huckleberries and pick over carefully, discarding any imperfect fruit. Line a pie tin with pastry and fill with berries. Combine sugar, flour, salt, and nutmeg to taste, and sprinkle over berries. Cover with a top crust and slit in several places to allow steam to escape. Bake in a hot oven, 450° F., for 10 minutes, then reduce heat to 350° F. and continue baking for about 30 minutes longer.

## LEMON PIE I

| | |
|---|---|
| 1 cup sugar | Juice and grated rind of 1 lemon |
| 2 eggs, well beaten | |
| 1 tablespoon flour | 1 cup boiling water |
| 2 tablespoons molasses | 1 unbaked pastry shell |
| ½ recipe Sweet Dough (see Index) | |

Combine ingredients and mix well. Pour mixture into unbaked pastry shell. Cut the Sweet Dough into strips and arrange them on top. Bake in a moderate oven, 350° F,. for about 30 minutes.

*Mrs. Jesse Renninger*

## LEMON PIE II

| | |
|---|---|
| Juice and grated rind of | 1 cup light molasses |
| 1 lemon | 2 cups water |
| 1 cup sugar | 2 tablespoons flour |
| 1 unbaked pastry shell | |

Combine lemon juice, grated rind, sugar, molasses and water. Mix well. Bring to a boil and add the flour. Pour mixture into unbaked pastry shell and place strips of following dough on top. Bake in a moderate oven, 350 F., for about 30 minutes.

**Dough**

| | |
|---|---|
| 1 cup sugar | 1 teaspoon baking soda |
| ½ cup butter and lard | 1 teaspoon cream of tartar |
| 1 egg, well beaten | 7 teaspoons water |
| ½ teaspoon lemon juice or vanilla | |

Cream together the sugar and shortening, and add the egg. Combine the baking soda and cream of tartar and dissolve in the water. Add to first mixture with lemon juice or vanilla. Roll out thin on lightly floured board and cut into 1-inch strips.

*Mrs. Jonas Martin*

## LEMON PIE III

| | |
|---|---|
| 1 cup sugar | 1 tablespoon butter |
| 2 tablespoons cornstarch | Juice of 1 lemon |
| 2 cups boiling water | Grated rind of ½ lemon |
| 2 eggs, separated | 1 baked pastry shell |
| 3 tablespoons powdered sugar | |

Mix together the sugar and cornstarch and gradually stir in the boiling water. Cook in the top of a double boiler over boiling water until mixture thickens, stirring constantly. Stir a small amount of mixture into beaten egg yolks and return to heat to cook for about 1 minute longer. Add butter, lemon juice and grated rind. Cool. Pour mixture into baked pastry shell. Beat egg whites with powdered sugar until stiff enough to form a peak. Spread meringue over top of pie. Bake in a moderate oven, 350° F., for about 15 minutes to brown the meringue.

*Mrs. Eva Haines*

## LEMON PIE IV

| | |
|---|---|
| 2 eggs, well beaten | 2 tablespoons flour |
| 1½ cups sugar | Juice of 2 lemons |
| 3 cups water | 1 recipe Basic Pastry |
| | (see Index) |

Combine the eggs, sugar, and water and mix well. Add the flour and lemon juice. Beat until thoroughly blended. Line a pie tin with pastry and pour mixture into tin. Cover with a top crust. Bake in a moderate oven, 350° F., for about 35 minutes.

*Grandma von Nieda*

## MINCEMEAT

| | |
|---|---|
| 3 pounds lean cooked beef, chopped fine | 1 pound chopped citron |
| 4 cups brown sugar | 3 pounds apples, diced |
| 1 pound raisins | 1¼ pounds suet, chopped fine |
| 1 pound currants | ¼ pound candied orange peel, sliced fine |
| 1 pound almonds, chopped | Juice and grated rind of 2 oranges |
| ¼ pound candied lemon peel, sliced fine | Juice and grated rind of 2 lemons |
| ½ tablespoon cloves | 1 pint brandy |
| ½ tablespoon cinnamon | 1 quart whisky |
| ½ tablespoon allspice | 1 tablespoon salt |
| ½ tablespoon grated nutmeg | |

Combine all ingredients and mix well. Place in an earthen crock, cover with a cloth, and place lid on top. Set aside in a cool place for 3 weeks. Taste mixture, and if needed, more salt and spices may be added. In earlier days rum was the preferred liquor. Let stand for one month altogether before using. Use 2 cups of mincemeat for each pie. Mince pie is always baked with an upper crust. Bake at 450° F. for 15 minutes, then reduce to 325° F. for 30 more minutes.

## GREEN TOMATO MINCEMEAT

| | |
|---|---|
| 1 peck green tomatoes, coarsely chopped | 4 cups white sugar |
| 1 cup suet, ground | 2 tablespoons cloves |
| 1½ pounds seedless raisins | 2 tablespoons cinnamon |
| Rind of ½ orange, ground | 1 tablespoon nutmeg |
| 4 cups brown sugar | 2 tablespoons salt |
| | 1 cup vinegar |
| 1 cup hot water | |

Place the tomatoes in a kettle, cover with cold water, and bring to a boil. Drain. Repeat process twice, being sure to drain well the last time. Combine with other ingredients and bring to a boil, stirring constantly. Pour into hot, sterilized jars and seal. Makes 4 quarts. Use 2 cups of mincemeat for each pie.

## MINCE PIE

The following old recipe was translated from the German recipe book of a Pennsylvania German housewife who kept house in Lancaster from 1767 to 1811. The 20th century housewife may not find it practicable, but it remains as interesting testimony to our early Pennsylvania German cuisine.

Cook tender in slightly salted water a fresh beef tongue and let it cool in the liquor it was boiled in. When cold, skin it, take about two-thirds its bulk of fresh kidney tallow (suet) and cut all fine with the rocking knife. Now weigh this, and take the weight of it in seeded raisins and in cleaned currants. Take the weight of all these in good sour pippins cut fine, 1 whole nutmeg grated, ½ ounce of each of ground cinnamon and cloves, the grated rind and juice of two lemons, 1 handful each of candied orange and lemon peel cut fine, a glass of currant jelly. Wet with the best of cider and sweeten to taste with soft sugar. Put in a big crock, cover with a cloth and when it begins to "crack" it is ready to use. Serve pies hot, and just before serving, put a tablespon full of brandy in the vent of each one. (Of course the cider is to crack, not the crock!)

## PRUNE PIE

Cook 1 pound prunes in 1 cup water. After cooking add 1½ cups sugar, ½ teaspoon vanilla, juice of 1 lemon and 6 tablespoons flour. Bake in 2 pieshells, either with lid or lattice.

## PLUM PIE

| | |
|---|---|
| 1 recipe Basic Pastry | 3 cups greengage plums, halved |
| (see Index) | 1 cup sugar |
| 2 tablespoons corn meal | 1 teaspoon cinnamon |
| 2 teaspoons powdered sugar | |

Line a pie tin with pastry and sprinkle the corn meal over the pastry. Place the plums in the pie tin and sprinkle the sugar and cinnamon over the top. Cover with top crust. Bake in a moderate oven, 350° F., for about 35 minutes. Remove, and sprinkle top crust with the powdered sugar.

## OLD-FASHIONED PUMPKIN PIE
### (Kaerbseboi)

| | |
|---|---|
| 1 recipe Basic Pastry | ½ cup brown sugar |
| (see Index) | 1 tablespoon flour |
| 2 cups uncooked pumpkin | Cinnamon |
| 3 tablespoons light molasses | Butter (optional) |

Use only the field pumpkin — the orange-colored *Feldkaerbse* used on Hallowe'en. Line a pie tin with pastry. Slice the pumpkin in ½-inch cubes and combine with the molasses and brown sugar. Use the so-called "eating" molasses and not the cooking molasses. Dredge the pastry shell with the flour and pour in pumpkin mixture. Sprinkle cinnamon over the top and dot with butter, if desired. Cover with top crust. Bake in a hot oven, 400° F., for 30 minutes, then reduce heat to 375° F. and bake 20 minutes longer, or until syrup oozes out of top crust. You will have a delicious old-fashioned pumpkin pie. This pie deserves our respect. It is probably the patriarch of all pumpkin pies.

*Gertrude Meyers Hillenhand*

## RAISIN PIE

### (Roseine Boi — the funeral pie)

No Pennsylvania German funeral feast was complete without raisin pie, hence it became popularly known as "funeral pie." In the earlier days raisins were looked upon as a rare and exotic fruit, which lent tone to the occasion. How informal and commonplace a function, how without dignity and reverence for the departed when there was no raisin pie to solemnize the post-mortuary feast!

| | |
|---|---|
| 1 recipe Basic Pastry | ¼ cup flour |
| (see Index) | 1 tablespoon vinegar |
| 1½ cups seeded raisins | Butter |
| ¾ cup brown sugar | Cinnamon |

Soak raisins in cold water for 3 hours. Line pie plate with pastry. Drain raisins. Mix raisins with sugar, flour and vinegar. Pour into pastry shell. Dot with butter and sprinkle with cinnamon. Cover with top crust and perforate it with fork. Bake 15 minutes at 450° F., reduce to 350° F. and continue baking for 30 minutes.

## RAISIN TART

| | |
|---|---|
| 1 cup seedless raisins | Juice of 1 lemon |
| 3 tablespoons flour | Grated rind of lemon |
| ¼ teaspoon salt | 1 unbaked pastry shell |
| 1 cup sugar | ½ recipe Sweet Dough |
| | (see Index) |

Wash raisins and soak in water for 2 hours. Drain. Mix with flour, salt, sugar, lemon juice and grated rind. Cook in top of double boiler over boiling water for 15 minutes, stirring occasionally. After cooling, pour mixture into unbaked pastry shell. Place strips of Sweet Dough over top. Bake in a hot oven, 450° F., for 15 minutes, then reduce to 350° F. and continue baking 25 minutes longer.

## RHUBARB PIE

| | |
|---|---|
| 1 recipe Basic Pastry | 3 cups sliced rhubarb |
| (see Index) | ½ teaspoon cinnamon |
| 2 tablespoons flour | ½ teaspoon nutmeg |
| ¾ cup sugar | |

Butter

Line pie tin with pastry and sprinkle 1 tablespoon flour over bottom. Mix sugar, remaining flour and rhubarb, and pour into pastry. Dot with butter, sprinkle with cinnamon and nutmeg and cover with top crust. Bake in hot oven, 450° F., for 20 minutes, reduce to 350° F., and bake 25 miutes longer.

Variation: Instead of top crust cover with twisted strips made of ½ Sweet Dough recipe (see Index).

## STRAWBERRY PIE

| | |
|---|---|
| 1 recipe Basic Pastry | 1 cup sugar |
| (see Index) | ½ cup flour |
| 3 cups hulled strawberries | Butter |

Line a pie tin with pastry. Sprinkle with ¼ cup flour. Combine strawberries, sugar and other ¼ cup flour. Pour into pastry shell and dot with butter. Cover with top crust and slit crust to allow the steam to escape. Bake in a hot oven, °450 F., for 10 minutes, then reduce heat to 350° F. and continue baking for about 30 minutes.

## GREEN TOMATO PIE

| | |
|---|---|
| 3 cups diced green tomatoes | 1 teaspoon cinnamon |
| 1 cup brown sugar | 2 tablespoons molasses |
| ¼ cup flour | Butter |

1 recipe Basic Pastry (see Index)

Line a pie tin with pastry and place tomatoes in pastry shell. Mix sugar, flour and cinnamon and sprinkle top of tomatoes. Dot generously with butter. Pour molasses over all. Cover with top crust. Bake in hot oven, 450° F., for 20 minutes, reduce to 350° F., and bake 25 minutes longer.

# CUSTARD PIES

### EGG CUSTARD PIE

| | |
|---|---|
| 3 eggs, slightly beaten | Pinch of salt |
| ½ cup sugar | 2 cups scalded milk, lukewarm |
| ¼ teaspoon nutmeg | ½ teaspoon vanilla |

1 unbaked pastry shell

Combine eggs with sugar, nutmeg, and salt. Gradually add the milk, mixing well. Add vanilla. Pour mixture into unbaked pastry shell. Bake in a hot oven, 450° F., for 10 minutes, then reduce heat to 350° F. and bake 25 to 30 minutes longer, or until inserted knife comes out clean.

## APPLE CUSTARD PIE

2 cups sweetened applesauce     ¼ teaspoon cinnamon
2 eggs, well beaten     ⅛ teaspoon nutmeg
1 unbaked pastry shell

Combine applesauce, eggs, cinnamon and nutmeg and mix well. Pour mixture into unbaked pastry shell. Bake in a hot oven, 400° F., for 10 minutes, then reduce heat to 350° F. and bake 25 to 30 minutes longer, or until inserted knife comes out clean.

## APPLEBUTTER CUSTARD PIE

3 eggs, slightly beaten     2 cups scalded milk, lukewarm
½ cup sugar     ½ cup applebutter
¼ teaspoon nutmeg     ½ teaspoon vanilla
Pinch of salt     1 unbaked pastry shell

Combine eggs with sugar, nutmeg, and salt. Gradually add the milk and mix well. Stir in the applebutter, and add the vanilla. Pour mixture into unbaked pastry shell. Bake in a hot oven, 450° F., for 10 minutes, then reduce heat to 350° F. and bake 25 to 30 minutes longer, or until inserted knife comes out clean.

*Mrs. Jesse Renninger*

## CARROT CUSTARD PIE

1 cup mashed cooked carrots     2 tablespoons melted butter
2 cups scalded milk, lukewarm     1 teaspoon grated nutmeg
3 eggs, well beaten     ¾ cup brown sugar
1 recipe Basic Pastry (see Index)

Combine mashed carrots, milk, eggs, butter, nutmeg and sugar and whip until smooth and creamy. Line a pie tin with pastry and pour mixture into pastry shell. Bake in hot oven, 450° F., for 15 minutes, then reduce heat to 350° and bake for 25 minutes longer, or until inserted knife comes out clean.

## CHERRY CUSTARD PIE

3 eggs, slightly beaten     1½ cups scalded milk,
½ cup sugar     lukewarm
Pinch of salt     1½ cups sweet cherries, pitted
1 teaspoon butter     1 unbaked pastry shell

Combine the eggs, sugar, salt, and butter. Gradually add the lukewarm milk and mix well. Place cherries in unbaked pastry shell and pour custard mixture over cherries. Bake in a hot oven, 450° F., for 10 minutes, then reduce heat to 350° and bake for 35 to 40 minutes longer, or until knife inserted in custard comes out clean.

## COCONUT CUSTARD PIE

| | |
|---|---|
| 3 eggs, separated | 2 cups scalded milk, lukewarm |
| 3 tablespoons flour | ½ teaspoon vanilla |
| ½ cup sugar | 1 cup shredded coconut |
| 1 tablespoon butter | 1 unbaked pastry shell |

Beat egg yolks and combine with flour, sugar, butter. Gradually add the lukewarm milk and mix well. Add vanilla and coconut. Fold in egg whites, beaten stiff. Pour mixture into unbaked pastry shell. Bake in a hot oven, 450° F., for 10 minutes, then reduce heat to 350° and bake for 35 to 40 minutes longer, or until an inserted knife comes out clean.

*Mrs. Eva Haines*

## LEMON CUSTARD PIE

| | |
|---|---|
| 4 eggs, separated | 1 tablespoon ice water |
| 6 tablespoons sugar | 1 tablespoon lemon juice |
| ¼ teaspoon salt | 5 tablespoons confectioners' |
| 1 lemon | sugar |
| 1¼ cups milk | 1 unbaked pastry shell |

Beat yolks of eggs slightly, add 6 tablespoons sugar and ⅛ teaspoon salt, grated rind of lemon and milk. Pour mixture into pastry shell and bake in hot oven, 450° F., for 10 minutes, then reduce heat to 350° F. and bake 30 minutes longer, or until inserted knife comes out clean. Remove from oven, cool slightly and prepare meringue as follows: Add ⅛ teaspoon salt and ice water to egg white and beat until light; then add lemon juice and beat mixture until it holds its shape. Cover pie with meringue, return to slow oven and bake about 10 minutes until it turns a light brown.

## LEMON SPONGE PIE I

| | |
|---|---|
| 1 cup sugar | 2 eggs, separated |
| 3 tablespoons flour | Juice and grated rind of |
| ½ teaspoon salt | 1 lemon |
| 1 cup scalded milk, lukewarm | 1 unbaked pastry shell |

Combine the sugar, flour, and salt. Gradually add the lukewarm milk and mix well. Beat egg yolks and stir into mixture. Add lemon juice and grated rind. Beat egg whites until stiff and fold into mixture. Pour into an unbaked pastry shell. Bake in a moderate oven, 350° F., for about 40 minutes.

## LEMON SPONGE PIE II

| | |
|---|---|
| ½ cup butter | Grated rind and juice of |
| 1 cup sugar | 1 lemon |
| 1 tablespoon cornstarch | 1 cup scalded milk, lukewarm |
| 3 eggs, separated | 1 unbaked pastry shell |

Cream together the butter, sugar, and cornstarch. Add 1 egg yolk at a time, beating well after each addition. Stir in the grated rind and juice of a large lemon. Stir in the milk. Beat the egg whites until stiff and fold into mixture. Pour into an unbaked pastry shell. Bake in a moderate oven, 350° F., for about 40 minutes.

## PEACH CUSTARD PIE

| | |
|---|---|
| 4 cups sliced peaches | ½ teaspoon cornstarch |
| 1 unbaked pastry shell | ¾ cup sugar |
| 2 eggs, well beaten | 2 cups scalded milk, lukewarm |
| Nutmeg | |

Place the peaches in an unbaked pastry shell. Combine eggs, cornstarch and sugar. Gradually add the milk and mix well. Pour custard mixture over the peaches and sprinkle nutmeg on top. Bake in a hot oven, 450° F., for 10 minutes, then reduce heat to 350° F. and bake for 25 to 30 minutes longer, or until inserted knife comes out clean.

## PUMPKIN CUSTARD PIE

| | |
|---|---|
| 1 cup cooked mashed pumpkin | 1 teaspoon grated nutmeg |
| ¾ cup brown sugar | 1 teaspoon cinnamon |
| 2 tablespoons butter | ½ teaspoon ginger |
| ¼ teaspoon salt | 3 eggs, well beaten |
| 1 tablespoon flour | ¾ cup milk |
| 1 unbaked pastry shell | |

Blend and cream pumpkin, sugar, butter, salt, flour and spices. Add eggs and milk, beat thoroughly and pour into unbaked pastry shell. Bake 20 minutes at 450° F., then reduce to 350° F. and bake 25 minutes, or until set.

*Mrs. Preston A. Barba*

## POTATO CUSTARD PIE

| | |
|---|---|
| 1 medium-sized potato, pared | ½ cup scalded milk, lukewarm |
| 2 tablespoons butter | Juice and grated rind of |
| ¾ cup sugar | ½ lemon |
| 2 eggs, separated | 1 unbaked pastry shell |

Boil and mash the potato. Add the butter and sugar and mix well. Cool. Beat the egg yolks and add to potato mixture together with milk and lemon juice and rind. Mix thoroughly and fold in the egg whites, beaten stiff. Pour mixture into unbaked pastry shell. Bake in a moderate oven, 350° F., for about 25 minutes.

## RHUBARB CUSTARD PIE

| | |
|---|---|
| 1½ cups rhubarb, cut fine | 3 tablespoons flour |
| 1 unbaked pastry shell | 1 teaspoon ginger |
| 3 eggs, separated | ¾ teaspoon salt |
| 1 cup sugar | 1 cup scalded milk, lukewarm |
| 1 tablespoon butter | ¾ cup powdered sugar |
| 1½ tablespoons lemon juice | |

Place rhubarb in unbaked pastry shell. Combine egg yolks, sugar, and butter and mix well. Add the flour, ginger, and ½ teaspoon of the salt. Gradually add the milk and mix well. Pour mixture over the rhubarb. Bake in a hot oven, 450° F., for 10 minutes, then reduce heat to 350° F. and bake 25 to 30 minutes longer, or until inserted knife comes out clean. Remove from oven. Make a meringue by beating egg whites with powdered sugar until stiff enough to form a peak. Gradually beat in lemon juice, 1 drop at a time. Cover pie with meringue and brown lightly in oven.

*Mrs. Preston A. Barba*

## SORREL PIE

### (Sauerambel Boi)

An almost forgotten pie. Once widely used by our Pennsylvania German forefathers both as a vegetable and as pie filling, sorrel (*Rumex Acetosa*) deserves to be reestablished in our cookery. If you like rhubarb pie you will like sorrel pie.

| | |
|---|---|
| 2 cups chopped sorrel leaves | 2 teaspoons flour |
| 1 recipe Basic Pastry | ¾ cup sugar |
| (see Index) | Cinnamon |
| Butter | |

Wash young sorrel leaves in hot water and chop fine. Line pie pan with pastry and sprinkle lightly with flour. Fill with sorrel, sprinkle with sugar and cinnamon and dot with butter. Cover with top crust and perforate. Bake in hot oven, 450° F., for 15 minutes, then reduce heat to 350° F. and bake 20 minutes longer. Serves 6.

*Mrs. Irwin Maurer*

Variation: Use brown sugar, juice of ½ lemon and a bit of grated lemon rind. Otherwise proceed as above.

*Mrs. Stanley Arthur*

## BUTTERSCOTCH PIE

| | |
|---|---|
| 1 cup brown sugar | 3 eggs, separated |
| ¼ cup water | ¼ cup butter |
| 3 tablespoons flour | 1 teaspoon vanilla |
| 2 cups scalded milk | 1 baked pastry shell |

3 tablespoons powdered sugar

Mix together the sugar, water, and flour. Gradually stir in the milk and cook in top of double boiler over boiling water until mixture thickens, stirring constantly. Stir a small amount of mixture into the beaten egg yolks. Pour into milk mixture and cook about 2 minutes longer. Add butter and vanilla. Cool. Pour mixture into baked pastry shell. Beat egg whites until stiff and sweeten with a little powdered sugar. Place meringue on pie and brown in a moderate oven, 350° F., for about 15 minutes.

## CREAM PIE

| | |
|---|---|
| 2 egg whites, beaten stiff | Sugar |
| 2¼ cups heavy cream | 1 teaspoon vanilla or lemon juice |

1 unbaked pastry shell

Fold beaten egg whites into the cream. Sweeten to taste with sugar. Add flavoring. Pour mixture into an unbaked pastry shell. Bake in a moderate oven, 350° F., for about 25 minutes, or until delicately browned.

## SOUR CREAM PIE

| | |
|---|---|
| 1 cup sour cream | 1 tablespoon flour |
| 1 tablespoon butter, melted | ½ teaspoon nutmeg |
| 2 tablespoons sugar | 1 teaspoon vanilla or lemon juice |
| 2 eggs, separated | 1 unbaked pastry shell |

Combine the cream, butter, and sugar. Beat the egg yolks and add to mixture. Sift together the flour and nutmeg and stir into the mixture. Add flavoring. Pour mixture into an unbaked pastry shell. Bake in a hot oven, 400° F., for about 20 minutes. Remove from oven. Beat egg whites until stiff and spread over top of pie. Return to oven and bake until delicately browned.

## LOVE PIE

### (A Mennonite Recipe)

| | |
|---|---|
| 6 tablespoons flour | 2 cups milk |
| 6 tablespoons sugar | 1 unbaked pastry shell |

Cinnamon

Combine the flour and sugar and mix well. Add the milk and stir until well mixed. Pour mixture into an unbaked pastry shell and sprinkle with cinnamon to taste. Bake in a hot oven, 400° F., for about 25 minutes.

*Miss Caroline Plank*

## MAPLE PIE

½ recipe Basic Pastry      Maple sugar
  (see Index)           Butter

Line a pie tin with rather thick pastry. Sprinkle generously with maple sugar and dot with butter. Bake in a hot oven, 400° F., for about 15 minutes.

## MONTGOMERY PIE

| | |
|---|---|
| 1 cup molasses | Grated rind and Juice of |
| ½ cup water | 1 lemon |
| 1 egg, well beaten | 3 tablespoons flour |
| | 1 cup sugar |

1 unbaked pastry shell

Combine the molasses, water, egg, and grated rind and lemon juice. Mix well. Combine the flour and sugar and add to first mixture. Pour mixture into unbaked pastry shell and top with following batter. Bake in a moderate oven, 350 F., for about 25 to 30 minutes.

**Batter**

| | |
|---|---|
| 1 cup sugar | 2 cups flour |
| ½ cup butter | 2 teaspoons baking powder |
| 2 eggs, separated | Pinch of salt |

½ cup milk

Cream together the sugar and butter, and add the beaten egg yolks. Mix well. Sift together the flour, baking powder, and salt. Add alternately with the milk to creamed mixture. Beat the egg whites until stiff but not dry. Fold into mixture.

## SLAB-DAB

| | |
|---|---|
| ½ recipe Basic Pastry | 3 tablespoons rich milk |
|   (see Index) | Butter |
| ⅓ cup brown sugar | Cinnamon |

Line a pie tin with pastry (the pastry should extend only halfway up the side of the tin). Place brown sugar and milk in pastry shell. Dot with butter and sprinkle cinnamon on top. Bake in a hot oven, 400° F., for aoout 15 minutes.

## WALNUT PIE

| | |
|---|---|
| 1 cup brown sugar | 2 tablespoons flour |
| 1 cup molasses | 1 cup chopped Black walnuts |
| 2 eggs, separated | ¾ cup warm water |
| 2 unbaked pastry shells | |

Combine brown sugar, molasses, beaten egg yolks, flour, nuts, and water. Mix well. Beat egg whites until stiff and fold into mixture. Pour mixture into pastry shells. Bake in a moderate oven, 350° F., for about 30 minutes.

## COCONUT TART

| | |
|---|---|
| 1½ cups cubed dry bread | 1½ cups shredded coconut |
| 1 unbaked pastry shell | 3 tablespoons sugar |
| Milk | |

Sprinkle the cubes of dry bread over bottom of unbaked pastry shell. Add coconut and sugar. Add enough milk to fill the pastry shell. Bake in a moderate oven, 350° F., for about 35 minutes.

## LEMON TART

| | |
|---|---|
| Grated rind of 1 lemon | 1 cup molasses |
| 1 cup sugar | 2 cups cold water |
| ½ cup flour | 2 unbaked pastry shells |

Combine ingredients and boil for a few minutes. Cool until a skin has formed on top of mixture. Pour into unbaked pastry shells and top with following batter. Bake in a moderate oven, 350° F., for about 30 minutes.

**Batter**

| | |
|---|---|
| 1 cup sugar | 2¼ cups flour |
| ¼ cup butter | 1 teaspoon baking powder |
| 1 egg, well beaten | 1 cup milk |

Cream together the sugar and butter, and add the egg. Mix well. Sift together the flour and baking powder. Add alternately with the milk to creamed mixture. Drop 4 tablespoons of batter on top of each pie, keeping each spoonful separate from the others. Utilize rest of batter to bake a thin cake in greased layer cake tin.

*Miss Mollie Gable*

## RHUBARB TART

| | |
|---|---|
| 1½ cups rhubarb, cut fine | 2 eggs, separated |
| 1 cup sugar | 2 unbaked pastry shells |
| 2 tablespoons flour | 1 tablespoon powdered sugar |

Combine rhubarb, sugar, flour and beaten egg yolks. Place mixture in unbaked pastry shells. Bake in a moderate oven, 350° F., for about 35 minutes. Remove from the oven. Beat egg whites with powdered sugar until stiff enough to form a peak. Spread meringue on top of pies and return to oven for about 15 minutes until delicately browned.

*Miss Emma Gable*

## SALEM TARTS

½ recipe Basic Pastry
  (see Index)
1 cup powdered sugar

1 tablespoon melted butter
8 egg yolks, well beaten
Juice and grated rind of
  1 lemon

Line 6 tart pans, or gem pans, with pastry. Combine the sugar, butter, and beaten egg yolks. Mix well. Add the lemon juice and grated rind. Pour mixture into tart shells. Bake in a hot oven, 450° F., for about 15 minutes. Chopped citron may be added, if desired.

## SCHNITTELS
### (Literally: Small Cuts)

1 recipe Basic Pastry
  (see Index)
1 cup brown sugar

⅓ cup butter
Cinnamon

Roll out dough ¼ inch thick on lightly floured board. Cut into 4-inch squares. On each square place 1 tablespoon brown sugar, 1 teaspoon butter, and sprinkle with cinnamon. Wet edges with cold water and fold over to form triangle. Pinch edges together and prick top with a fork. Place on greased baking sheet. Bake in a hot oven, 450° F., for about 15 minutes. Makes approximately 1 dozen tarts.

*Mrs. J. Max. Hark*

## DIE VERBABBELT SUSS

### (Tell-tale Susan)

Friday's big baking usually ended with a left-over bit of pastry, which was hastily fitted into a pie tin or baking dish and the following poured into it.

1½ tablespoons flour
1½ tablespoons brown sugar

¾ cup milk
1 tablespoon butter

Cinnamon

Mix flour, sugar and milk and pour into pastry. Dot with butter and sprinkle with cinnamon. Bake in a hot oven. — The little ones at mother's apron strings wait eagerly for this pretty postlude. Other names in the vernacular are *Millich Flitscher* and *Fress es graad*.

*Mrs. Arthur D. Graeff*

# Desserts

*Was batt en scheeni Schissel wann nix drin iss?*
A pretty dish with colors bright may be the housewife's pride,
But what's the good of it unless there's something good inside?

## GOETTERSPEISE

### (Ambrosia)

| | |
|---|---|
| 1 teaspoon cornstarch | Spongecake or lady fingers |
| 2 cups wine | Macaroons, cut fine |
| 3 eggs, separated | 1 teaspoon powdered sugar |
| 3 tablespoons sugar | Spiced almonds |

Mix the cornstarch with a little water to form a smooth paste. Heat the wine and add the egg yolks, sugar, and cornstarch. Stir until thickened. Place pieces of spongecake or lady fingers and the macaroons in the bottom of a pudding dish and pour in the wine mixture. Chill. Beat egg whites with powdered sugar until stiff. Spread meringue over top of pudding and sprinkle generously with sliced almonds. Brown in a moderate oven, 350°F., for about 10 minutes. Chill and serve.

## HULLABALOO

| | |
|---|---|
| 2 oranges | 1 cup sugar |
| 1 lemon | Fresh snow or shaved ice |

Mix together the juice of the oranges and the lemon and the grated rind of 1 orange. Add the sugar. Thicken to the consistency of sherbet with freshly fallen snow or shaved ice. Press into a mold and serve immediately.

## BAKED PEARS

Wash firm, tart pears in amount desired, removing the blossom end but keeping the stems intact. Place them in a pan with a small quantity of water and bake until soft. Remove from oven, pour molasses over pears, and return to oven until molasses boils. Serve hot or cold.

## RICE WITH CINNAMON SAUCE

⅔ cup rice                            3 tablespoons sugar
2½ tablespoons flour                  ½ teaspoon cinnamon
                    1½ cups milk

Boil the rice in salted water until tender. Drain and cool. Mix together the flour, sugar, and cinnamon. Bring milk to a boil and gradually add the mixture of dry ingredients, stirring constantly. Boil for 5 minutes. Pour while hot over the cold rice. Serves 4.

*Miss Rose Wiest*

## BLACKBERRY MUSH

1 quart blackberries                  ¾ cup sugar
⅓ cup water                           3 tablespoons cornstarch
                    ½ teaspoon vanilla

Wash and pick over the blackberries, discarding imperfect ones. Add water and boil until berries are soft. Mash through a strainer. Add the sugar and cornstarch and return to heat to boil until thick, stirring constantly. Add the vanilla and chill. Serve with cream. Serves 6.

*Mrs. Oborn Levis*

Other berries or peaches may be used instead of blackberries, if desired.

## FIG PUDDING

3 tablespoons quick-cooking          2½ cups water
   tapioca                           ½ pound figs
2 tablespoons butter                  1 cup sugar
Pinch of salt                         1 teaspoon vanilla
                    1 cup chopped nuts

Combine the tapioca, butter, salt, and 2 cups of the water. Cook in top of double boiler over boiling water until thick and clear. Cut the figs into small pieces and combine with the sugar and remaining ½ cup water. Cook until thick. Combine with tapioca mixture and mix well. Flavor with vanilla. Cool and sprinkle top with chopped nuts. Serve with cream. Serves 6.

## COFFEE CUSTARD

4 cups milk                           6 eggs, separated
½ pound coffee, freshly ground        1 cup powdered sugar

Bring the milk to a boil, add the coffee and cover tightly. Let stand for 30 minutes and strain through a fine sieve. Beat together 6 egg yolks and 3 egg whites, and add the sugar. Combine with coffee mixture. Strain again and pour mixture into 6 custard cups. Place cups in pan of hot water. Bake in a moderate oven, 350°F., for about 1 hour or until inserted knife comes out clean. Serves 6.

## LEMON CUSTARD

| | |
|---|---|
| 1 cup sugar | 3 tablespoons flour |
| 2 eggs, well beaten | Juice and grated rind of |
| 2 cups milk | 1 lemon |

½ cup melted butter

Mix the sugar, egg, and flour. Add the lemon juice and grated rind, and melted butter. Pour mixture into 6 small custard cups. Place cups in pan of hot water. Bake in a moderate oven, 350°F., for about 25 to 30 minutes, or until inserted knife comes out clean. Chill. Serves 6.

## ORANGE CUSTARD

| | |
|---|---|
| 6 oranges | 6 egg yolks, well beaten |
| Sugar | 2 cups scalded cream or milk |

Squeeze oranges, strain the juice and sweeten to taste with sugar. Place in top of double boiler and cook over boiling water until the sugar is dissolved, removing the scum as it rises to the surface. Remove from heat and when nearly cold add the egg yolks and cream or milk. Place over boiling water once more and stir until mixture thickens. Pour into mold or individual cups and chill. Serves 4 to 6.

## GRANDMA NETTY'S GERMAN PUFFIES

| | |
|---|---|
| 2 cups scalded milk | 4 tablespoons flour |
| 2 tablespoons butter, melted | 4 eggs, well beaten |

Powdered sugar

Mix together the milk, butter, and flour, and gradually add the eggs. Beat thoroughly. Pour mixture into 4 custard cups and place cups in pan of hot water. Bake in a moderate oven, 350°F., for about 25 to 30 minutes, or until inserted knife comes out clean. Sift powdered sugar over top of each custard. Chill and serve with cream. Serves 4.

## BREI

### (Pap)

| | |
|---|---|
| 3 tablespoons flour | 1½ cups scalded milk |
| 2 tablespoons sugar | 2 tablespoons brown sugar |

Mix the flour with a small quantity of the milk. Add the sugar and the remaining milk. Place in top of double boiler and cook over boiling water until the consistency of a soft custard. Pour into a serving dish and sprinkle top with the brown sugar. Chill and serve. Serves 2.

## APPLE SNOW

| | |
|---|---|
| 10 medium-sized apples | 1 wineglass wine |
| 1½ cups sugar | 4 egg whites |

Pare and core the apples, and cut them into small pieces. Add 1 cup of the sugar and the wine. Cook apples until tender and force through a fine sieve. Beat egg whites with remaining ½ cup sugar until stiff, Fold into apple mixture. Turn into a greased baking dish and place in a pan of hot water. Bake in a moderate oven, 350°F., for about 30 minutes, or until firm. Serve at once. Serves 6.

## QUINCE SNOW

| | |
|---|---|
| 5 quinces | 1 cup sugar |
| 5 egg whites, beaten stiff | |

Pare and grate the quinces, add the sugar and a small amount of water. Cook until tender. Fold in beaten egg whites and turn mixture into greased baking dish. Place in a pan of hot water. Bake in a moderate oven, 350°F., for about 30 minutes, or until firm. Serves 4 to 6.

## RASPBERRY SNOW

### (Hembeere Schnee)

| | |
|---|---|
| 1 cup raspberry jelly | 8 egg whites, beaten stiff |
| ½ cup sugar | Sugar |

Beat jelly and gradually add the sugar. Fold in beaten egg whites. Turn mixture into a greased baking dish and with a broad knife swirl the top of mixture, bringing to a peak in the center. Sprinkle lightly with sugar and flick a few drops of water on top. Place in pan of hot water. Bake in a slow oven, 300°F., for about 1 hour. Remove and serve immediately. Serves 6 to 8.

*Das Neue Gothaische Kochbuch, Gotha, 1804*

## APPLE SOUFFLE

| | |
|---|---|
| 4 eggs, separated | ⅓ cup butter, melted |
| 1 cup applesauce | 3 tablespoons sugar |
| 1 cup fine bread crumbs | Cinnamon |

Beat egg yolks until thick and light. Add other ingredients and mix well. Fold in egg whites, beaten stiff and pour mixture into a greased baking dish. Place in pan of hot water. Bake in a moderate oven, 350°F., for about 30 to 45 minutes, or until firm. Serves 6.

*Henriette Davidis: Praktisches Kochbuch*

## SOUR CREAM SOUFFLE

| | |
|---|---|
| 4 eggs, separated | 4 tablespoons sugar |
| 1 pint thick sour cream | ½ teaspoon cinnamon |
| 2 tablespoons flour | 1 teaspoon vanilla |

¼ teaspoon salt

Beat egg yolks until thick and light, and combine with sour cream. Mix flour, sugar, and cinnamon, and stir into sour cream. Fold in egg whites, beaten stiff with vanilla and salt. Pour mixture into a greased baking dish. Place in pan of hot water. Bake in a moderate oven, 350°F., for about 45 minutes, or until firm. Serves 6.

*Henriette Davidis: Praktisches Kochbuch*

## APPLE and SWEET POTATO PUDDING

| | |
|---|---|
| ¾ cup mashed sweet potatoes | 2 tablespoons butter, melted |
| 2 eggs | 1 teaspoon nutmeg, mace, and |
| 1½ cups thick applesauce | cinnamon, mixed |

Powdered sugar

Beat eggs until light and gradually stir in the mashed sweet potatoes and applesauce. Add the butter and spices. Mix thoroughly. Turn mixture into a greased baking dish. Bake in a moderate oven, 350°F., for about 1 hour. Cool and sprinkle generously with powdered sugar. Serve with cream. Serves 4.

## BAKED PUMPKIN

| | |
|---|---|
| 2 cups mashed cooked pumpkin | 1 cup milk |
| ⅛ pound almonds, ground fine | 4 eggs, separated |
| ¼ pound butter, melted | 3 tablespoons sugar |
| ½ cup fine bread crumbs | Pinch of mace |
| ½ cup cream | Pinch of salt |

Combine mashed pumpkin ,almonds and butter. Beat until foamy. Add bread crumbs and mix well. Combine cream, milk, and egg yolks, beat until well mixed and add to pumpkin mixture. Beat egg whites with the sugar, mace, and salt until stiff enough to form a peak. Fold into pumpkin mixture. Turn into a greased baking dish. Bake in a slow oven, 300° F., for about 1 hour, or until firm. Serves 6.

## BERRY PUDDING

| | |
|---|---|
| ½ pound butter | 4 eggs, separated |
| 2 cups brown sugar | 2 cups sifted flour |

1 quart blackberries or huckleberries

Cream together the butter and sugar, and add the beaten egg yolks. Mix thorougthly. Stir in the flour and mix well. Beat egg whites until stiff and

fold into batter. Turn into a greased baking dish. Make a depression in
the center of dough and turn in the berries. Bake in a moderate oven, 350° F.,
for about 45 minutes. Serve while hot with hard sauce. Serves 6 to 8.

## ROTE GRUETZE
### (Cranberry Pudding)

Wash and pick over the desired amount of cranberries. Cover with water,
add a little cinnamon, and boil until cranberries are soft. Strain through
cheesecloth. To each quart of juice, add 4 tablespoons cornstarch and 4
tablespoons sugar, mixed to a paste with a little cold juice. Boil the juice,
stirring constantly until mixture thickens. Pour into a mold and chill. Serve
with sugar and cream.

## HUCKLEBERRY PUDDING

| | |
|---|---|
| 1 teaspoon baking soda | 1 egg, well beaten |
| 1 tablespoon warm water | 1½ cups sifted flour |
| 1 cup dark molasses | 1 pint huckleberries |

Dissolve the baking soda in the warm water and beat into the molasses.
Add the egg and the flour and beat until well mixed. Dust the huckleberries
lightly with flour and stir into the mixture. Pour into a greased loaf pan.
Bake in a moderate oven, 350°F., for about 45 minutes, or until done. Serve
hot with cream or hard sauce. Serves 6.

## LEMON RICE PUDDING

| | |
|---|---|
| 1 cup cooked rice | 4 eggs, separated |
| 2 tablespoons butter | Juice and grated rind of |
| 4 cups scalded milk | 1 lemon |
| 4 tablespoons sugar | |

Combine the rice, butter, and milk, and sweeten to taste. Add the beaten
egg yolks and the grated lemon rind. Place in a greased baking dish. Beat
egg whites with the sugar until stiff enough to form a peak. Add the lemon
juice. Spread over top of mixture to form a meringue. Bake in a mdoerate
oven, 350°F., for about 15 to 20 minutes to brown. Serves 6.

## QUAKER'S PLUM PUDDING
### (From an old Lancaster County almanac)

| | |
|---|---|
| 2 cups raisins | 4 cups scalded milk |
| 6 slices bread, buttered | ½ teaspoon cloves |
| 5 eggs, well beaten | ½ teaspoon cinnamon |
| Pinch of salt | |

Boil the raisins in a small amount of water to plump them. Lay them in
a greased baking dish in alternate layers with the buttered bread until dish is

filled to within 1 inch of top. Stir the eggs into the milk, add the spices and salt, and pour mixture over the bread and raisins. Bake in a moderate oven, 350°F., for about 20 to 25 minutes. Serve hot with the following sauce.
**Wine Sauce:**

| | |
|---|---|
| 2 eggs, well beaten | 1½ cups sugar |
| 2 tablespoons melted butter | 2 tablespoons milk |
| ½ cup sherry | |

Combine the eggs, melted butter, and sugar, and beat to a froth. Place bowl in a pan of hot water and gradually add the milk and sherry to the mixture. Serve while hot.

### PRUNE SOUFFLE

| | |
|---|---|
| ¾ pound prunes | 4 egg whites, beaten stiff |
| Sugar | |

Cook the prunes with sugar to taste. When soft remove the pits and force prunes through a food chopper, using a coarse blade. Cool. Fold egg whites into prune mixture and turn into a greased baking dish. Bake in a moderate oven, 350°F., for about 20 minutes. Chill and serve with whipped cream. Serves 6.

### COTTAGE PUDDING

| | |
|---|---|
| 1 cup brown sugar | ½ teaspoon baking soda |
| 1 egg, well beaten | 1 teaspoon cream of tartar |
| ¼ teaspoon nutmeg | 2 cups flour |
| 1 tablespoon butter | 1 cup milk |

Combine the sugar, egg, and nutmeg, and add the butter. Mix well. Sift the baking soda and cream of tartar with the flour and add to first mixture alternately with the milk. Pour into greased cake tins. Bake in a moderate oven, 350°F., for about 30 minutes. The cake should be about 2 inches thick. Cut into squares and serve with Wine Sauce (see Quaker's Plum Pudding). Serves 6.

### CRACKER PUDDING

| | |
|---|---|
| 4 large soda crackers | 1 cup raisins |
| 2 cups scalded milk | 1 cup light cream |
| ½ cup sugar | 1½ tablespoons melted butter |
| 1 teaspoon cinnamon | 1 teaspoon vanilla |
| ⅛ teaspoon salt | 2 eggs, well beaten |

Place crackers in the scalded milk, cover the pan, and set aside to cool. Add the remaining ingredients and mix well. Turn into a greased baking dish. Bake in a slow oven, 300°F., for about 1 hour, or until firm. Serve with hard sauce. Serves 4 to 6.

*Mrs. John Dyson*

### CORN-MEAL PUDDING

| | |
|---|---|
| 2 cups corn meal | 1 teaspoon salt |
| 4 cups milk | 1 tablespoon butter, melted |
| 1 cup molasses | 4 eggs, well beaten |

Scald the corn meal with the milk, and add the molasses and salt. Cool. Add the butter and eggs and mix well. Pour into a greased baking dish. Bake in a slow oven, 300°F., for about 2 hours. Serve with the following sauce. Serves 6.

**Sauce:**

| | |
|---|---|
| 2 eggs, separated | 2 cups milk |
| ⅔ cup sugar | |

Beat the egg whites lightly and stir into the milk. Bring mixture to a boil. Beat egg yolks with sugar and stir into milk mixture. Cook until mixture thickens. Serve while hot.

## STEAMED PUDDINGS

### APPLE PUDDING
#### (From an old Pennsylvania German almanac)

| | |
|---|---|
| 1 cup diced apples | Cinnamon |
| 1 cup chopped suet | Cloves |
| 1 cup bread crumbs | 1 cup currants |
| 1 cup brown sugar | 3 egg whites, beaten stiff |
| 12 almonds, chopped fine | 1 wineglass brandy |

Combine the apples and suet and mix well. Add the bread crumbs, sugar, almonds, and spices to taste. Stir in the currants. Fold in the beaten egg whites and add the brandy last. Turn into a well-greased mold, cover, and steam for 3 hours. Cool and serve. Serves 6.

### APPLE POTPIE I

| | |
|---|---|
| 4 cups sifted flour | 6 medium-sized apples |
| ¼ pound lard | ¾ cup sugar |
| ¼ teaspoon salt | 1 teaspoon cinnamon |
| Cold water | ¼ cup butter |

Mix together the flour, lard, and salt, and add just enough cold water to make dough hold together. Roll out on a lightly floured board and cut into 2-inch squares. Pare the apples and cut them into eighths. Place alternate layers of dough squares and apples in a kettle. Sprinkle each layer of apples with sugar and cinnamon. Top with layer of dough squares and dot with butter. Add water to half fill the kettle, cover, and simmer until apples are soft. Serve with milk or cream. Serves 6 to 8.

## APPLE POTPIE II

Place a layer of sweet, unpared apples, cut in quarters, in the bottom of a kettle. Add a layer of bread dough. Cover with a tight fitting lid and steam for about 30 minutes. Serve with sweetened milk.

*Carrie Haas Troutman*

## BACHELOR'S PUDDING
### (From an old Lancaster County almanac)

| | |
|---|---|
| 3 eggs | ½ cup sugar |
| Lemon juice | 1 cup apples, chopped fine |
| Nutmeg | 1 cup currants, chopped fine |

1 cup grated bread crumbs

Beat the eggs and add lemon juice and nutmeg to taste. Add remaining ingredients and mix thoroughly. Turn into a well-greased mold, cover, and steam for about 3 hours. Serve with Wine Sauce (see Index). Serves 4 to 6.

## PLUM PUDDING FOR THE MILLION
### (Taken from a 100-year-old almanac)

"Take half a pound of flower [flour], half a pound of currants, half a pound of grated carrots, half a pound of grated potatoes, a quarter of a pound of suet, and a little seasoning. Mix them together and boil them in a basin an hour and a half. You will then have an excellent plum pudding for a trifle more than a sixpence! Just try the experiment."

## PENNSYLVANIA PLUM PUDDING

| | |
|---|---|
| 2 teaspoons baking powder | 2 eggs, well beaten |
| 1 cup chopped beef suet | 1 cup milk |
| 1 cup seeded raisins | 1 cup molasses |
| ½ cup currants | ½ cup corn meal |
| ¼ cup citron, sliced fine | 1 cup bread crumbs |
| Flour | ½ teaspoon salt |
| Chopped almonds | ½ teaspoon nutmeg |

Mix together the eggs, milk, and molasses. Mix together the corn meal, bread crumbs, salt, nutmeg, and baking powder, and combine with egg mixture. Add chopped suet and the fruit. Mix well. Add enough flour to form a stiff batter. Turn into a well-greased mold, cover, and steam for about 3 hours. Turn out and sprinkle almonds on top. Serve while hot with the following sauce. Serves 6 to 8.

Sauce:

| | |
|---|---|
| 2 egg whites | 1 cup powdered sugar |
| 1 teaspoon lemon juice | ½ cup butter (scant) |

Cream together the sugar and butter. Add the egg whites one at a time, beating until foamy. Add the lemon juice. Chill.

## SUET PUDDING

| | |
|---|---|
| 2 cups sugar | 2 teaspoons baking powder |
| 2 eggs, well beaten | 1 teaspoon cinnamon |
| 1 cup milk | 1 cup raisins |
| 3 cups flour | 1 cup currants |
| 1 cup ground suet | |

Combine the sugar and eggs and mix well. Add the milk alternately with the sifted dry ingredients and mix well after each addition. Stir in the fruit and suet and mix well. Turn into a well-greased mold, cover, and steam for about 3 hours. Then unmold and place in a warm oven for a few minutes to dry. Serve with the following sauce. Serves 8.

**Sauce:**

| | |
|---|---|
| 1 cup powdered sugar | 1 egg |
| 1½ tablespoons butter | 1 teaspoon vanilla |

Cream together the sugar and butter, and add the egg. Beat until foamy. Season with vanilla. Rum or brandy may be substituted for the vanilla, if desired.

## STEAMED WALNUT PUDDING

| | |
|---|---|
| 1 cup sugar | 3½ cups sifted flour |
| ½ cup butter | ½ teaspoon nutmeg |
| 2 eggs, separated | ½ teaspoon cinnamon |
| 1 teaspoon baking soda | ¼ teaspoon cloves |
| ½ cup maple syrup | Pinch of salt |
| 1 cup milk | ¾ cup seeded raisins |
| ½ cup chopped walnuts | |

Cream together the sugar and butter, and add the beaten egg yolks. Mix well. Dissolve the soda in the maple syrup and add to creamed mixture. Add the milk alternately with the flour and spices, mixing well after each addition. Add salt, raisins and chopped nuts. Beat egg whites until stiff and fold into mixture. Turn into a well-greased mold, cover, and steam for about 3 hours. Serve hot with the following sauce. Serves 8 to 10.

**Sauce:**

| | |
|---|---|
| 1 cup powdered sugar | 1 egg white |
| 2½ tablespoons butter | ¾ teaspoon lemon extract |

Cream together the sugar and butter. Add the egg white and beat until foamy. Flavor with the lemon extract. Chill.

## FRIED FRUIT PIES

| | |
|---|---|
| 1 teaspoon salt | ½ cup butter and lard |
| 2 cups flour | ⅓ cup cold water |

**Stewed fruit**

Sift the salt and flour together. Rub the shortening into the mixture, add the water, and mix just enough to form a fairly stiff dough. Turn out onto a floured board and roll out quite thin. Cut dough into 4-inch rounds. Place 1½ tablespoons sweetened stewed fruit (applesauce, prunes, apricots, or peaches) on one-half of each round of dough and fold over to form a semi-circle. Moisten the edges and press together with a fork. Fry in deep, hot fat, 370° F., for 3 to 4 minutes or until golden brown. Drain on absorbent paper. Makes about 14 fruit pies.

## BAKED APPLE DUMPLINGS

| | |
|---|---|
| 2 cups flour | ¾ cup milk (about) |
| 3 teaspoons baking powder | 4 medium-sized apples, halved |
| ½ teaspoon salt | 1 cup brown sugar |
| 4 tablespoons shortening | Cinnamon |

Sift together the flour, baking powder, and salt and cut in the shortening. Add enough of the milk to form a fairly stiff dough, though not as stiff as pie pastry. Roll out on a lightly floured board and cut dough into 8 rounds. Place ½ apple on each round and sprinkle with some brown sugar and cinnamon to taste. Moisten edges of dough with cold water and draw edges up over apple, pinching edges together. Place on baking pan, folded side down and prick dough in several places with a fork. Mix ½ cup of the brown sugar with ¼ cup water and pour over the dumplings. Bake in a hot oven, 450° F., for 20 minutes, then reduce heat to 350° and continue baking for 10 minutes longer, or until apples are tender. Serve with sweetened milk.

*Elizabeth Gorr Moll*

## APPLE DUMPLINGS

| | |
|---|---|
| ¾ pound grated white bread | 1 tablespoon butter, melted |
| 4 eggs, separated | 1 cup diced apples |
| 2 cups milk | 1 teaspoon grated lemon rind |

To the grated bread add the beaten egg yolks and mix well. Add the milk and stir until blended. Add the butter, apples, and lemon rind. Beat egg whites until stiff and fold into mixture. Shape into dumplings and drop into salted, boiling water. Cover and steam for 15 minutes, without uncovering. Serve with rich sweetened milk. Serves 6.

*Henriette Davidis: Praktisches Kochbuch*

### CHERRY DUMPLINGS

| | |
|---|---|
| 1 pound pitted cherries | 1/8 teaspoon cloves |
| 1/2 cup sugar | 1 tablespoon butter, melted |
| 1 teaspoon grated lemon rind | 3 eggs, well beaten |
| Grated dry bread | |

Combine cherries and sugar with lemon rind and cloves. Cook until tender, adding no water during cooking process. Cool. Add butter, the beaten eggs, and enough grated dry bread to form dumplings that will hold together. Experiment by dropping 1 dumpling in boiling salted water. Steam from 5 to 10 minutes, depending on size of dumpling. Serve with sweetened rich milk.

*Henriette Davidis: Praktisches Kochbuch*

### CARAMEL DUMPLINGS

| | |
|---|---|
| 1¼ cups flour | 1/3 cup milk |
| 1½ teaspoons baking powder | 1/2 teaspoon vanilla |
| 1/3 cup sugar | 1½ cups brown sugar |
| 1/8 teaspoon salt | 1½ cups boiling water |
| 3 tablespoons butter | 1/8 teaspoon salt |

Sift together the flour, baking powder, sugar, and salt. Cut in the butter. Add the milk and vanilla. Mix thoroughly. Combine remaining ingredients in a saucepan and bring mixture to a boil. Drop batter from a teaspoon into boiling syrup, cover, and simmer for 20 minutes. Serves 6.

### PEACH DUMPLINGS

| | |
|---|---|
| 1 tablespoon butter | 1 cup flour |
| 1 cup sugar | 2 teaspoons baking powder |
| 2 cups hot water | 1/2 teaspoon salt |
| 2 cups sliced peaches | 1 cup milk |

Combine the butter, sugar, hot water in a saucepan and bring to a boil. Cook until a syrup forms. Add the peaches and bring to a boil again. Sift together the dry ingredients and add the milk. Drop from a tablespoon into the boiling peach mixture, cover, and steam for 20 minutes. Serve while hot. Serves 6.

### OFFE SCHLUPPER

#### (The Oven Sneak!)

| | |
|---|---|
| 2 cups flour | Pinch of salt |
| 2 teaspoons baking powder | 1 egg |
| 2 tablespoons sugar | 2/3 cup milk (about) |
| 1 cup fruit | |

Sift together the flour, baking powder, sugar and salt. Break the egg into a measuring cup and fill cup with milk. Stir into the dry ingredients and beat until smooth. Add 1 cup of fruit (whatever berries in season, or thinly sliced peaches, apples, etc.). Turn into a greased baking dish. Bake in a moderate oven, 350°F., for about 30 minutes. Serve with sugar and milk. Serves 4 to 6.

*Mrs. Harry Hess Reichard*

## FRUIT PUDDING

| | |
|---|---|
| ⅓ cup sugar | 1 teaspoon baking powder |
| ⅓ cup butter | ⅓ cup milk |
| 1 egg, well beaten | 1 cup sugar |
| 1 cup flour | 1 quart fruit |

Cream together the sugar and butter, and add the egg. Mix well. Sift together the flour and baking powder, and add alternately with the milk to creamed mixture. Beat well after each addition. Sprinkle the cup of sugar over the fruit. Turn batter into a greased 8-inch-square baking pan. Pile the sugared fruit (cherries, blackberries, peaches, or plums) on top of batter. Bake in a moderate oven, 350°F., for about 40 minutes. Serve with heavy cream. Serves 4 to 6.

## DRAUWEKUCHE
### (Grape Cake)

| | |
|---|---|
| ½ recipe Moravian Cake | 2 cups ripe grapes (local) |
| (see Index) | 1 egg |
| ¼ cup melted butter | ½ cup cream |
| ½ cup bread crumbs | 1 cup sugar |

Make up dough as directed. Press out as thin as possible in a large square or rectangular pan, about 2 inches deep. Brush dough with melted butter and sprinkle lightly with bread crumbs. Spread grapes on dough. Bake in a moderate oven, 350°F., for about 20 minutes. Then mix egg, cream and sugar, beat well, and pour over the top. Put back into oven and continue baking for another 10 minutes. Serves 6.

Cherries, gooseberries or currants may be substituted for the grapes, according to their season.

## PEACH DELIGHT

| | |
|---|---|
| 1 cup flour | ⅓ cup milk |
| 2 teaspoons baking powder | 1 cup sliced peaches |
| 1 teaspoon salt | ½ cup brown sugar |
| 2 tablespoons sugar | ½ teaspoon cinnamon |
| 1 egg, well beaten | 1 teaspoon lemon juice |
| 2 tablespoons butter | |

Sift together the flour, baking powder, salt, and sugar. Add the egg and milk and beat until thoroughly mixed. Pour batter into a greased square baking pan. Combine remaining ingredients and place on top of batter. Bake in a moderate oven, 350°F., for about 35 minutes. Cut in squares and serve while hot. Serves 6.

*Miss Mollie Gable*

### STRAWBERRY SHORTCAKE

| | |
|---|---|
| 4 cups flour | 1 tablespoon butter, melted |
| 1 teaspoon salt | 2 cups milk (about) |
| 2 teaspoons baking powder | 2 quarts strawberries |

Sugar

Sift together the flour, salt, and baking powder, and add the butter. Stir in enough milk to form a soft batter. Turn into a greased cake pan. Bake in a moderately hot oven, 375°F., for about 20 minutes, or until done. Wash and hull strawberries and crush them, reserving a few whole berries for decoration. Sweeten to taste with sugar. Split the cake crosswise. Spread half of the berries over the lower section, arrange other section of cake on top, and spread with remaining crushed berries. Serves 6.

Sugared peaches may be substituted for the strawberries, if desired.

Variations: Pineapple Shortcake: Substitute crushed pineapple for the strawberries and sprinkle zwieback crumbs between the layers also.

Rhubarb Shortcake: Combine 2 cups of stewed, sweetened rhubarb with 1 cup of ground dates and use as substitute for strawberries.

### LEMON SAUCE FOR PUDDING

| | |
|---|---|
| 1 tablespoon cornstarch | 1 cup boiling water |
| 3 tablespoons sugar | 1 teaspoon butter |
| ¼ teaspoon salt | 1 tablespoon lemon juice |

Grated rind of ½ lemon

Mix together the cornstarch, sugar, and salt. Add the boiling water slowly, stirring constantly. Cook in the top of a double boiler, over boiling water, until the mixture thickens. Add the butter, stir until melted, and then add the lemon juice and rind. Serve hot or cold, as desired.

### ORANGE SAUCE FOR PUDDING
#### (From a 100-year-old almanac)

| | |
|---|---|
| 2 cups orange juice | 5 cups powdered sugar |

4 tablespoons melted butter

Combine orange juice and powdered sugar. Cook over low heat until thick and syrupy. Skim off any scum which rises to the surface. Add the melted butter. Serve hot or cold, as desired.

# Candies

*Mann un Weib*
*Sin ee Leib —*
*Awwer zwee Maage!*

A man and his wife
Are one through life —
But they have two stomachs!

As a people the Pennsylvania Germans are little given to "sweets." The confections made in their kitchens offer little that is unusual. They are for the most part new world adaptations. One notable exception is *marzipan* (known also in English as marchpane), an almost forgotten confectionary that certainly deserves to be restored. It is known throughout the Mediterranean countries, probably because one of its two main ingredients is the almond. Among German people generally it is the main sweetmeat of the Christmas season. A commercialized imitation of marzipan, without the almond paste, of crystalized sugar, hard and tasteless, pressed into molds of animal and flower forms, with tiny colored pictures stuck upon them, were common in the second half of the 19th century as Christmas tree decorations. The name for these cheap and gaudy imitations is distorted into *Matzebäume* in Weygandt's The Dutch Country. The name "marzipan" points to Latinic origin. In popular etymology it is derived from *marcipanis*, the bread of Mark. We shall not venture to inquire whether Mark had a sweeter tooth than the other evangelists. There is the possibility that this confection was first marketed from Venice, whose patron saint is Mark.

## MARZIPAN

| | |
|---|---|
| 2 pounds of confectioner's sugar | 2 pounds ground almonds |
| | 2 teaspoons almond extract |

Rosewater

Mix sugar and almonds. Add the almond extract and sufficient rosewater to form a paste that will allow itself to be molded easily. Be very careful not to get it too wet. Now the skillful hands will fashion the paste into all sorts of shapes and figures: strawberries, apples, peas in open pods, carrots, potatoes, with the aid of coloring matter; or in the forms of pretzels and miniature bread rolls, to be browned slightly in the oven; or rolled in balls or oblongs to be dipped into chocolate; or again, if you possess old *springerle* molds, these can be used to imprint designs upon the flattened out almond paste, in which instance the paste must be sprinkled with flour, then browned in the oven.

Please note that this confection is neither boiled nor baked. In metropolitan centers almond paste can sometimes be purchased in bakeshops and delicatessen stores at Christmas time. Better it is to grind the almonds, adding a few bitter almonds, if procurable. In whatever form the paste is molded, be sure to place carefully in a tight container until used.

## MORAVIAN MINTS

2 cups sugar                    ½ cup hot water
14 drops oil of peppermint

Combine the sugar and water and boil for exactly 10 minutes. Add the oil of peppermint and beat until slightly cloudy. Pour into small round tins, about 1¼ inches in diameter. Wintergreen, anise or other flavoring may be substituted for oil of peppermint, if desired.

## COCONUT CREAMS

1 cup shredded coconut          1 egg white, beaten stiff
2½ cups confectioners' sugar    ½ teaspoon vanilla

Combine the coconut and sugar and gradually add to the beaten egg white. Add the vanilla. Knead for about 15 minutes, until smooth and creamy. Shape into small balls and set aside to stiffen. If desired, half an English walnut may be pressed into the top of each ball while still soft.

Variation: Melt ½ square of chocolate with ½ teaspoon of paraffin and roll the small balls in mixture until thoroughly coated. Place on waxed paper to dry.

## COCONUT BLOCKS

1 pound sugar                   ½ cup water
1½ cups grated coconut

Combine sugar and water in an agate kettle. Bring to a boil and add grated coconut. Continue boiling, stirring constantly, until mixture spins a thread when dropped from the spoon. Remove from heat and beat until creamy. Pour onto a buttered platter and mark into squares while still warm.

*Mrs. Robert Seaber*

## MAPLE CANDY

| | |
|---|---|
| 2 cups brown sugar | 2 tablespoons butter |
| ½ cup milk | 2 cups crushed peanuts |

Vanilla

Combine the sugar, milk, and butter and cook over low heat until a small amount forms a soft ball when dropped into cold water. Remove from heat, add the vanilla, and beat rapidly for about 5 seconds. Add the crushed peanuts while beating the mixture. Pour mixture into buttered pans and cut into squares while still warm.

## MAMMY BENDER'S CANDY

| | |
|---|---|
| 2½ cups soft white sugar | ½ cup vinegar |
| ½ cup water | |

Combine the ingredients and boil until a small amount forms a soft ball when dropped into cold water. Remove from the heat and let stand until cool enough to handle. Oil the finger tips slightly and fold or gather the candy into a ball. Pull candy with finger tips until candy is white. Then twist and cut into 1- to 2-inch pieces.

## "MOSIES"

| | |
|---|---|
| 4 cups brown sugar | ½ cup water |
| 1 tablespoon butter | 1 cup chopped nuts |

Combine the sugar, butter, and water and boil until a small amount forms a hard ball when dropped into cold water. Remove from heat and beat until creamy. Add the chopped nuts. Pour into buttered pans.

*Mrs. J. Max. Hark*

## BUTTERSCOTCH CANDY

| | |
|---|---|
| 2 tablespoons butter | 1 tablespoon vinegar |
| 1 cup brown sugar | ⅓ cup water |
| 2 cups molasses | Pinch of baking soda |

Combine the ingredients and cook until a small amount cracks when dropped into cold water. Pour into a buttered pan and allow to cool slightly before cutting into squares.

## MOLASSES CANDY

| | |
|---|---|
| 1 cup brown sugar | 1 teaspoon vinegar |
| 1 cup New Orleans molasses | 1 ounce melted butter |

Combine sugar, molasses and vinegar, bring to a boil, add the melted butter and boil until a small amount hardens when dropped into cold water Pour into buttered tins, cool and crack into pieces.

*Mrs. Lloyd A. Moll*

## OLD-FASHIONED MOLASSES TAFFY

| | |
|---|---|
| 2 tablespoons butter | 1 tablespoon vinegar |
| 1 cup brown sugar | ⅓ cup water |
| 2 cups New Orleans molasses | Pinch of baking soda |

Combine the ingredients and boil until a small amount cracks when dropped into cold water. Pour into a buttered pan and allow to cool enough for handling. Oil the finger tips and take up a small amount of the candy at one time. Pull until it becomes light in color. Twist and cut into 1-inch pieces.

## OLD-FASHIONED CARAMELS

| | |
|---|---|
| 2 cups brown sugar | 4 squares unsweetened |
| 2½ tablespoons butter, melted | chocolate |
| 2 tablespoons molasses | 1 cup nuts |
| ½ cup condensed milk | 1 teaspoon vanilla |

Combine the sugar, butter, molasses, and milk and bring to a boil. Cut the chocolate into small pieces and add to mixture. Stir constantly until chocolate is melted. Continue boiling until a small amount forms a firm ball when dropped into cold water. Remove from heat and add the nuts and vanilla. Pour mixture into a buttered pan. Cut into squares while still warm and then set aside to cool.

## POPCORN BALLS

| | |
|---|---|
| 10 large ears popcorn | 1 tablespoon molasses |
| 2½ cups soft white sugar | 1 tablespoon butter |
| 1 tablespoon vinegar | 1 teaspoon baking powder |
| 1 cup boiling water | |

Pop the corn and remove any half-popped or entirely unpopped kernels. Place the thoroughly popped corn in a large dish. Combine the sugar, vinegar, molasses and butter. Dissolve the baking powder in the boiling water. Combine the two mixtures and boil for 20 minutes without stirring. When the syrup spins a thread, pour it over the popcorn, mix thoroughly and shape quickly into balls.

## POPCORN CAKE

| | |
|---|---|
| 4 quarts popped corn | 2 tablespoons butter |
| 4 cups molasses | 3 cups mixed nuts |

Place the popcorn in a large pan and add the nuts. Boil the molasses and butter until the mixture spins a thread. Pour syrup over the popcorn and mix thoroughly. Pound vigorously with a wooden mallet until hard and firm. Slice or break into pieces.

*Mrs. J. Max. Hark*

## HOREHOUND CANDY

2 cups brown sugar                    2 tablespoons horehound tea

Make a strong tea of fresh or dried horehound. While the tea is still hot, place the sugar in a heavy frying pan and place over low heat. Stir constantly until the sugar melts and begins to bubble. Add the hot tea and continue boiling, stirring constantly, until a small amount cracks when dropped into cold water. Pour into a buttered pan, allow to cool, then crack in pieces.

## PEANUT BRITTLE

2 cups granulated sugar               2 cups peanuts, chopped fine

Place the sugar in a heavy frying pan and place over low heat, stirring constantly until the sugar melts. Remove from the heat and stir in the peanuts. Spread thin on a buttered baking sheet. Cool and break into pieces.

*Courtesy*, The Historical Society of York County, Pa.
THE REV. DR. MUHLENBERG IS LAYING THE CORNER STONE OF THE
GERMAN LUTHERAN CHURCH ABOVE, WHILE COLONEL SPANGLER
IS MAKING CHERRY BOUNCE BELOW.
From a drawing by the Pennsylvania German folk artist Lewis Miller (1796-1882)

# Beverages

*En goldner Gruck macht der Wei net siess!*

A golden jug sweetens not the wine

Wine had gladdened the hearts of our Rhenish and Palatine ancestors ever since Roman colonists had introduced the grape in the first centuries of the Christian era. The many thousands who in the 18th century left the vine-clad hills of their native land for Pennsylvania no doubt also entertained hopes of establishing vineyards there. Various attempts were made but without notable success. The use of sour table wines in the colonies was not common, so that any extensive viniculture was commercially unwarranted. In urban centers distilleries and breweries had been established at an early time. But distilled drinks were dispensed chiefly in taverns. A notable exception was rum from the West Indies which had easy access through the port of Philadelphia and as "Dramm" found its way into hinterland households where it was used to cover the annual mince meat, to break winter colds in the form of hot grogs and toddies, for Easter Monday eggnogs and in harvest time, "when," as the Reverend Provost Israel Acrelius (see Cider Royal) points out, "the laborers most frequently take a sup, and then immediately a drink of water, from which the body performs its work more easily and perspires better than when rye whiskey or malt liquors are used."

But it was cider in its various forms that came most nearly being a happy substitute for the sour wines of the Fatherland. Orchards bore apples in such abundance that it became a problem to market them in the early days of inadequate transportation and distribution unless distilled into brandy. But large quantities were consumed at home in the pressing of cider, to be used for cooking, for conversion into vinegar and for fall and winter drinking. It was drunk in all stages, but especially preferred when it began to show "the white feather" in the first stage of fermentation. Late cider of superior quality was sometimes boiled, slightly sweetened and flavored with root of sassafras or with wintergreen, or juniper berries, closed tightly in cask or barrel and put aside in a cool place for use at Christmas time.

Small beers and mead were also frequently brewed in Pennsylvania German homes of an earlier generation and were favored hot weather drinks. Also, the head of an hospitable household would hardly have considered provisions for the winter complete without some home-made fruit wines, syrups, vinegars or cordials to set before the Christmas or New Year callers when his *Hausfraa* proudly served her assortment of Christmas cookies.

The Pennsylvania Germans were never great tea drinkers, although they liked to brew "tea" of dried mint leaves and other herbs for their winter suppers. Coffee became the general table beverage and in many homes continues to be served with all meals. Since "store" tea has always been used sparingly, our Pennsylvania history records no incident comparable to that of the Boston Tea Party. However, when in 1765 high taxes, which were imposed upon the imported coffee bean, forced the price to a height the frugal Pennsylvania German considered unjust and prohibitive, he remonstrated in his own way. Rye could be bought for 2 cents a pound and roasted rye made a good substitute. In fact the patriotic Heinrich Miller, early printer and publisher of *Der Philadelphia Staatsbothe* (the same who did the biggest scoop of colonial times by being the first to announce to the world the Declaration of Independence in his paper for July 5, 1776) offered in his paper No. 168 (April 11, 1765) the following recipe for making a good coffee substitute:

"Take a quantity of rye meal and roast it until it turns light brown. Take an equal amount of water and of milk and cook it with the roasted rye meal as one would with chocolate. Remove it from the fire and add beaten egg yolk, one yolk for every two people."

The following recipes, aside from their historic interest, are not beyond practical use in the modern kitchen. No doubt others could be added, but these are offered in the proud belief that no more extensive list has yet appeared. They are forthright folksy drinks that have nothing in common with the fin-de-siécle mixed drinks of our day.

## ANISE CORDIAL

Pour 1 quart of proof brandy on ¼ pound of aniseed, ½ ounce cumin (caraway) seed and ½ ounce dried lemon peels. Let it draw for 48 hours. Add a quart of water and filter it. Dissolve 1½ cups of sugar in 1½ cups of water and bring to a boil. When cool add to the liquor, filter through blotting paper and bottle. — In the absence of good brandy 2 quarts of rye may be substituted.

Adapted from *Die Wahre Brantewein-Brennerey; oder, Brantwein-Gin- und Cordialmacher-Kunst; etc. Gedruckt bey Salomon Meyer, York, Pa., 1797.*

## APPLE WINE
### (From Baer's Almanac, Lancaster, 1871)

"*To Make Pure Wine of Apples:* Take pure cider made from sound ripe apples as it runs from the press: put sixty pounds of common brown sugar into fifteen gallons of the cider, and let it dissolve; then put the mixture into a clean barrel, and fill the barrel up to within two gallons of being full with clean cider; put the cask in a cool place, leaving the bung out three or four weeks."

## APRICOT WINE

| | |
|---|---|
| 1 pound dried apricots | 2 lemons, sliced thin |
| 4 quarts warm water | 2 oranges, sliced thin |
| 6½ cups granulated sugar | 1 tablespoon ginger |
| 2¼ cups brown sugar | 1½ cups seeded raisins |

½ yeast cake

Wash the apricots thoroughly, changing the water several times. Dry and halve them. Place in a large crock and add the warm water, reserving ½ cup. Stir in the sugar, fruit, and ginger. Dissolve the yeast cake in the remaining water and add. Mix well, cover, and let stand for 30 days, stirring every 2nd day. At the end of the time, strain and bottle.

## BLACKBERRY WINE

| | |
|---|---|
| 4 quarts blackberries, mashed | Brown sugar |
| 2 quarts cold water | Egg whites |

Combine blackberries and cold water and let mixture stand for 24 hours. Strain, and measure the juice. To each gallon of juice add 6 cups brown sugar and 2 egg whites, mixed with a little water. Place liquid in a jar, cover with a cloth, and place a weight on top. Remove scum each day until fermentation has ceased. Bottle.

## GRANDFATHER BUTE'S BLACKBERRY WINE

| | |
|---|---|
| 4 quarts blackberries | 2 quarts boiling water |

5 cups sugar

Combine blackberries and boiling water and let stand for 24 hours. Strain, and add the sugar. Pour liquid into a 1-gallon jug and fill to the top with water. Remove scum each day until fermentation has ceased. Bottle.

## BLACKBERRY CORDIAL

| | |
|---|---|
| 2 quarts blackberries | 2 tablespoons cinnamon |
| 3 cups sugar | 1 tablespoon cloves |
| ½ ounce nutmeg | 2 tablespoons allspice |

2 cups brandy

Combine the blackberries, sugar, and spices. Boil together for 5 to 10 minutes. Cool, strain, and add the brandy. Bottle.

## CARDAMOM CORDIAL

Pour 1 quart of rectified spirits or proof brandy over a mixture of ½ ounce crushed cardamom seeds, ⅛ ounce dried lemon peels, ⅛ ounce cinnamon bark, 20 grams of cloves. Set aside and let it draw for 48 hours, after which add 1 quart of water and filter. Dissolve 1 cup of sugar in a pint of water, bring to a boil, let it cool and add to the liquor. Filter once more through blotting paper and bottle.

Adapted from *Die Wahre Brantewein-Brennerey, etc. York, Pa., 1797.*

## SHAM CHAMPAGNE

### (From Baer's Almanac, Lancaster, 1880)

| | |
|---|---|
| 10 quarts boiling water | 1 teaspoon tartaric acid |
| 1 lemon, sliced | 3 cups sugar |
| 1 ounce ginger root | 1 cup Liquid Yeast (see Index) |

Pour the boiling water over the lemon, ginger root, tartaric acid, and sugar. When lukewarm, stir in the yeast. Cover with cheesecloth and let mixture stand all day in the sun. "When cold in the evening, bottle, cork and wire it, then place it on the floor of the cellar. In forty-eight hours it will be ready for use, and will pay the trouble of making it."

## DOMESTIC CHAMPAGNE

### (From Baer's Almanac, Lancaster, 1882)

Gather the desired amount of grapes when only partially ripe, pound them in a large tub, and to every quart of pounded fruit add 2 quarts of water. Let the mixture stand for 2 weeks, then strain, and to every gallon of liquor add 3 pounds of loaf sugar. When sugar is dissolved, pour the wine into a cask and allow it to work. When it is finished working, place in the cellar, and in 6 months it will be ready to bottle. Be sure to wire the corks securely.

## KIRSCHEN-BRANDWEIN

### (Cherry Bounce)

| | |
|---|---|
| 6 pounds ripe sour cherries | 3 pounds sugar |
| 6 pounds black oxheart cherries | 2 gallons whisky |

Place the sour cherries and black cherries in a large wooden tub or vat. Pound them until the stones are crushed. Stir in the sugar and place mixture in a stone jug. Pour whisky, a good double-distilled type, over the cherries. Stir or shake the mixture daily for 1 month. At the end of 3 months strain the liquid and pour into bottles. The older one lets it get, the better!

*Die Geschickte Hausfrau, Harrisburg, Pa., 1852.*

### CHERRY CORDIAL
#### (Kaersche Gaartschel)

Mash 1 pound of cherry pits. Add ½ ounce of cinnamon bark, ¼ ounce of whole cloves, 20 grams of coriander seeds. Over this mixture pour 4 quarts of proof brandy and set in a warm place for a week. Strain carefully. Dissolve ¾ pound of sugar in a quart of water, bring to a boil, let it cool and add to the liquor. Filter through blotting paper and bottle.

Adapted from *Die Wahre Brantewein-Brennerey, etc., York, Pa., 1797.*

### WILD CHERRY WINE

| 1 quart wild cherries | 6 cups sugar |
|---|---|
| 2 cups whisky | |

Combine the ingredients and place in a 1-gallon jug. Fill the jug with water and set in a warm place. When fermentation ceases, strain, and pour liquid into bottles.

*Mrs. Jonas Martin*

### POTENT CIDER
#### (An Old-Time Recipe)

| 40 gallons cider | 20 pounds raisins |
|---|---|
| 40 pounds sugar | 10 pounds honey |

Combine ingredients, mix well, and pour into a clean barrel, leaving bung out until fermentation has ceased. Close tightly. The cider will then be ready for use. *Er hockt sich hart uff die Aagedeckel.* It sits down heavily on one's eyelids!

*William F. Yoder*

### CIDER WINE

| 1 gallon cider | 4 cups sugar |
|---|---|
| 1 pound chopped raisins | |

Combine ingredients and place mixture in a 2-gallon jug. Fill the jug with water. Cork loosely and place in a cool spot for 3 weeks. Strain and bottle.

### MULLED CIDER

| 1 quart cider | 6 eggs |
|---|---|
| 1 teaspoon whole cloves | Sugar |
| Nutmeg | |

Combine cider and cloves and bring to a boil. Break the eggs into a pan and add sugar to taste. Beat eggs and sugar thoroughly. Pour boiling cider over the egg mixture, then pour back into pan in which cider was boiled. Pour back and forth until foam rises. Then pour into punch glasses and sprinkle nutmeg on top.

*Die Geschickte Hausfrau, Harrisburg, Pa., 1852.*

## CIDER ROYAL

*Seidereil,* our dialect corruption of Cider Royal, is today little more than a name, although remembered with fond respect by a few of the older generation. Cornelius Weygandt, in his delightful meanders in pursuit of this elusive drink (see his The Plenty of Pennsylvania, 1942) apparently did not come upon a source of information, all the more important because of its early date. The Rev. Israel Acrelius, Provost of the Swedish congregations on the Delaware (1749-56), possessed of a healthy interest in mundane matters, journeyed about in the adjacent territory, visiting the Dunkers in Ephrata in 1753 and the Moravians in Bethlehem in 1754. Upon his return to Sweden he published his invaluable "Description of the Former and Present Condition of the Swedish Churches in what was Called New Sweden, afterwards New Netherland, but at the present Time Pennsylvania, etc., Stockholm, 1759" in which he did not disdain including a chapter entitled "Drinks Used in North America." In it the Reverend Provost lists 48 items, numbers 15 and 16 of which read as follows:

15. Cider Royal is so called when some quarts of brandy are thrown into a barrel of cider along with several pounds of muscovado sugar, whereby it becomes stronger and tastes better. If it is then left alone for a year or so, or taken over the sea, then drawn off into bottles, with some raisins put in, it may deserve the name of apple-wine.

16. Cider Royal of another kind, in which one-half is cider and the other mead, both freshly fermented together.

## CARAWAY CORDIAL
### (Kümmel Aquavit)

Pour 1 quart of rectified spirits or proof brandy over a mixture of ¼ pound caraway seed, 1 ounce of fennel seed, 1 ounce of aniseed and 1 ounce of grated lemon peel and let it stand for 24 hours. Then add 1 quart of boiled water and filter. Dissolve 1½ cups of sugar in a cup of water, bring to a boil, let it cool and add to the filtered liquor. Filter once more through blotting paper and bottle.

Adapted from *Die Wahre Brantewein-Brennerey, etc., York, Pa., 1797.*

## CURRANT WINE

This is a literal copy of a recipe, at least 125 years old, bearing the name of Johannes Trombauer and found in an old saddlebag among a collection of sermon outlines.

"A—Recipe for 30 gals.

8 gals. currant juice
Then put the Bung in your cask and leave the air-hole open until the end of
6 gals. of good brown sugar, dissolve, let it ferment 3 weeks or 1 month.

Oct. and leave it on the seddiment till Spring before you tap it of [off]. Then begin the opperation on a clear day.

### "B—Currant Wine

After the sap is measured take ⅔ water and 3 lbs. of best drye brown sugar. The mixing must be done before it begins to ferment."

## CURRANT SHRUB

| | |
|---|---|
| 6 cups sugar | 2 cups rum |
| 1 quart currant juice | Juice of 1 lemon |

Combine the sugar and currant juice. Bring to a boil and skim off any scum which forms on the surface. Add the rum and lemon juice. Bottle.

*Mrs. Conrad Hermsted*

## DANDELION WINE I

| | |
|---|---|
| 2 quarts boiling water | 4 cups sugar |
| 2 quarts dandelion flowers | Juice of 3 lemons |

Pour the boiling water over the dandelion flowers and let stand for 48 hours. Strain, and add the sugar and lemon juice. Pour into jug. Let stand in a warm place. As liquid ferments, add water to maintain the original level. When fermentation ceases, bottle the liquid.

## DANDELION WINE II

| | |
|---|---|
| 2 quarts dandelion flowers | 2 oranges, grated |
| 4 pounds sugar | 4 quarts boiling water |
| 2 lemons, grated | 1 yeast cake |

Pick the flowers in the morning while the dew is still on them. Combine dandelion flowers, sugar, grated lemons and oranges. Pour boiling water over all. Let stand until mixture is lukewarm. Crumble yeast cake and add to mixture. Let stand for 4 hours. Strain, and pour liquid into a 2-gallon jar. When fermentation ceases, strain again and pour into bottles.

*Mrs. Harry Hess Reichard*

## ELDERBERRY WINE

| | |
|---|---|
| 4 quarts elderberries | 4 quarts water |
| 3 pounds sugar | |

Combine ingredients and place mixture in a crock. Let it stand for 8 days. Strain and return liquid to the crock. Let it stand until fermentation ceases, maintaining the original level of liquid by adding sugar water when needed. Bottle.

*Mrs. Samuel A. Taylor*

## ELDERBERRY CHAMPAGNE

4 quarts water　　　　　　　　　1 quart elderberry blossoms
4 pounds sugar　　　　　　　　　1 egg white, beaten stiff
　　　　　　　　1 yeast cake

Combine water and sugar and bring to a boil. Pour over the elderberry blossoms. Cool and add the beaten egg white. Crumble the yeast cake and stir into mixture. Let mixture stand for 3 days. Strain and pour into a stone jug. When fermentation ceases, bottle.

*Catherine Haller Bomgardner* (Courtesy Dr. Arthur D. Graeff)

## GRAPE WINE

7½ cups sugar　　　　　　　　　2½ quarts warm water
　　　　　　1½ quarts grapes, stemmed

Dissolve the sugar in the water and pour mixture over the grapes. Let stand in a warm place for 6 weeks. When fermentation has ceased, strain, and bottle.

## POTATO WINE

4 large potatoes, pared　　　　　1 yeast cake
4 cups raisins　　　　　　　　　2 quarts cold water
　　　　　　　6 cups sugar

Force the potatoes and raisins through a food chopper, using a coarse blade. Dissolve the yeast cake in a small amount of warm water and add to potato mixture. Add the cold water and sugar. Place mixture in a crock and let stand for 10 days. Strain, and return liquid to crock to ferment for 5 days. Bottle.

*Miss Mollie Gable*

## QUINCE CORDIAL
### (Kwitte Gaartschel)

1 pint quince juice　　　　　　　¼ ounce cinnamon stick
1¼ pounds sugar　　　　　　　　1 quart brandy

Combine quince juice, sugar, and cinnamon stick and bring to a boil. Remove cinnamon stick and pour boiling mixture into brandy. Filter and bottle.

## RHUBARB WINE

Cut fine the desired amount of rhubarb. Cover with water and boil until mushy. Strain and measure liquid. To each quart of liquid add 6 cups of sugar and the juice of 3 lemons, oranges, or grapefruit. Pour into a jug and let stand in a warm place to ferment, adding water to maintain the original level. When fermentation ceases, bottle the liquid.

## STRAWBERRY WINE

4 pounds strawberries                    6 cups sugar

Boil the strawberries until soft, strain, and add the sugar.  Place in a 1-gallon jug and add enough water to fill the jug.  Place in a warm spot to ferment, and when fermentation ceases, strain and bottle.

*Mrs. Jonas Martin*


## SPRUCE BEER

Handful of hops, equal ½ cup          1 pint molasses
2½ gallons water                      1 tablespoon essence of spruce
1 tablespoon white ginger             1 cup Liquid Yeast (see Index)
                        Raisins

Combine water and hops and boil until the hops sink to bottom of pan. Strain the liquid and when lukewarm add white ginger, molasses, and essence of spruce.  (If essence of spruce is not available you may use branch tips of spruce and boil them in the first water with the hops.)  Add the yeast and let it stand for 2 days.  Place 3 to 4 raisins in each bottle used and pour liquid from jug into bottles.

*Die Geschickte Hausfrau, Harrisburg, Pa., 1852.*


## PIPSISSEWA BEER

5 gallons water                       1 teaspoon allspice
3 pounds sugar                        1 teaspoon cloves
1 teaspoon ginger                     1 yeast cake
                  Oil of wintergreen

Boil the water for 5 minutes.  Cool to lukewarm and add the sugar and spices.  Crumble the yeast cake and add.  Place in hot sun all day.  Strain and flavor with wintergreen, as desired.  Bottle and seal.

Pipsissewa is an Indian name for wintergreen.

*Joseph B. Diehl*


## SUMMER DRINK

(From Baer's German Almanac, Lancaster, 1877)

4 ounces raw ginger root              5 pounds sugar
3 ounces cream of tartar              5 gallons boiling water
8 lemons, sliced thin                 1 cup Liquid Yeast (see Index)
                  1 slice toasted bread

Combine the ginger root, which has been well bruised, and cream of tartar. Add the lemons, sugar and mix well.  Pour the boiling water over mixture. Let stand until lukewarm, stirring to dissolve the sugar.  Add the yeast, turned out on the toasted bread. Cover with a cloth and let stand for 12 hours. Strain and pour into bottles, filling only ⅔ full. Fasten corks with wire or twine. Store in a very cool place and let stand for 2 days before serving.

### SOMMER BIER
#### (Summer Mead)

| | |
|---|---|
| 1 gallon hot water | 1 ounce hops |
| 5 pounds honey | ½ cup brandy |
| 1 lemon, sliced | |

Combine water and honey and boil for 45 minutes, skimming frequently. Place hops in a muslin bag and add to mixture. Boil for 30 minutes longer. Strain and pour into a large crock and let stand for 4 days. Then pour liquid into a keg or large jug and add brandy and sliced lemon and close tightly until used.

*Die Geschickte Hausfrau, Harrisburg, Pa., 1852.*

### MEAD I

| | |
|---|---|
| 12 quarts water | 2 teaspoons cinnamon |
| 3 pounds sugar | 2 teaspoons cream of tartar |
| 2 cups Liquid Yeast (see Index) or 2 yeast cakes | ½ nutmeg, grated |

Combine ingredients and place in hot sun for 1 day. Strain and pour into bottles. Fasten corks securely. Store in a cool place and let stand for several days before serving.

*Mrs. Tilghman Doll*

### MEAD II

| | |
|---|---|
| 8 cups sugar | 1 ounce ginger |
| 1 gallon honey | 1 ounce cinnamon |
| 1 ounce allspice | 1 cup Liquid Yeast (see Index) |
| 12 cloves | 10 gallons water |

Boil together the sugar and honey, skimming occasionally when scum forms on the surface. Tie the allspice, cloves, and ginger in a muslin bag and place in the mixture. Boil for 10 minutes longer. Add the cinnamon just before removing mixture from the heat. Cool and add the yeast and water. Set in a warm place for 24 hours. Strain and fill into bottles or other vessels that can be corked securely. Store in a cool place for several days before serving.

## CURRANT SYRUP

10 pounds currants                    1 pound sour cherries
                       Sugar

Combine the fruit and press it to squeeze out the juice. Let juice stand for 24 hours. Pour off carefully and strain through cheesecloth. Measure the juice and to each pint add 1 pound of sugar. Boil and skim occasionally as scum rises to the surface. Pour into bottles and seal.

## RHUBARB SYRUP

2 quarts diced rhubarb                2 pounds sugar

Combine diced rhubarb with 1 pound of the sugar and simmer over a low heat for 20 minutes. Strain. Add remaining sugar to the liquid and boil for 15 minutes. Pour into bottles and seal.

*Mrs. Harry Hess Reichard*

## GRAPE JUICE

6 pounds Concord grapes,              1 quart water
    stemmed                          1½ cups sugar

Simmer the grapes in the water until soft. Place in cheesecloth bag to drain. Add the sugar to the juice and bring to a boil. Pour into sterilized bottles and seal.

## RASPBERRY VINEGAR

4 quarts raspberries                  4 cups vinegar
                       Sugar

Combine 2 quarts of the raspberries with the vinegar and let mixture stand for 24 hours. Strain and add remaining raspberries. Let stand for 24 hours longer. Strain and measure. To each pint add 2 cups of sugar. Bring to a boil quickly. Bottle and seal. To be used in iced water.

*Mrs. Conrad Hermsted*

## STRAWBERRY NECTAR

1 quart strawberries                  Juice of 1 orange
Juice of 1 lemon                      3 pints water
                   1¼ cups sugar

Mash the strawberries and add the fruit juice and water. Let stand for 3 hours. Strain and add the sugar. Chill before serving.

### EASTER MONDAY EGGNOG

| | |
|---|---|
| 1 cup sugar | 6 cups heavy cream |
| 6 eggs, separated | 1¼ cups brandy or rum |

Nutmeg (optional)

Beat together the sugar and egg yolks and combine with the cream. Beat until thick. Add the brandy and fold in the egg whites, beaten stiff. Sprinkle with nutmeg, if desired. Chill.

### SHERRY EGGNOG

| | |
|---|---|
| 1 egg, separated | 2 wineglasses sherry |
| ½ cup milk | Cracked ice |
| 2 teaspoons sugar | Nutmeg (optional) |

Beat the egg yolk until light and add the milk, sugar, and sherry. Add cracked ice and shake thoroughly. Fold in the egg white, beaten stiff. Sprinkle with nutmeg, if desired.

### MILK PUNCH

| | |
|---|---|
| 1 egg | 1 tablespoon brandy |
| 1 cup milk | Sugar |

Nutmeg (optional)

Beat the egg until light and frothy. Add the milk and strain mixture through a fine sieve. Add the brandy and enough sugar to sweeten as desired. Sprinkle nutmeg on top, if desired. Chill before serving.

### RHUBARB COCKTAIL

| | |
|---|---|
| ½ cup Rhubarb Syrup (see Index) | 1 teaspoon lemon juice |
| 1 cup water | 1 egg white, beaten stiff |
| | Cracked ice |

Combine ingredients and shake vigorously until well blended. Makes 4 glasses of an unusual and delicious cocktail.

*Mrs. Harry Hess Reichard*

### MINT CORDIAL

Pick two quarts of leaves of spearmint, preferably in the month of May. Pour over them two quarts of rectified spirits or proof brandy and let them draw for 48 hours. Strain the liquor from the leaves. Dissolve in it three pounds of white rock candy and bottle.

## ORANGE CORDIAL

### (Pomeranzen Aquavit)

Pour 2 quarts of proof brandy over 1 pound of dried orange peels. Add a small piece of yellow sandalwood or a pinch of saffron as coloring matter. Let stand for 48 hours, after which filter. Add two more quarts of brandy. Now dissolve 1 pound of sugar in a pint of water, bring to a boil, let it cool and add to the liquor. Filter once more through blotting paper and bottle.

Adapted from *Die Wahre Brantewein-Brennerey; oder, Brantwein-Gin- und Cordialmacher-Kunst; etc. Gedruckt bey Salomon Meyer, York, Pa., 1797.*

## PEACH BRANDY

| | |
|---|---|
| 1 pound dried peaches | 1 quart warm water |
| 1 pound brown sugar | 1 yeast cake |

Put peaches through the meat grinder. Mix peaches, sugar and water and let stand in a warm place for 8 days. Then strain and add the yeast, dissolved in a small quantity of warm water. Let stand another 8 days, filter and bottle.

*From Mrs. Mary Baumgartner Shepler's book of recipes collected in the Dauphin-Cumberland area a century ago.*

*Luschdich gelebt un selich gschtarwe*
*Iss em Deiwel sei Rechling verdarwe.*

A merry life and at death salvation
Spoils the devil's calculation.

# Index

Almond Points, 188
Ambrosia (conserve), 113
Ambrosia (dessert), 213
Angel Cake, 153
Anise Cookies, 184
Anise Cordial, 234
*Apfelstrudel*, 196
Apple Cream Cake, 155
Apple Crumb Pie, 194
Apple Custard Pie, 205
Apple Dumplings, 223
Apple Fritters, 106
Apple Jelly, 113
Apple Pancakes, 101
Apple Pie, 194, 195
Apple Potpie, 220, 221
Apple Pudding, 220
Apple Tart, 195
Apple Whorl, 196
Applebutter, 116
Applebutter Pie, 197
Applebutter Custard Pie, 205
Applesauce Cake, 147
Apple-Sweet Potato Pudding, 217
A.P.'s, 179
Apricot Wine, 235
*Armer Mann* Cake, 148
Asparagus Soup, 24

Ball Cheese, 62
*Ballekaes*, 62
Basic Pastry, 193
Bachelor's Pudding, 221
Batter
  Fritter, 105, 106
  Pancake, 99, 101
Beans
  Baked, 69
  Baked Lima, 73
  Green, 69
  *Kraut*, 69
  *Schnitzel*, 68

Sour, 122
Soup, 24
Stew, 69
Beef Loaf, 46
Beer, 241, 242
Bellylaps, 184
*Belsnickelkuche*, 185
Berry Pudding, 217
Big Valley Bran Muffins, 19
Biscuits
  Cream, 18
  Potato, 17
  Raised, 17
  "Tante" Betty's Buttermilk, 18
Black Cake, 156
Blackberry Cordial, 235
Blackberry Mush, 214
Blackberry Wine, 235
Bran Bread, 14
Brandied Peaches, 119
Brandy, Peach, 245
*Brauni Mehl Supp*, 25
*Brauni Wasser Supp*, 24
Brown Hermit Cookies, 169
Breads
  Bran, 14
  Corn Cake, 20
  Crumb Corn Cake, 103
  Dunker Communion, 15
  Homemade, 13
  Nut, 15
  Nut and Raisin, 15
  Oatmeal Loaf, 13
  *Oschder Brot*, 14
  Raisin, 14
  Rusks, 21
  Steamed Corn, 20
Bread and Butter Pickles
  (Cucumber), 127
Bread Filling for Fowl, 56
Bread Griddle Cakes, 102
*Brei*, 215

Brown Hermit Cookies, 169

Brown Sauce, 58

Brown Spice Cookies, 189

Buckwheat Cakes, 102

Buns
  Moravian Love-Feast, 16
  Hot Cross, 21
  Raised Sweet, 21
  Spanish, 151

Burdock, 8

Butter Balls, 37

Butter Dumplings, 37
Buttermilk Waffles, 104

Butterscotch Candy, 229

Butterscotch Cookies, 161

Butterscotch Custard Pie, 209

*Buttersemmeln,* 134

*Buweschenkel,* 93


Cabbage
  Coleslaw, 83, 84
  Pepper, 127
  Pickled Red, 122
  Red, 70
  *Sauerkraut,* 78-80
  Slaw, Hot, 84
  Sour, 70
  *Weisskraut,* 70


Cake
  See also Cupcakes

  Angel, 153
  Applesauce, 147
  Apple Cream, 155
  *Armer Mann,* 148
  Black, 156
  Caramel, 148
  Cheese, Sweet, 65
  Chocolate, 155, 156
  Cider, 149
  Citron, 153
  Cocoa, 139
  Coconut, 156

Cake—*Continued*
  Coffee, 134
  Crumb, 142
  Custard Sponge, 154
  Delicate, 158
  Dried-Apple, 147
  *Ebbelschnitz,* 147
  *Eepies,* 135
  Feather, 149
  Fruitcake, 180-182
  Funny, 139
  Gingerbread, Walnut, 149
  Gingerbread, Soft, 150
  Hickory Nut, 150
  Honey Bread, 182
  *Hunnichbrot,* 182
  *Hutzelbrot,* 182, 183
  Ice Cream, 157
  King's, 152
  Lady Baltimore, 157
  *Lebkuchen, Weiche,* 150
  *Lebkuchen,* White, 176
  Lemon, 150
  Loaf, 151
  Marble, 151
  Molasses, 140
  Moravian, 141
  Moravian Sugar, 140
  Orange, 157
  Potato Sponge, 154
  Pound, 152
  Queen's, 152
  *Riwwelkuche,* 142
  Rotation, 159
  *Schwarz,* 156
  Schwenkfelder, 142
  Scripture, 159
  Shoofly, 142, 144
  Shellbark, 158
  Spanish Bun, 151
  Spice, 152
  Sponge, 154
  *Streisel,* 145
  Straw, 159
  *Strietz,* 183
  Sweet Cheese, 65

Calf's Head, Baked, 48

Calf's Head Soup, 25

Candies
  Butterscotch, 229
  Coconut Blocks, 228
  Coconut Creams, 228
  Horehound, 231
  Mammy Bender's, 229
  Maple, 229
  *Marzipan,* 227
  Molasses, 229
  Moravian Mints, 228
  "Mosies," 229
  Old-fashioned Caramels, 230
  Old-fashioned Molasses Taffy, 230
  Peanut Brittle, 231
Cantaloupe, Pickeled, 123
Cantaloupe, Spiced, 123
Caramel Cake, 148
Caramel Dumpling, 224
Caraway Cordial, 238
Cardamom Cordial, 236
Carrot Custard Pie, 205
Carrot Marmalade, 117
Carrot Salad, 84
Catchfly, 7
Champagne, Domestic, 236
Cheese
  Balls, 62
  Cake, 65
  Cottage, 61, 62
  Custard Pie, 64
  Egg, 63
  Pie (Peach), 65
  Pot, 62
  *Schmierkaes,* 61, 62
Cherries, Pickled, 123
Cherry Bounce, 236
  Cordial, 237
  Custard Pie, 205
  Dumpling, 214
  Jam, 117
  Pie, 197
Chestnut Soup, 25
Chestnut Stuffing
  for Poultry, 56
Chicken-Corn Pie, 53

Chicken-Corn Soup, 26
Chicken Corn-Meal Pie, 53
Chicken-Noodle Soup, 26
Chicken Potpie, Saffron, 52
Chicken Salad, 87
Chili Sauce, 129
Cigar Maker's Dutch Turkey, 41
Chocolate
  Cake, 155
  Cookies, 162
  Drop Cakes, 166
  Kisses, 170
Chow-chow, 123, 124
Christmas Cookies
  Almond Points, 188
  Anise, 184
  A.P.'s, 179
  Bellylaps, 184
  *Belsnickelkuche,* 185
  Brown Spice, 189
  Cinnamon Stars, 185
  *Eepies,* 179
  Fruit, 187
  Fruitcakes, Little, 190
  Ginger Nuts, 187
  *Leckerli,* 176
  *Mandelspitzen,* 188
  Moravian, Brown, 185
  Moravian, White, 187
  *Pefferniss,* 177
  Sand Tarts, 188
  Slap Jacks, 188
  Soft, 189
  *Speculatius,* 189
  *Springerle,* 177-179
  *Zimmtsterne,* 185
Christmas Doughnuts, 190
Cider
  Mulled, 237
  Potent, 237
  Royal, 238
Cider Cake, 149
Cider Soup, 26
Cinnamon Stars, 185
Citron Cake, 153
Cocoa Cake, 139

Coconut
  Blocks, 228
  Cake, 156
  Creams, 228
  Custard Pie, 206
  Molasses Cookies, 168
  Snaps, 164
  Tart, 211
Coffeecake, Baking Powder, 135
Coffee Custard, 214
Coffee Wreath, 134
Coleslaw, 83, 84
Cookies
  Butter, 164
  Butterscotch, 161
  Chocolate, 162
  Coconut Molasses, 168
  Coconut Snaps, 164
  Filled, 163
  Gingersnaps, 163
  Heifer Tongues, 164
  Honey, 165
  Jumbles, 165
  Peanut, 162
  Rice, Small, 165
  *Rinnszung*, 164
  *Schpritz*, 162
  Shrewsbury, 166
  Sour Cream, 161
  Squirt, 162
  Sugar Snaps, 164
  Walnut, English, 163
Cordials
  Anise, 234
  Blackberry, 235
  Caraway, 238
  Cardamon, 236
  Cherry, 237
  *Kaersche Gaartschel*, 237
  *Kwitte Gaartschel*, 240
  Mint, 244
  Orange, 245
  Quince, 240
Corn
  Cake, 20
  Chowder, 27

Corn—*Continued*
  Dried, 71
  Fritters, 108
  Griddle Cakes, 103
  Muffins, 19
  Pie, 71
  Pudding, 71
  Relish, 124
Corn-meal Mush, 111
Corn-meal Pudding, 220
Corn Salad, 7
Cottage Cheese, 61, 62
Cottage Cheese Custard Pie, 64
Cottage Pudding, 219
Crabapples, Spiced, 125
Cracker Pudding, 219
Cranberry Pudding, 218
Cream Custard Pie, 209
Cream Schnitzel, 149
Cress, Water, 6, 8
Cress, Winter, 7
Crullers, 138, 139
Crumb Cake, 142
Crumbs, Sweet, 194
Cucumber Pickles, 127, 128
  Relish, 125
  Rings, 125
Cucumbers, Spiced, 126
Cucumbers, Stewed, 72
Cupcakes
  Ginger, 172
  Little Crumb, 171
  Small Sponge, 172
  Snowball, 172
  Spoon, 171
Curd Dumplings, 64
Currant
  Catsup, 126
  Cookies, 166
  Jelly, 118
  Pie, 198
  Shrub, 239
  Wine, 238
Custard Filling, 153
Custard Pie
  Apple, 205

Custard Pie—*Continued*
  Applebutter, 205
  Butterscotch, 209
  Carrot, 205
  Cherry, 205
  Coconut, 206
  Cottage Cheese, 64
  Egg, 204
  Lemon, 206
  Lemon Sponge, 207
  Onion, 74
  Peach, 207
  Pumpkin, 207
  Potato, 207
  Rhubarb, 208

Dandelion Greens, 5
Dandelion Salad, 85, 88
Dandelion Wine, 239
Date and Nut Cookies, 170
Delicate Cake, 158
*Die Verbabbelt Suss*, 212
Dock Greens, 7
Dock Salad, 89
Dough, Sweet, 193
Doughnuts, 135, 137
*Drauwekuche*, 225
*Drechderkuche*, 109, 110
Dressings (see Salad)
Dried-apple Cake, 147
Drop Cookies
  Chocolate, 166
  Coconut Molasses, 168
  Currant, 166
  Date and Nut, 170
  Hermits, Brown, 169
  Kisses, Chocolate, 170
  Kisses, Nut, 170
  Kisses, Shellbark, 170
  Kisses, Vanilla, 170
  Love, 166
  Macaroons, Almond, 171
  Macaroons, Hickory Nut, 171
  Molasses, 168
  Oatmeal, 168
  Raisin, 167

Drop Cookies—*Continued*
  Rocks, 169
  Sponge, 167
  Spunigal, 167
  Taylor, 169
  Walnut, Black, 168
Duck, Roast, 55
  Apple, 223
  Caramel, 224
Dumplings
  Cherry, 224
  Curd, 64
  Green, 95
  Hairy, 95
  *Hooriche*, 95
  Liver, 37, 96
  Peach, 224
  Potato, 96
  *Schneeballe*, 97
  Snowballs, 97
  *Schnitz un Gnepp*, 50
  *Schwowe* (Swabian), 97
  Sponge, 97
  Yeast, 98
Dunker Communion Bread, 15
Dunker Love-feast Soup, 27
*Dunkes*, 133

*Ebbelkuche*, 195
*Ebbelschnitz Kuche*, 147
*Eepies Cake*, 135
*Eepies* Cookies, 179
Eggnog, Easter Monday, 244
Eggnog, Sherry, 244
Eggs in Beet Juice. 126
Egg Bread, 111
Egg Cheese, 63
Egg Drops, 37
Eggplant, 72
Egg Pancakes, 101
Elderberry Blossom Fritters, 106
Elderberry
  Champagne, 240
  Jelly, 118
  Pie, 198
  Wine, 239

Endive Salad, 88
Escalloped Potatoes, 76

*Fassnachtkuche*, 135, 137
Feather Cake, 149
Fig Pudding, 214
Filled Cookies, 163
Flannel Cakes, 103
*Fleeschboi*, 39
Force Meat Balls, 38
Fried Bread, 110
Fried Fruit Pies, 223
Fritters
  Batter, 105, 106
  Apple, 106
  Corn, 108
  *Drcchderkuche*, 109, 110
  Elder Blossom, 106
  Funnel, 109, 110
  Grapeleaf, 107
  Locust Blossom, 107
  Nunspuffs, 107
  Onion, 108
  Peach, 107
  Rice, 109
  Rye-meal, 109
  Snowballs, 107
  *Strauben*, 109
  Washington, 108
Fruitcake, 180-182
Fruitcakes, Little, 190
Fruit Cookies, 187
Fruit Pudding, 225
Funnel Cakes, 109, 110
Funny Cake, 139

Garters, 146
*Gebratene Kalbsleber*, 48
General Washington's Soup, 27
German Fried Potatoes, 75
*Gfillder Grautkopp*, 46
*Gfillde Nudle*, 94
*Gfillder Seimaage*, 40
Gingerbread, Walnut, 149
Gingerbread, Soft, 150
Ginger Cupcakes, 172

Ginger Nuts, 187
Ginger Pears, 120
Ginger Snaps, 163
Ginger Tomatoes, 122
*Goetterspeise*, 213
Gooseberry Pie, 199
Grandma Netty's German Puffies, 215
Grandfather Bute's
  Blackberry Wine, 235
Grape Cake, 225
  Mormalade, 118
  Pie, 199
  Syrup, 243
  Wine, 240
Greens, 5-9
Green Pea Soup, 29
Griddle Cakes
  Bread, 102
  Buckwheat, 102
  Corn, 103
  Flannel, 103
  Rice, 104
*Gritzel-Grotzel*, 83
*Grumbeere Balle*, 76
*Grumbeere Fillsel*, 57
*Gschmelzte Nudle*, 91

*Haasekuche*, 54
*Haffekaes*, 62
Hairy Dumplings, 95
Ham and Egg Cutlets, 49
Ham and Noodles in Casserole, 51
Ham with Lima Beans, 51
*Hasenpfeffer*, 54
Hazelnut Cookies, 188
Heifer Tongues, 164
Herbs, 1-4
Herb Soup, 28
Hickory Nut Cake, 150
Homemade Bread, 13
Homemade Sausage, 42
Honey Bread, 182
*Hooriche Gnepp*, 95
Horehound Candy, 231
Horseradish in Milk, 59
Horseradish Sauce, 58

Hot Cabbage Slaw, 84
Hot Endive Dressing, 87, 88
Huckleberry Pie, 199
Huckleberry Pudding, 218
Hullabaloo, 213
*Hunnichbrot*, 182
*Hutzelbrot*, 182, 183

Ice Cream Cake, 157
Icing
  Apple, 155
  Caramel, 148
  Coconut, 156
  Fruit and Nut, 157
  Orange, 158
  Vanilla, 157, 158, 159

Jam
  Cherry, 117
  Peach and Plum, 119
  Rhubarb, 121
  Strawberry, 121
Jelly
  Apple, 113
  Currant, 118
  Elderberry, 118
  Quince, 120
  Tomato, 121
Johnnycake, 20
Jerusalem Cherry
  Pie, 198
  Preserved, 118
Jumbles, 165

*Kaersche Gaartschel*, 237
*Kaffee Kranz*, 134
Ketchup, 128
King's Cake, 153
*Kipfels*, 32
*Kirschen-Brandwein*, 236
Kisses, 170
*Kukelhopf*, 140
*Kuttelfleck*, 44
*Kwitte Gaartschel*, 240

Lady Baltimore Cake, 157

*Latwerg*, 116
*Lebkuchen*, 175
*Lebkuchen, Weiche*, 150
*Lebkuchen*, White, 176
*Leckerli*, 176
Lemon
  Butter, 118
  Cake, 150
  Custard, 215
  Custard Pie, 199-201
  Rice Pudding, 218
  Sauce, 226
  Sponge Pie, 206
  Tart, 211
Lentil Soup, 28
Lettuce, Wild, 7, 89
Lima Beans, 73
Little Crumb Cupcakes, 171
Liver Cakes, 49
Liver Dumplings, 37, 96
Loaf Cake, 151
Locust Blossom Fritters, 107
Love Drop Cookies, 166
Love Pie, 209

Macaroons, Almond, 171
Macaroons, Hickory Nut, 171
Mammy Bender's Candy, 229
*Mandelspitzen*, 188
Maple Candy, 229
Maple Pie, 210
Marble Cake, 151
Marrow Dumplings, 38
*Marzipan*, 227
*Maultaschen*, 92, 93
Mead, 242
Meat and Cabbage Rolls, 47
Meat and Fish Salad, 87
Meat-filled Peppers, 47
Meat Pie, 39
Meat Sauces (see Sauces)
Meat Stuffings (see Stuffings)
Milk Punch, 244
Mince Pie, 202
Mince Pie, Green Tomato, 201
Mint Cordial, 244

Mixed Salad, 85
Molasses Cake, 140
Molasses Candy, 229
Molasses Drop Cookies, 168
Molasses Pie, 209
Montgomery Pie, 210
Moravian Cake, 140
Moravian Mints, 228
Moravian Sugar Cake, 140, 141
Moravian Cookies, Brown, 185
Moravian Cookies, White, 187
"Mosies," 229
Muffins
  Big Valley Bran, 19
  Corn, 19
  Peanut, 18
  Raised Breakfast, 19
  Rice, 19
Mush, Corn-meal, 111
Mush, Fried, 111
Mustard
  Pickles, 128
  Salad Dressing, 89
  Sauce, 59

Nettle Greens, 8
Noodles, 91
Nudle
  Gfillde, 94
  Gschmelzte, 91
  Wasserschpatze, 92
Nunspuffs, 107
Nut Bread, 15
Nut and Raisin Bread, 15

Oatmeal Drop Cookies, 168
Oatmeal Loaf, 13
Offe Schlupper, 224
Ohrfeige, 104
Old-fashioned Caramels, 230
Old-fashioned Molasses Taffy, 230
Onion Fritters, 108
Onion Pie, 73
Onion Custard Pie, 74

Orange Cake, 158
  Cordial, 245
  Custard, 215
  Sauce, 226
Oschder Brod, 14
Oyster Stew, 28

Pancake Batter, 99
Pancake Soup, 29
Pancakes
  Apple, 101
  Berries, 101
  Cherry, 101
  Chives, 101
  Egg, 101
  Ohrfeige, 104
  Plum, 101
Pannhaas, 43
Pap, 215
Parsnips, 74
Pastry, Basic, 193
Pastry for Meat Dishes, 193
Pea Potage, 29
Peas, Sugar, 74
Peach
  Cheese Pie, 65
  Delight, 225
  Dumplings, 224
  Fritters, 107
Peaches, Spiced, 119
Peanut Cookies, 162
Peanut Muffins, 18
Pear Butter, 119
Pears, Baked, 213
Pears, Pickled, 126
Pepper Cabbage, 127
Pepper Pot, 30
Pepper Relish, 127
Peppers, Cabbage-filled, 127
Piccalilli, 128
Pickles
  Bread and Butter, 127
  Mustard, 128
  Sweet, 128
Pickelfleesch, 40

Pie

Apple, 194, 195
Applebutter, 197
Apple Crumb, 194
Apple on Cabbage Leaves, 195
Apple Whorl, 196
Cherry, Sour, 197
Cherry, Jerusalem, 198
Chicken-Corn, 53
Chicken, Corn-Meal, 53
Corn, 71
Cream, 209
Currant, 198
Custard (see Custard)
Elderberry, 198
Gooseberry, 199
Grape, 199
Huckleberry, 199
Lemon, 199-201
Lemon Sponge, 206
Love, 209
Maple, 210
Meat, 39
Mince, 202
Molasses, 210
Montgomery, 210
Onion, 73
Peach Cheese, 65
Plum, 202
Pumpkin, 202
Rabbit, 53
Raisin, 203
Rhubarb, 204
Roseine, 203
Sauerambel, 208
Schnitz, 196
Schnitz Crumb, 197
Shoofly, 143
Slab-dab, 210
Sorrel, 208
Sour Cream, 209
Strawberry, 204
Sweet Cheese, 65
Tarts (see Tarts)
Tomato, Green, 204

Pie—Continued

Walnut, 211
Yuddekaersche, 198
Pig's Knuckles and Sauerkraut, 41
Pig's Stomach, Stuffed, 40
Pipsissewa Beer, 241
Plantain Greens, 8
Plum (Peach and) Jam 119
Plum Pudding,
for the Million, 221
Pennsylvania, 221
Quaker's, 218
Pokeweed Greens, 8
Popcorn Balls, 230
Popcorn Cakes, 230
Pot Cheese, 62
Potato Balls, 76
Biscuits, 17
Cakes, 77
Dumplings, 96, 97
Dumplings, Small, 38
Pie with Sausage, 42
Pudding, 77
Salad, 85, 86
Soups, 31, 32
Wine, 240
Potatoes
Baked, 76
Escalloped, 76
German Fried, 75
Sour, 77
Potpie, 51
Apple, 220, 221
Chicken, 52
Lazy, 52
Veal, 52
Pot Pudding, Aunt Ellie's, 44
Pound Cake, 152
Pretzel Soup, 33
Pudding
Apple-Sweet Potato, 217
Aunt Ellie's Pot, 44
Corn, 71
Cottage, 219
Cracker, 219

Pudding—*Continued*
  Cranberry, 218
  Fig, 214
  Fruit, 225
  Huckleberry, 218
  Lemon Rice, 218
Pudding, Steamed
  Apple, 220
  Apple Potpie, 220
  Bachelor's, 221
  Plum Pudding, 221
  Suet, 222
  Walnut, 222
Pumpkin, 202
Pumpkin Custard, 207
Punch, Milk, 244

Quaker's Plum Pudding, 218
Queen's Cake, 152
Quince Cordial, 240
  Honey, 120
  Jelly, 120
  Quince-Apple Honey, 120
Quinces, Spiced, 121

Rabbit Pie, 53
Raised Biscuits, 17
Raised Breakfast Muffins, 19
Raised Rolls, 16
Raisin Bread, 14
  Drop Cookies, 167
  Pie, 203
  Tart, 203
Raspberry Vinegar, 243
Rhubarb Cocktail, 244
  Custard Pie, 208
  Jam, 121
  Marmalade, 121
  Pie, 204
  Syrup, 243
  Tart, 211
Rice Cookies, 165
  Fritters, 109
  Griddle Cakes, 104
  Muffins, 19
  Waffles, 105

Rice with Cinnamon Sauce, 214
*Rinnszung*, 164
*Riwwelsupp*, 33, 34
*Riwwelkuche*, 142
Rocks (Drop Cakes), 169
*Rolitsches*, 45
*Roseine Boi*, 203
Rotation Cake, 159
*Rote Gruetze*, 218
Roulades, 47
Rusks, 21
Rye Meal Fritters, 109

Salads
  Cabbage Slaw, 84
  Carrot, 84
  Chicken, 87
  Coleslaw, 83, 84
  Cress, 8
  Cucumber, 85
  Dandelion, 85
  Dock, 7, 89
  Hot Cabbage Slaw, 84
  Meat and Fish, 87
  Mixed, 85
  Potato, 85, 86
  Raw Vegetable, 87
  Sorrel, 7, 89
  Spinach, 86
  Tomato, 86
  Turnip-Top, 86
  Wild Corn Salad, 7
  Wild Lettuce, 7, 89
Salad Dressings
  Dandelion, 88
  Dutch, 88
  Hot, 87, 88
  Hot Endive, 88
  Mustard, 89
  Sour Cream, 89
  Sweet-Sour, 90
  Without Cream, 90
Salem Tarts, 212
Sally Lunn, 20
Sand Tarts, 188

Sauces, Meat
  Brown, 58
  Horseradish, 58
  Horseradish in Milk, 59
  Mustard, 59
  Sorrel, 59
  Tomato, 59
*Sauerambel Boi,* 208
*Sauerkraut,* 78-80
*Sauerkraut* and Spareribs, Baked, 41
*Sauerkraut un Schpeck,* 41
*Sauerer Rindsbraten,* 45
Sausage Cakes, 42
Sausage Wreath, 42
*Schmierkaes,* 61
*Schnecke,* 142
*Schneeballe,* 97
*Schnittels,* 212
*Schnitz un Gnepp,* 50
*Schnitz* Pie, 196
*Schnitz* Crumb Pie, 197
*Schnitzel,* Cream, 49
*Schnitzel, Wiener,* 49
*Schpritz Kuche,* 162
*Schwarz* Cake, 156
Schwenkfelder Cake, 142
*Schwowegnepp,* 97
Scrapple, 43
Scripture Cake, 159
Sham Champagne, 236
Shellbark Cake, 158
Shellbark Macaroons, 171
Shepherd's Purse, 7
Shoofly Pie, 143, 144
Shrewsbury Cakes, 166
Slab-dab Pie, 210
Slap Jacks, 188
Snails, 142
Snicker Doodles, 184
Snowballs (Dumplings), 97
Snowballs (Fritters), 107
Soft Cookies, 189
*Sommer Bier,* 242
Soufflés
  Apple, 216
  Prune, 219

Sour Cream, 217
Sorrel, 7
Sorrel Soup, 34
Sorrel Pie, 208
Soups
  Bean, 24
  *Brauni Mehl,* 25
  *Brauni Wasser,* 24
  Calf's Head, 25
  Chestnut, 25
  Chicken-Corn, 25
  Chicken-Noodle, 26
  Cider, 26
  Corn Chowder, 27
  Dunker Love-Feast, 27
  Gen. Washington's, 27
  Green Pea Soup, 29
  Herb Soup, 28
  Lentil, 28
  Oyster Stew, 28
  Pancake, 29
  Pea Potage, 29
  Pepper Pot, 30
  Potato, 30, 31
  Pretzel, 33
  *Riwwel,* 33
  Sorrel, 34
  Spinach, 34
  Split Pea, 30
  Tomato, 34, 35
  Tomato, Cream of, 35
  Tomato, Yellow, 35
  Veal, 35
  Vegetable, 36
  Vegetable, 36
Soup Garnishes
  Butter Balls, 37
  Butter Dumplings, 37
  Egg Drops, 37
  Force Meat Balls, 38
  Liver Dumplings, 38
  Marrow Dumplings, 37
  Mock Peas, 37
  Small Potato Dumplings, 38
Sour Cream Cookies, 161
Sour Potato Soup, 77
Souse, 44
Soused Tripe, 44

*Speculatius,* 189
Spice Cake, 152
Spinach Soup, 34
Split Pea Soup, 30
Sponge Cake, 153, 154
Sponge Drop Cakes, 167
Sponge Dumplings, 97
*Springerle,* 177-179
Spunigal Drop Cakes, 167
Squab, Roast, 55
Steamed Cabbage and Meat Loaf, 46
Steamed Corn Bread, 20
Steamed Dumplings, 94
Straw Cake, 159
Strawberry Jam, 121
         Nectar, 243
         Pie, 204
         Shortcake, 226
*Streiselkuche,* 145
Strickle Sheets, 145
*Strietz,* 183
*Strumpfbaender,* 146
Stuffed Beef Heart, 48
Stuffings
    Bread Filling for Fowl, 56
    Chestnut Stuffing for Poultry, 56
    *Grumbeere Fillsel,* 57
    Pig's Stomach Filling, 57
    Potato Filling, Berks County, 57
    Stuffing for Goose or Duck, 55
    Turkey Filling, 56
Suet Pudding, 222
Sugar Peas, 74
Sugar Snaps, 164
Summer Drink, 241
Sweet Cheese Cake, 65
Sweet Pickles, 128
Sweet Potatoes, Baked, 77
Syrups, 243

"Tante" Betty's Buttermilk Biscuits, 18
Tarts
    Apple, 195
    Coconut, 211
    Lemon, 211
    Raisin, 203
Tarts—*Continued*

Salem, 212
*Schnittels,* 212
*Verbabbelt Suss, die,* 212
Taylor Drop Cakes, 169
Telltale Susan, 212
Tomato
    Catsup, 128, 129
    Jelly, 121
    Pickle, Green, 130
    Pickle, Ripe, 130
    Preserves, 122
    Salad, 86
    Sauce, 59
    Soup, 34, 35
Tomatoes, 80, 81
    Dilled, 129
    Ginger, 122
Turkey Filling, 56
Turnip *Kraut,* 81
Turnip-Top Salad, 86
Veal Potpie, 52
Veal Soup, 35
Vegetable Soup, 36
Vienna Rolls, 17
Waffles
    Buttermilk, 104
    Corn, 105
    Rice, 105
    Yeast, 105
Walnut Cookies, 163, 164
Walnut Pie, 211
Walnut Preserve, 122
Walnuts Pickled, 130
Walnuts Spiced, 131
Walnut Pudding, 222
Washington Fritters, 108
*Wasserschpatze,* 92
*Wiener Schnitzel,* 49
Wild Corn Salad, 7
Wild Lettuce, 7, 89
Yeast, Potato, 12, 98
Yellow Tomato Soup, 35
*Yuddekaersche,* Preserved, 118
*Yuddekaersche,* Pie, 198
*Zimmtsterne,* 185
*Zitterli,* 44
    Rhubarb, 211

BLUE HILLS
AND
SHOOFLY PIE

in Pennsylvania Dutchland

ANN HARK

Blue Hills and Shoofly Pie
ISBN 1-61646-291-4

Cherokee Cooklore
ISBN 1-61646-257-4

American Indian Cooklore
ISBN 1-61646-280-9

www.ingramcontent.com/pod-product-compliance
Lightning Source LLC
Chambersburg PA
CBHW031317280626
47169CB00019B/1931